BROWN UNIVERSITY STUDIES

THE JUNKER IN THE PRUSSIAN ADMINISTRATION UNDER WILLIAM II, 1888-1914

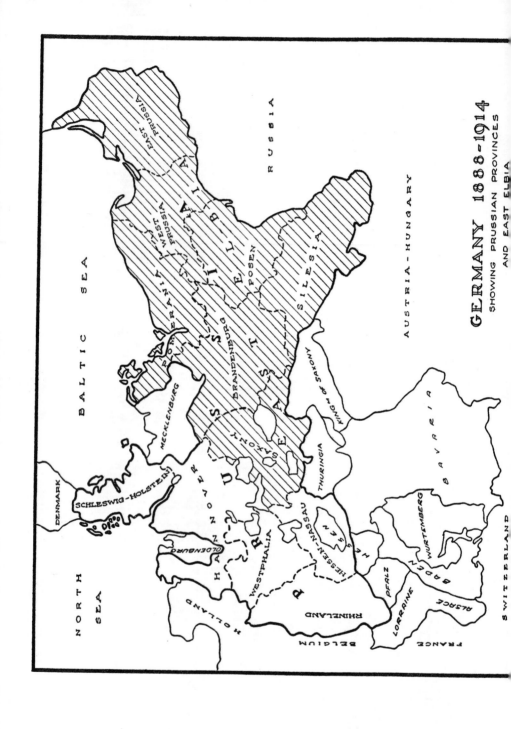

GERMANY 1888–1914

SHOWING PRUSSIAN PROVINCES
AND EAST ELBIA

THE JUNKER

*In the Prussian Administration
Under William II, 1888-1914*

BY

LYSBETH WALKER MUNCY

NEW YORK

Howard Fertig

1970

PRINTED IN THE UNITED STATES OF AMERICA
BY NOBLE OFFSET PRINTERS, INC.

To My Father and Mother

Preface to the 1970 Edition

WHEN I began preparing the materials for this book more than twenty-five years ago, under the guidance of Hans Rothfels, the subject was relatively new and unexplored. Since then, some interesting monographs and articles have been written on the relationship of the Prussian aristocracy and bureaucracy, notably by Hans Rosenberg. More has also been published on the character of the Prussian and the German administrative personnel. But the field still calls for further intensive and extensive studies. If my book has proved of interest and value to others, I attribute this not so much to the novelty of the subject as to the wise counsel of Hans Rothfels, to whom I remain deeply indebted.

Were I to revise this book now I would modify some of the statements, especially those on the character of non-Junker officials holding office in the five western provinces. My later research on the character of the *Landraete* in the Rhine Province, as well as in Pomerania from 1890 to 1933, leads me to realize that *Landraete* from western Prussia did not necessarily represent a different political and social strain. In fact they may have been even more faithfully committed to the policies of the Prussian ministry than the independent and assertive Junkers of East Elbia. *Landraete*, because of their position as leaders of the *Kreis* government, were, in the west as in East Elbia, almost invariably chosen from the area and in line with local views and interests. They might be bourgeois, even Catholic. But the Ministry of the Interior would make certain that they were conservative, loyal to the monarch and the ministry. They were not liberal, nor Centrist. I hope later to be able to publish substantial evidence in support of these conclusions as a part of my current work on the *Landraete*. Other members of the higher administration from *Regierungsrat* to *Regierungs-*

Praesident fall more naturally into the category of professional, mobile, politically non-partisan and inactive administrators, whatever their place of origin.

It is perhaps supererogatory to mention one final passage which is glaringly dated: the concluding speculations on the possible future of the Junkers and their political influence. We now know with certainty that the total defeat of Germany in 1945 carried the Junkers down into the pit. The occupation of East Elbia by the Russians and the Poles, the dissolution of Prussia, the new character of political life in both West and East Germany leave the Junkers of interest only to the historians—but of great interest to them!

L.W.M.

Sweet Briar College
Sweet Briar, Virginia
August, 1969

PREFACE

THE many and oft-repeated generalizations and complaints about the degree and extensiveness of the Junker's influence over the Prussian administration seem to warrant scrutiny. This study is an inquiry into the capacity for political power which the Junkers derived from officeholding. It examines their habitual attitude toward the administration, the kind and variety of careers which they tended to pursue in the service, and the correspondence between these careers and the economic and social position of the men who held office. The political potentialities of the Junker official have been estimated as carefully as possible on the basis of the number of Junkers holding office, the political character of the various offices and the distribution of the Junkers among them. It will appear from these analyses that the usual assumptions regarding the numbers of Junkers in office are greatly exaggerated but that due to a variety of special factors the Junker officials nonetheless possessed a high degree of political influence.

The basic materials for such a study are available in the *Handbuch ueber den Koeniglich preussichen Hof und Staat* and the *Gothaische Genealogische Taschenbuecher;* memoirs, contemporary accounts, biographies and other works serve to enrich the bare account set forth in these annual handbooks.

In discussing the Prussian administration, it has been impossible to avoid the use of a number of technical terms and, since many of them defy translation, I have included a glossary after the text which gives both the untranslated terms with their definition and the translated terms with the original German expression. A full bibliography is appended to the text and references in footnotes have been abbreviated, a number in parenthesis after the name of each work cited referring to the corresponding title in the bibliography.

I welcome the opportunity to express my gratitude to the people, unfortunately too many to enumerate completely, who thru their gracious interest in the undertaking and their specific comments and suggestions have helped me in the writing of this book.

My sincere thanks are due to Professor Hajo Holborn of Yale University for his constant willingness to help me and his excellent advice. I wish to thank Professor Sinclair W. Armstrong of Brown University for the encouragement which led me to undertake this work originally. To Professor Theodore Collier of Brown University I am deeply indebted for the warm understanding and the careful criticism of form and style which he has always gladly given me. Professor Sidney B. Fay and Dr. Heinrich Bruening of Harvard University were kind enough to read the completed manuscript and offer some suggestions.

I gratefully acknowledge my special debt to Professor Hans Rothfels of Brown University for the inspiration of his scholarship and his invaluable counsel. His wise and cordial discussions have given added insight and joy to every part of my work.

For aid in editing the manuscript and reading the proofs I wish to thank Professor H. B. Van Hoesen of Brown University and Mrs. R. W. Hathaway, Jr., of the Brown University Library.

My thanks are also due to the staff of the Widener Library for the courtesy and hospitality extended to me at all times during the preparation of this work.

Finally, I am grateful to Brown University for the grant which it gave me to investigate this subject, for the inclusion of this book in the Brown University Studies and for the aid which the University has given to make its publication possible.

LYSBETH W. MUNCY

Sweet Briar College,
Sweet Briar, Virginia,
July 15, 1944.

TABLE OF CONTENTS

THE JUNKER IN THE PRUSSIAN
ADMINISTRATION UNDER WILLIAM II, 1888-1914

1

HISTORICAL DEVELOPMENT OF THE JUNKER

IN STUDYING the Junker we are dealing with a distinct social type. Our first task, therefore, is to become acquainted with him and to know and recognize his peculiar characteristics. A description of the typical Junker will also serve to indicate to the reader what considerations have guided the writer in calling certain nobles Junkers and rejecting others. Moreover, to be acquainted with the Junker's character and temperament is to know something, if only in a general way, of the nature of the Junker's political interests and his capacity for promoting them.

The Junker character is the product of a long historical process extending from the first permanent settlements in the Mark Brandenburg in the 12th and 13th centuries. Therefore the best way in which to introduce the modern Junker is to describe his development from his origins down to the end of the 19th century and to fit together, piece by piece, the mosaic of his personality by dwelling on those phases in his history and the history of Prussia which contributed new traits to his character.

EARLY SETTLEMENTS IN EAST ELBIA

The Junker[1] was the country squire of Prussia's seven[2] eastern provinces. He belonged to the lesser landed nobility and spent most of his time living at home on his knight's estate or *Rittergut* which he cultivated himself and from which he derived

1. The term "Junker" originally referred to the younger son of a noble family, see Grimm (71) *Deutsches Woerterbuch*, v. 4, Part 2, p. 2399. Generally it was this younger son who left home to serve the prince at the Court or in the army.

2. The province of Saxony has been included along with the six provinces east of the Elbe because the Altmark, the original home of the Junkers, was transferred from Brandenburg to the province of Saxony in 1815, also because there were some Junkers resident in the other sections of that province as well. Therefore the term "East Elbia" when used thruout this work will refer to the province of Saxony as well as to those six provinces lying east of the Elbe.

his income. His relatively small holdings together with the poor quality of the light, sandy soil yielded him only a small, often a meager income, so that, altho he might live comfortably in the style of a gentleman farmer, generally speaking he could not acquire affluence or afford the luxury of life at Court. For the same reason he welcomed the opportunity to send his younger sons into salaried positions in the government service, both military and civil.

The monotonous, dreary landscape which is typical of the flat, sandy plains and moors east of the Elbe and which is not without its melancholy charm may have had a formative influence upon the Junker character. The Junker loved his heaths and moors even though he had to struggle with their poor, thin soil, and perhaps he drew from them some of the toughness, robustness and bluntness which he might not have acquired in a softer, gentler and more luxuriant landscape.

The Junkers were originally knights from western Germany who settled in East Elbia. In the 12th century, under the leadership of Albert the Bear and Henry the Lion, they moved into the territory along both banks of the Elbe, which later became the Mark Brandenburg, and into Pomerania and established the first permanent German settlements in these hostile Slav lands.[3] The native Slavs were either reduced by the sword or reconciled to German domination. Their property rights were taken from them and title to all the land was assumed by the prince. The prince then made grants of land to knights, barons, bishops and peasants alike in return for a few simple taxes. Both the prince and the knights made systematic efforts to persuade peasants from western Germany to migrate to the east and settle on their lands. They offered them the free, heritable tenancy of a tract of land in return for the payment of a small money rent and some few commodities to the landlord, the Church tithe and the nominal public taxes and services due the prince.[4] These generous terms made a great appeal to the unfree and depressed peasants of the west. Hardy and ambitious tillers of the soil from

3. Mecklenburg was also conquered and settled by the Germans at this time. For an account of the early colonization of East Elbia see James W. Thompson (118) *Feudal Germany*, pp. 493-520; Karl Lamprecht (92) *Deutsche Geschichte*, v. 3, pp. 364-366.

4. Thompson (118) pp. 508, 511-13, 519, note 1; Lamprecht (92) v. 3, p. 366.

Westphalia, the Rhineland, Holland, Flanders and other western territories migrated to Brandenburg and Pomerania to take advantage of the simpler and freer life on the frontier. Thus villages of free peasant tenants were established on the prince's land or on the lands of nobles alongside the nobles' own estates.

A similar settlement of German knights and German peasants took place in the 13th century farther east, in Prussia, where the Teutonic Knights had been called upon by Conrad of Masovia to subdue the heathen Pruzzen. Many of the old Pruzzen were slain by the Knights but some few noble families survived and intermarried with the German nobles so that even at the end of the 19th century certain Junker families such as the Perbandts,[5] the Gaudeckers,[6] the Sauckens[7] and the Ostaus[8] could speak with pride of their descent from heathen Pruzzen. The Teutonic Knights, altho not owning property individually, were able during the two centuries of their rule to extend German settlements westward toward Pomerania and the German nobles who thus moved into the intervening territory of Pomerelia laid out their estates alongside the estates of native Kaschube noble families.[9]

Thus the Junkers were among the original German colonizers of East Elbia and they became the indigenous nobility of eastern Prussia. They antedated the Hohenzollerns in Brandenburg by two hundred years or more and in the 19th century many old Junker families were proud to boast that they were there "before the Hohenzollerns."[10] Yet they were a new and young nobility when compared with the nobility of western Europe, even of western Germany, and they had the vigour of a young stock.[11]

5. *Taschenbuch der Uradeligen Haeuser* (12) 1913, p. 489; *Jahrbuch des deutschen Adels* (15) v. 2.
6. *Jahrbuch des deutschen Adels* (15) v. 3.
7. *Ibid.; Uradeligen Haeuser* (12) 1913, p. 608.
8. *Jahrbuch des deutschen Adels* (15) v. 2; *Uradeligen Haeuser* (12) 1900.
9. The Kaschubes are a small Slav group, related to the Poles, living on the shore of the Baltic between the Vistula and the Oder.
10. Frederick William IV writes as follows in a letter presenting Bismarck to Franz Josef, "Er gehoert einem Ritter-Geschlecht an, welches laenger als mein Haus in unseren Marken sesshaft, von jeher und besonders in ihm seine alten Tugenden bewaehrt hat." Otto von Bismarck (22) *Gedanken und Erinnerungen*, v. 1, p. 103.
11. For a detailed account of the origins of the Junker stock see Hans Rosenberg (175) "The Rise of the Junkers in Brandenburg-Prussia, 1410-1653," *Am. Hist. R.*, 1943-44, pp. 4-14.

The inevitable consequence of the close proximity of Germans and Slavs in the eastern borderlands was frequent intermarriage and the mingling of these two racial strains.[12] Slavic traits appeared in the physique, the manner, the speech and especially in the family names of the East Elbian Germans. German names were Slavicized and Slavic names Germanized.[13] Hence we find among the good, old Junker families the names of Itzenplitz in the Kurmark, Jagow, in the Uckermark, and Selchow in the Neumark. The Massows, Zastrows, Bonins, and Zitzewitzes of Pomerania have Slavic names[14] and the von Borckes were originally a pure Wendish family.[15] The Krockows, Puttkamers and Thaddens are descendants of very old Pomerelian noble families of Slavic origin.[16] Rudolf Nadolny goes so far as to propose the thesis that this mixture of Slavs and Germans produced a new Slavic-German ethnic type peculiar to East Elbia.[17] Certainly it is true that by his mingling with the Slav the Junker early acquired certain Slavic characteristics which were an

12. Thompson (118) p. 517, claims that the Slav population of Brandenburg was already admixed with German when Albert the Bear took over the territory. He writes, "what little population there was in Brandenburg at Albert's accession was mixed German and Slav, a forecast of the future social composition of the country." Hans Lothar von Schweinitz (39) *Denkwuerdigkeiten*, v. 1, pp. 1-2, refers to the Slavic influences in Silesia as well as in the Mark and Pomerania, ". . . auch im eigenen Charakter spuerte ich oft und deutlich die slawischen Einfluesse, welche so lange Zeit hindurch auf meine Vorfahren eingewirkt hatten. Spaeter, als ich mit Pommern und Brandenburgern, die doch auch slawisch-deutsche Mischvoelker sind, in Potsdam in naehere Beruehrung trat, erkannte ich den grossen Unterschied zwischen den Provinzen. . . ."

13. Rudolf Nadolny (103) *Germanisierung oder Slavisierung?*, pp. 199-204. Thompson (118) p. 463, note 1, states that in general *-itz, -in,* and *-zig* are Slavonic endings and place names with these suffixes show the Slavonic influence. Since Junkers often took their family names from the places where they lived they often acquired Slavic names thus. Theodor von Schoen refers to *-ow* and *-itz* as indications of a Slavic character. Writing in the 19th century and claiming the old Pruzzen as non-Slavs, von Schoen says, "In Ostpreussen ist alles rein germanisch und alle Herren in 'ow' und 'itz' (Zeichen des Slaventums) sind sehr spaet erst eingewandert. . . . Pommern und die Mark und Posen sind unsere slawischen Provinzen, Schlesien nur zur Haelfte." From a letter to Bruenneck, November 1, 1844, see Hans Rothfels (113) *Theodor von Schoen . . .*, p. 89.

14. See *Uradeligen Haeuser* (12); *Briefadeligen Haeuser* (13); *Graeflichen Haeuser* (10); *Jahrbuch des deutschen Adels* (15), 3 vols., *passim.*

15. Hermann von Petersdorf (106) *Hans von Kleist-Retzow*, p. 19; *Graeflichen Haeuser* (10) 1914, p. 139. "Borcke" is the Wendish name for "wolf."

16. A. O. Meyer (172) "Hans von Kleist-Retzow," *Pommersche Lebensbilder,* v. 1, p. 221; *Gothaische Genealogische Taschenbuecher.*

17. Nadolny (103) p. 198.

added feature that distinguished him from the nobles of western and southern Germany.

PERIOD OF THE STAENDESTAAT

Some of the most characteristic qualities of the Junker were acquired by him in the four centuries from his first settlements in the east to the reign of the Great Elector. In this period of the territorial and the *Staendestaat,* while a series of weak princes ruled their scattered lands in patrimonial fashion and lived largely from their own domains, the noble landowner was free to expand and flourish and in these centuries the Junker struck the roots of his economic, social and political power deep into the soil of the eastern marches. At the opening of the 15th century, following a period of anarchy, the nobles of the Mark felt strong and proud enough to resist the rule of the new Count Hohenzollern. Under the leadership of the von Quitzow family they rose up against the new Margrave. Altho he was able to break their resistance he could not accomplish any real subjugation of the nobles. Instead he was obliged to reach a compromise with them by which they accepted his princely rule but kept their local privileges.[18]

These privileges pertained largely to the control which the noble landlords had been able to extend over the peasants living on and around their estates as they turned gradually from fighting and plundering to farming for a livelihood. The light, sandy soil of the eastern plains made possible only an extensive form of agriculture. Moreover, the objective of the East Elbian aristocratic farmers was from the first commercial farming on a large scale. They raised grain for export in order to secure a profit and in the 16th century they forced a weak Elector to transfer from the cities to the nobles the exclusive right to export grain.[19] Hence they early developed a system of capitalistic agriculture, but they founded it on a semi-feudal social basis.[20] In order to acquire extensive estates for large-scale grain production and, even more important, to ensure themselves a cheap and permanent labor supply the noble landlords gradually

18. Otto Hintze (167) "Die Hohenzollern und der Adel," *Hist. Z.,* 1914, p. 497.
19. *Ibid.,* p. 500; Sidney B. Fay (163) "The Hohenzollern Household and Administration in the Sixteenth Century," *Smith College Studies in History,* 1916, p. 7.
20. Hintze (167) *Hist. Z.,* 1914, pp. 109-10.

spread the coils of their large estates around the surrounding peasant
holdings. They turned peasants' obligations from money dues into
personal service[21] and stretched and extended these service dues at
every possible occasion until they had reduced their peasant tenants
to a state of serfage (*Leibeigenschaft*) where they remained until
they were emancipated by Freiherr vom Stein in 1807.[22] In this way
the East Elbian peasant lost the relatively free position which his
ancestors had enjoyed when they first colonized the Mark. The
Junker by turning to the cultivation of his own estates and by binding
the peasant more closely to the soil reversed the developments in the
west, where the nobles slowly gave up the farming of their lands and
rented them to their peasants who were gradually emerging from
serfdom.

Junker landlords incorporated peasant holdings, even whole villages, into their own estates, often on the scantiest pretexts.[23] As these
peasant villages passed under the control of the noble landlord they
lost all vestige of independence and self-government. For the Junker
was only too eager to extend his authority over the peasant families
and villages which he annexed, and weak princes, pressed by the need
for ready money, gradually sold their rights of administration to the
lords of the manors or simply granted to them the rights which they
had already usurped. Moreover, the local noble still retained the
authority vested in him under the feudal system because of the great
distances from the prince's Court and because of the need to protect
the surrounding countryside. He continued to exercise these powers
after the need for protection had disappeared and they enhanced his
semi-public role of local administrator.

In these ways the Junker acquired the right to administer justice,

21. Georg von Below (159) "Adel," *Handwoerterbuch der Staatswissenschaften*,
v. 1, p. 45.

22. Guy Stanton Ford (66) *Stein* . . ., p. 179. "The peasants' status in the
eastern provinces was a devolution since the middle of the sixteenth century from
a condition more distinctly one of independence and untrammelled possession of
the land to something for which the courts, the pamphleteers and the reformers
of the eighteenth century had revived the hateful old German word *Leibeigenschaft*
(slavery)."

23. This process of annexation was known as *Bauernlegen*. During the Thirty
Years' War when large areas were depopulated the nobles simply annexed the
lands without inhabitants.

to exercise police power, to appoint the village magistrates and later the pastor.[24] He also acted as local tax administrator and collected the scot (*Schoss*) levy from his peasants. The noble himself, except in East Prussia, was free from the scot as to his person, his buildings and his fields.[25] From his manor house the nobleman actually ruled over all the peasants on whom he had any claim or pretense of a claim and treated them as his subjects.[26]

In this manner evolved the characteristic economic, social and administrative institution of the rural east—the *Gutsherrschaft*. It is to be clearly differentiated from the *Grundherrschaft* of western Germany, where the noble landlords did not farm their land themselves but leased it, often on the basis of hereditary tenure, to peasants for money rents and then lived from their ground rents with little concern for agriculture or peasant activities.[27] For the *Gutsherr* of the east with his immediate control over his lands and the very lives of his peasants it soon became a habit to command, to make decisions freely and independently and to assume full responsibility for all those under his personal jurisdiction—traits essential to the character of a real Junker. This whole transition of the eastern nobleman from knight to farmer and *Gutsherr* has been deftly summarized by Otto Hintze in the following words:

"Thus the land-owning nobility east of the Elbe was from the 15th century a class of cultivating gentlemen farmers who now frequently demanded compulsory service from their bound peasants in place of dues and who developed in themselves thru these activities a business capacity and a habit of dominating, commanding and disposing which were not characteristic to the same degree of the west and south German nobility who lived from their ground rents. In this manner evolved the type of the East Elbian Junker which was so definitely differentiated from the west German type of nobleman."[28]

24. Conrad Bornhak (52) *Preussisches Staatsrecht*, v. 2, pp. 180-82.
25. Carl Brinkmann (161) "Wustrau: Wirtschafts und Verfassungsgeschichte eines brandenburgischen Ritterguts," *Staats- und sozialwissenschaftliche Forschungen*, 1911, p. 35.
26. Felix Priebatsch (173) "Die Hohenzollern und der Adel der Mark," *Hist. Z.*, 1902, p. 236.
27. Fay (163) p. 6, note 2, distinguishes between "the produce-yielding estates of the cultivating lords to the east of the Elbe and the rent-yielding estates of landlords in the south and west of Germany."
28. Hintze (167) *Hist. Z.* 1914, pp. 499-500.

It was not only on his own estate and in his own local community that the Junker developed the habit of authority and domination; he also learned the taste of power at the centre of the State during this early period. As in all countries in the age of the *Staendestaat* the nobles in Brandenburg-Prussia sought and acquired large powers over the prince and the central government. They attained this influence thru their strong position in the territorial Diets and their insistence upon their right to be the hereditary military and political advisers of the prince.[29] The reign of the Elector Joachim II (1535-1571), that pleasure-loving and extravagant prince, marked the apogee of the nobles' power over territorial affairs in Brandenburg. Hard-pressed financially, Joachim II frequently found himself obliged to ask the Estates to take over his debts. The Brandenburg nobles, prosperous from their grain trade, were able to use the power of the purse—a power usually possessed by burghers rather than nobles—to force the prince to grant them important privileges.[30] In addition to the extension of their control over their peasants the nobles exacted the right to appropriate, levy and administer their own taxes and to exercise a controlling voice in foreign affairs.[31] Altho Joachim's more thrifty successors were able to avoid further grants of political power to the nobles no prince until the Great Elector was able to break their hold on the central government or to destroy the dual system of rule by prince and Estates.

In the territorial Diets or *Landtage* the nobles theoretically shared their power with the other two Estates, the clergy and the burghers. Actually the landed nobility were able to dominate in the Diets, particularly after the conversion of Brandenburg-Prussia to Protestantism and the disappearance of the clergy as a separate Estate. In the Brandenburg Diet the noble landlords were the most powerful and numerous group and documents of the period show a tendency to refer to the whole Diet as "the knights" and "the nobility."[32]

The Junkers' assumption that they were the natural rulers in the land was enhanced by their complete control over the *Regierungen* or

29. Hintze (80) *Die Hohenzollern* . . . , p. 113.
30. Fay (163) p. 5.
31. *Ibid.*, pp. 9-11; Hintze (167) *Hist. Z.*, 1914, pp. 501-02.
32. Hintze (167) *Hist. Z.*, 1914, p. 500; Fay (163) pp. 29-30.

Governments which handled almost all of the administration in the provincial subdivisions of the territories.[33] These *Regierungen* grew up with the *Staendestaat* and they, too, enjoyed their greatest power in the 16th century. Independent of the central government and concerned entirely with *staendisch*[34] affairs, they had become the judicial and administrative authority within the provinces. It was customary for the offices of *Regierungsraete,* honorary posts without pay, to be filled by the sons of local noble families.[35]

Powerful and influential as the Junkers had become at Court, in the Diets and in the *Regierungen* they built up their most complete and exclusive control over the administration in the rural areas. Here they were at home. Here they were the natural and, indeed, the only available political leaders. Here they were able to erect on the basis of their dominion over their own estates a corporate control of the whole district. In Brandenburg they took over the collection of the land tax for the Estates, set up special tax offices and elected their own deputies to administer them.[36] In Pomerania and Magdeburg the Junkers developed *staendisch* institutions similar to those in the Mark. Here the heads of the *staendisch* tax administration were known as *Landraete.* In all of these territories it was the Circle or *Kreis,* the smallest general administrative unit for the countryside, which slowly emerged as the vital administrative centre and the stronghold of the local nobility. The Circle had been from its origins a communal association of knights and when the Thirty Years' War brought about the political disintegration of Brandenburg-Prussia these bodies of knights assumed the general administration of both

33. Hintze (78) *Behoerdenorganisation*, p. 202.

34. The term *staendisch* is used thruout as meaning of or pertaining to the feudal Estates and to the political and social principles basic to the feudal Estates system.

35. With the administrative reforms of Frederick William I the *Regierungen* were pushed aside by the new *Kriegs- und Domaenenkammern.* They lost their feudal character and administrative features and retained only their judicial functions. By the 19th century they had developed into the Provincial Supreme Courts. Hintze (78) *Behoerdenorganisation*, pp. 202-04, and his *Historische und Politische Aufsaetze* (79) v. 1, p. 48.

36. Hintze (168) "Der Ursprung des preussischen Landratsamts in der Mark Brandenburg," *Forsch. z. brandenburg. u. preuss. Gesch.,* 1915, p. 36. "Diese ritterschaftliche Verwaltung der Hufenschosskassen in den drei Hauptkreisen [Altmark, Mittelmark and Uckermark] enthaelt den wichtigsten Keim zur Ausbildung einer rein ritterschaftlichen Selbstverwaltung in den Kreisen ueberhaupt."

territorial and local matters. Sometimes the Circle Assemblies (*Kreis-versammlungen*) appointed an executive head called a Circle Director (*Kreisdirektor*). In many instances it was to this Circle Director that the Elector assigned the collection of the new land tax or *Contribution*. Altho this added function made the Circle Director, later known as *Landrat*,[37] an agent of the central government as well as head of the local, *staendisch* administration, his sympathies remained with the Circle and with his fellow Junkers and he continued to use his authority, including that vested in him by the Elector, to promote the interests of his own associates and his own class. The experience of complete control over all affairs, even the prince's administration, in their local districts led the Junkers to assume that this was their natural realm of authority and they acquired a possessive attitude toward all Circle matters.

In 1618 the Duchy of Prussia was joined to Brandenburg in personal union and the landed nobility of that isolated territory came under the nominal rule of the Elector. The noble landowners there had developed a high degree of self-government and they ruled Prussia as an oligarchy. The Diet was in full control of the administration and all rural offices were held by local nobles. It was decades before the Elector was able to assert his authority over the Prussian Estates.

In the age of the *Staendestaat* when the Prussian nobles possessed an authority over the central government parallel with that of the prince and complete control over local affairs together with their far-reaching powers as *Gutsherren* over their own estates they fortified their traits of self-assertion, self-confident domination and jovial self-sufficiency. Priebatsch asserts that the fundamental character of the Junker as he appeared in the 19th and 20th centuries was formed here in the 16th century:

"It was in this period that the character of the Brandenburg Junker as we know it first developed, that comfortable, patriarchal, naively inconsiderate trait, that belief in his calling in this land, that self-assurance toward those above him as well as those below."[38]

37. For a fuller description of the origins of the *Landratsamt* see Chapter V, p. 175ff.
38. Priebatsch (173) p. 239.

THE 17TH AND 18TH CENTURIES

The period of the *Staendestaat,* in particular the 15th and 16th centuries, marked the first phase in the evolution of the Junker. It was then that he attained his complete economic and social domination over his estate and his immediate locality and that he laid the foundations of his political power in Circle and province and at the centre of government. His relationship with a series of weak princes had developed an attitude of opposition and resistance to princely authority and the presumption of equality with the prince in the government of the State. There followed in the 17th and 18th centuries the second epoch in the development of the Junker, a period of struggle between these proud and independent nobles and a succession of strong Hohenzollern rulers who established an absolute regime in Brandenburg-Prussia and who finally succeeded in bringing the stubborn and recalcitrant nobles under the yoke of the State.[39] The Junker emerged from this contest a loyal and enthusiastic supporter of the Crown and this he remained ever after, but he also preserved much of his self-sufficient, domineering and obstinate spirit because of the powers which he still retained over Circle and *Gutsherrschaft.*

The reign of the Great Elector (1640-1688) marks the opening of the struggle between prince and nobles. Frederick William was determined to introduce an absolute rule in Brandenburg-Prussia and in particular to build up a standing army under his own control. To do this he had to destroy the power of the Estates—that is, of the nobles—over the central government. But he was not strong enough to overpower the Estates by a frontal attack; he was forced to bargain with them. The result was the famous compromise reached at the session of the Brandenburg Diet in 1653. The Great Elector persuaded the Diet to grant a six-year tax appropriation for his standing army but in return he was obliged to confirm to the nobles all the material, social and political rights which they had acquired over the peasants and peasant holdings in the course of centuries. This even

39. Hintze (167) *Hist. Z.,* 1914, pp. 495-96. "Dann folgt die zweite Epoche. . . . Das ist die Epoche des Kampfes und der Auseinandersetzung zwischen den Fuersten, die den Gedanken des militaerischen Grossstaats verfolgen, und dem Adel der Provinzen, der anfaenglich diesem Staatsgedanken widerstrebt, der aber schliesslich damit endet, sich rueckhaltlos in seinen Dienst zu stellen."

included an affirmation of the condition of serfdom. "In those places where it is in use and customary, serfage must by all means remain," decreed the Great Elector.[40] By this compromise, the cornerstone of all future relations between the Junkers and the Crown, the Junkers were guaranteed complete dominion over the local sphere. The far-reaching powers of the Junker in his *Gutsherrschaft* were made definite and explicit and the roots of his self-assertiveness and domineering habits were more firmly entrenched.

But the Junker's power at the centre of government began to slip from his hands. The Great Elector used the original grant of taxes by the Brandenburg Diet as the thin edge of the wedge to pry the nobles loose from the central government. In time he simply circumvented the old *staendisch* constitutions. His way was made easier by the spirit of narrow particularism in the Estates of the several territories, each defending its own rights and unwilling to join with the Estates of other territories in a common front against absolutism.[41] Frederick William handled the Estates' tax organization with skillful obliqueness. He gradually honeycombed the whole tax administration with his own loyal officials and then pushed the whole structure to one side in favor of his Electoral taxes, the excise tax and the *Contribution,* collected by his own men. This is only one example of the way in which he proceeded, very slowly, to replace the independent, feudal officials with servants of the Crown and thus to lay the first foundations of the Prussian bureaucracy. The Junker found himself excluded from the central administration unless he entered the service of the prince.

The Great Elector's prime achievement was, of course, the founding of the Prussian Army as a tool of absolutism and Prussian might. But by undermining the rights of the Estates and encroaching on the power of the nobles over the administration he was able to force their authority back from the centre of the State, down toward the Circles, and to clear the ground for the thoroughgoing absolutism which was to follow. Already by 1688 the old feudal, territorial foundations of the *Staendestaat* were giving place to the three pillars of the modern

40. Bernhard Erdmannsdoerffer (62) *Deutsche Geschichte . . .* , v. 1, p. 423.
41. L. Tuempel (120) *Entstehung des brandenburgisch-preussischen Einheits-staats . . .* , pp. 56-57.

Prussian State—the monarchy, the army and the bureaucracy. But the Junker, altho willing to accept an agreement which affirmed his local privileges, was still far from converted to whole-hearted support of the sovereign. On his estate and in his own locality he was as proud and unco-operative as ever[42] and his compromise with the Crown was rather in the nature of an armed truce.[43]

It was Prussia's second great Hohenzollern ruler, Frederick William I (1713-1740) who curbed the Junker's rebellious spirit and prepared him for that position of leadership in the King's service which he was later to assume. Frederick William I carried forward the reduction of the nobles' power at the centre of government by his reorganization and expansion of the standing army and the royal bureaucracy. Moreover, he continued his grandfather's policy of drawing the marrow from the old *staendisch* institutions. Altho he allowed the framework of the old Estates to remain standing he removed their power. "I leave the Junkers the wind from the Diet," wrote Frederick William I.[44] But as the King stretched his royal authority out from the centre into the rural areas he ran up against the old compromise between King and nobles which guaranteed to the latter dominion over the *Gutsherrschaft* and the local community. Here the Junker was still supreme, still free to satisfy his desire to direct and com-

42. Hintze says (79) *Historische und Politische Aufsaetze*, v. 1, pp. 161-62, "Das ist das Reich in dem der Junker wie ein kleiner Koenig herrscht, in dem er die Faehigkeit zu befehlen, zu disponieren, zu regieren ausgebildet hat, die ihn spaeter als Offizier und Beamten auszeichnet. Damals aber steht die Mehrzahl dieser kleinen Herren dem Staatsgedanken noch fremd und sproede gegenueber."

43. Frederick William I himself complains of the Junkers' haughty insubordination as he describes them province by province in his Political Testament: "In Preussen ist auch ein grosser adell . . . auf die finckische und Donaische familie mus mein Successor ein wachsahmes auge hahben sonsten sie mit mein Successor mit Regieren werden . . . die Pommersche wassallen seindt getreue wie Goldt. . . . Wahs die Neuemarck anlanget ist in allen stuecken wie die Pommern . . . aber Klagen tuhn die wassallen stetigl: absonderlich der Krossensche Kreis. . . . Wahs die Mittell und Ucker Marck betrifft sein die wassallen die getreueste von allen . . . die Altmerckische Vassallen sein schlimme ungehorsame leute die dar nichts mit guhten tuhn sondern Reweche sein und rechte leichtfertige lutte gegen Ihren Landesherren sein Mein lieber Successor mus sie den Daum(en) auf die augen halten und mit Ihnen nicht guht umbgehen . . . die Schullenburgische Alvenslehbensche Bismarck(sche) familien sein die vornehmste undt schlimmste . . . dit Knese(beck)-sche familie ist eine schlimme auch. Das Magdeburgische ist ein schoehnes landt und stette die wassallen wie die alte Mercker fast noch schlimmer." *Die politischen Testamente der Hohenzollern* (26) v. 1, pp. 103-05.

44. Erdmannsdoerffer (62) v. 2, p. 498.

mand. Even in the rural Circles the nobles were able to resist the penetration of the King's absolute rule and to retain a large measure of their feudal self-government.

Altho preserving his old traits of independence and imperiousness by his resistance to royal control in Circle and *Gutsherrschaft* the Junker nonetheless had impressed upon him by Frederick William I the quite new characteristics of submissiveness to the royal will and enthusiasm for the King's service thru his initiation into the Army Officers Corps and, to a lesser degree, into the royal bureaucracy. By his reform of the Officers Corps Frederick William I brought about a new relationship between the nobles and the Crown and caused a lasting transformation in the character of the Junker and his attitude toward the Prussian State. The King had hoped that their experience as Prussian army officers would break down the Junkers' haughty independence toward the Crown. At first the proud provincial landed nobility were very hostile to the King's plans and offered passive resistance to the drafting of its sons as army officers. But the strong-willed monarch did not shrink from the use of force against his recalcitrant nobles and sometimes sent sergeants and dragoons to drag the nobles' sons to the Cadet Schools.[45]

A milder form of "persuasion" was the economic advantage offered the often quite poor landed nobility of the eastern provinces by service in the Officers Corps. Frederick William I had founded Cadet Schools in Berlin, Magdeburg and Stolp where noblemen's sons could under comfortable and attractive circumstances receive free an education suitable to their social position. Later, as officers, they received an income which made them more or less independent of the family estate and in this way families were often freed from the burden of younger sons. Sons of wealthy landed noblemen did not feel the same economic compulsion to enter the royal service and were hence less closely attached to the Crown and more independent and sophisticated in their point of view.

Altho at first an unwelcome privilege and indeed even a very heavy and burdensome duty, service in the Prussian Officers Corps

45. Hintze (167) *Hist. Z.*, 1914, p. 511. See also Gustav Schmoller (177) "Die Entstehung des preussischen Heeres, 1640 bis 1740," *Umrisse und Untersuchungen . . .* , ch. iv, *passim*.

rapidly became a customary occupation and a cherished privilege for Junkers' sons. Even during the reign of Frederick William I there were but few Prussian noble families "which did not have one or more members in the profession of army officer."[46] Furthermore, altho the Officers Corps included members of the bourgeoisie in some branches, the profession as a whole acquired the predominant character of aristocratic gentility and exclusiveness.[47] Thus the Officers Corps was and continued to be the first and most effective training ground of Prussianism for the Junker. Here he learned unreserved devotion to his fatherland and his sovereign. From here he carried these qualities back home and impressed them on his own family and neighbors, until their indifference or hostility toward the rationalized State was transmuted into loyal acceptance. Militarism and the tradition of service in the King's uniform were woven into the central strand of the Junker's character. On the other hand, the Officers Corps, with its largely Junker personnel, became a central pillar in the structure of the Prussian State.

Frederick William's administrative reforms were hardly less important for the Junker's status and the evolution of his character. The new central administrative organ, the General Supreme Finance, War, and Domains Directory (*General Ober Finanz-, Kriegs- und Domaenendirektorium*) set up in Berlin in 1723, and the new provincial bodies, the Chambers for War and Domains (*Kriegs- und Domaenenkammern*), both collegial in organization, were staffed with royal officials. These men were notable for their unquestioning obedience to orders from above and their scrupulous observance of a rigid routine. In other words, they were bureaucratic officials. It is clear that this type of work which required complete submission to royal commands would be distasteful to the proud and stiff-necked Junker. And yet he gradually began to realize that once the civil administration of an absolute monarchy had been placed in the hands of a bureaucracy the only way to acquire a position of influence over affairs of State was *thru* the royal administration, that is to say, thru a large hold on, even a monopoly of, the new administrative offices. As he came to appreciate the possibilities for authority and influence

46. Erdmannsdoerffer (62) v. 2, p. 511.
47. *Ibid.*

in the new royal offices he began to seek high positions in the administration.

At the level of the Circle the Junker was not forced to give place to a new collegial royal administrative body. Instead the *Landrat*, the executive of the Circle's *staendisch* administration, was made the single agent of the Chamber of War and Domains in the next lowest sphere of government. On him fell the duties of tax collection, police administration and administration of justice for the Circle, the quartering of troops and the provision of an adequate supply of new recruits, etc. Thus the *Landrat* became much more of a royal official with responsibilities to the Crown. Yet he still retained his *staendisch* character as chairman of the Circle Assembly and head of the few remaining self-governing activities of the Circle. He was generally a local noble landlord who lived on his estate and carried on his administrative duties by frequent visits to the Circle capital. He never became a really bureaucratic official but kept his half-*staendisch*, half-amateur, half-honorary character.[48] In the office of *Landrat* the Junker retained some of his old political power.

If the Junkers failed to achieve as strong a position among the regular royal administrative officials as they did in the Officers Corps during the reign of Frederick William I the reason lies not only in their antipathy to submission to the commands of others, even the King, but also in Frederick William's mistrust of the recalcitrant and particularistic landed nobles. He frequently passed them by when choosing his royal bureaucratic officials and appointed middle class men instead. In the Altmark and Magdeburg he sometimes even infringed on the right of the nobles to elect their own *Landraete* and appointed his bourgeois candidate.[49] Yet, in spite of his mistrust and his desire to establish a thoroughly rationalized absolute monarchy, Frederick William I did not wish to exclude the Junkers from a place in the new royal army and bureaucracy. And indeed he could not do so because of the great residuum of feudal power still within the noble Estate. What he did do was to inaugurate among the antagonistic Junkers the tradition of service in the King's uniform and to instill into many of them loyalty and devotion to the Crown.

48. Tuempel (120) p. 133; Hintze (78) *Behoerdenorganisation,* pp. 260, 267.
49. Hintze (167) *Hist. Z.,* 1914, p. 513.

It was his contribution to train the Junkers and prepare them for that fuller participation in the royal service which they were to attain under his son, Frederick II.

By reaffirming the nobles' privileges and drawing them into closer co-operation with the Crown Frederick the Great moderated the highly rationalistic and absolutistic policies of his father[50] and transformed the old compromise of 1653, which had left the nobles sullen and antagonistic, into a genuine working partnership. He modified Frederick William I's policy of increasing the revenue, irrespective of the social cost, and took into consideration the social and political as well as the economic utility of his measures.[51] His object was to reconcile absolutism at the centre of the State with feudalism at the base and to establish mutually satisfactory and profitable relations between the Crown and the landed nobility.[52] This policy of Frederick II had the effect of fortifying and expanding the power of the Junkers both at home, on their patrimonial estates, and at the centre of government, thru their growing numbers and influence in the army and administration.[53] But an increase in the Junker's power was not the King's real objective, in spite of his natural affinity for the nobility. What Frederick II wanted primarily was an abundant and vigorous landed gentry to serve as a seed-bed for his Officers Corps and administrative officials.[54] In order to keep his nobles strong and flourishing Frederick II was willing to give them definite aids and advantages. He is reported to have once said that the race of old Prussian nobles was so good that it merited to be conserved.[55]

50. Walter L. Dorn (162) "The Prussian Bureaucracy in the Eighteenth Century," *Pol. Sci. Quar.*, 1932, p. 265.
51. *Ibid.*, p. 266; Hintze (167) *Hist. Z.*, 1914, p. 514.
52. Hugo Preuss (109) *Die Junkerfrage*, pp. 9-12. It is true that Frederick II also made some rather ineffectual attempts to prevent the nobles from making any further annexations of peasant lands.
53. Hintze (167) *Hist. Z.*, 1914, p. 514; Dorn (162) p. 266.
54. "Der Koenig von Preussen muesse einen zahlreichen und wohlhabenden Grundadel haben, der ihm Offiziere fuer seine Armee liefern koenne." Hintze (167) *Hist. Z.*, 1914, p. 514.
55. "Denn ihre Soehne sind es, die das Land defendieren; davon die Rasse so gut ist, dass sie auf alle Weise meritiert conserviert zu werden." Quoted by Hintze (167) *Hist. Z.*, 1914, p. 514. That Frederick's admiration for the landed nobility varied from province to province is evident from the following quotation from his Political Testament: "J'ai remarqué que les Prussiens ont l'esprit fin et délié, qu'ils ont de la souplesse. . . . Les Poméraniens ont un sens droit et de la naïveté; c'est

The Junkers took advantage of this attitude of Frederick II to consolidate and expand their power at home and at the centre. Their old capacity to command and dispose with freedom and authority was more firmly rooted by Frederick's reaffirmation of their social, economic and administrative privileges within their *Gutsherrschaften*. Moreover, these privileges were now reserved for nobles alone by Frederick's decree prohibiting burghers from acquiring real estate outside the city and nobles from engaging in business within the city. The Junkers' proud assumption that local administration was their own affair was also emphasized by Frederick's extension to the landed gentry of a wider degree of self-government within the Circles along the old, feudal lines and his encouragement of a closer connection between the *Landrat* and the *staendisch* corporate bodies. The Junkers' economic and financial stability was protected in part by the King's promotion of the founding of fideicommissa so that the nobles' estates could be preserved intact and by the establishment of *Landschaften* or aristocratic land credit institutions to provide noble landholders with easy credit.[56]

The greatest economic assistance which Frederick II gave to the Junkers and that which is most significant for their development was to employ them in the royal service. By greatly extending his father's policy of offering the Junkers salaried career positions in the Officers Corps and the civil administration he made it possible for them to add to the slender incomes from their frequently small and meagre estates. For Frederick II was anxious to preserve the nobility and to preserve it as a landed aristocracy. He did not want a purely court and service nobility, dependent on salaries from the royal exchequer

---

de toutes les provinces celle qui a produit les meilleurs sujets tant pour la guerre que pour les autres emplois; . . . La noblesse de l'Électorat est voluptueuse; elle n'a ni l'esprit des Prussiens ni le solide des Poméraniens. Celle de Magdeburg a plus de sagacité et a produit quelques grands hommes. Les Silésiens de la Basse-Silésie sont ce qu'on appelle de bons gens, un peu bêtes, ce qui n'est que la suite de la mauvaise éducation qu'ils ont reçue; ils sont vains, ils aiment le luxe, la dépense, les titres, et haïssent un travail suivi ou cette application austère que demande la discipline militaire. . . . Ceux de la Haute-Silésie ont la meme vanité avec plus d'esprit mais aussi moins d'attachement pour le gouvernement prussien à cause qu'ils sont tous catholiques et que la plupart de leurs parents établis sous la domination autrichienne." *Die politischen Testamente der Hohenzollern* (26) v. 2, pp. 30-31.

56. Hintze (167) *Hist. Z.*, 1914, p. 516. For a fuller treatment of the *Landschaften* see Chapter V, p. 199f.

and cut off from its connection with the land, and he realized that the Prussian gentry was unable to support itself from its estates alone. Hence he helped the nobles—but not for their own sakes—by giving them an added source of income, he helped himself by paying his propertied officials low salaries and he confirmed the historic connection between landholding and officeholding.

It is certainly true that under Frederick II both the Officers Corps and the bureaucracy acquired a distinctly aristocratic character. The Officers Corps, which had already been filled with Junkers' sons by Frederick William I, became almost exclusively aristocratic under his son.[57] In the bureaucracy, due to Frederick William I's lack of confidence in noble officials, the increase in the number of Junkers was much more striking. In the new province of Silesia, where the Prussian administrative system was but recently introduced, the ratio of nobles was particularly high.[58] In Brandenburg and Pomerania, noble and bourgeois elements were more nearly equal,[59] but this meant a decided increase in the aristocratic element over the previous reign. The office of *Landrat* from which the commoners had previously been excluded by custom was restricted exclusively to nobles by a decree in 1769.[60]

Why did the Junkers choose to enter the royal service in increasing numbers? Was the economic advantage suggested above the only or even the primary motive? Surely it was a powerful factor and some consider it to have been decisive.[61] But beyond the concrete economic advantages, the prospect of partnership with the King in the direction

57. Karl Demeter (59) *Das deutsche Heer und seine Offiziere*, p. 8, tells us that nine-tenths of all the officers of Frederick the Great's army were nobles, but that in the ranks of Major and above the ratio of nobles was even greater—689:22.

58. For instance, of 108 understudies taken into the Silesian Chambers from 1742 to 1806 some 70 were nobles and only 38, bourgeois. Dorn (162) *Pol. Sci. Quar.*, 1932, p. 264.

59. *Ibid.*, p. 265.

60. Ernst von Meier (101) *Die Reform der Verwaltungsorganisation unter Stein und Hardenberg*, pp. 87-93.

61. Dorn (162) pp. 263-64, seems to be of the conviction that the economic motive was foremost in leading Junker sons to enter a purely bureaucratic career, as contrasted with local, honorary offices. He points out that, due to the small incomes from their estates, the Junkers and their sons usually had to "eke out their incomes by some form of public employment." Demeter (59) pp. 65-66, also implies that it was economic need which led younger sons to enlist in the Officers Corps and he maintains, with substantiating evidence from the *Geheimes preussisches Staatsarchiv*, that the degree of the Junkers' participation in administrative offices was directly related to the size of their estates.

of the army and the government certainly offered a strong attraction to the Junkers. Their old presupposition that they were the rightful civil and military advisors of the prince made this partnership natural for them and the policy and predilection of the Hohenzollerns gave them their opportunity.

By the time of Frederick II we may even add that the process of education in the royal service which the landed nobles had been undergoing since the days of Frederick William I, in addition to instilling devotion to the sovereign, was already producing a social tradition which made military and government service a noble profession.

As in the Officers Corps the Junker in the bureaucracy had to pass thru a prescribed course of training in order to receive an appointment. This consisted of a period of apprenticeship in the Chambers of War and Domains and on the royal domains and of one or two regular examinations.[62] Altho practical in nature this bureaucratic education was such as to break down the refractory spirit of the Junker and make him an obedient servant of the State, responsive to the commands of his sovereign.

THE 19TH CENTURY

Under Frederick II, or perhaps rather under Frederick William II who lacked the will and energy to bridle their ambitions, the Junkers enjoyed a maximum of privilege and preferment with all the power and influence which flowed therefrom. But the French Revolution and the 19th century carried them forward into an age of liberalism which challenged their feudal concepts and undermined their position. This challenge and threat brought forth new traits in their character as well as accentuating many older ones. These changes result almost entirely from the fact that the Junker was placed on the defensive by the advance of the philosophy and practice of liberalism and of individual liberty and equality. New forces of nationalism, constitutionalism and representative government, industrial capitalism and a rising middle class, materialism and the predominance of the profit motive—all these destroyed the Junker's sense of security

62. Clemens von Delbrueck (58) *Die Ausbildung fuer den hoeheren Verwaltungsdienst in Preussen*, pp. 2-6.

and threatened to eliminate him entirely as a social type and a political power. He could no longer afford to be lofty and complacent, assured of his position as a member of the privileged Estate. Now he was forced down into the arena to compete economically, professionally and politically with the rising middle class and to struggle for his very survival.

In the course of this struggle which became more intense and bitter as the position of the landed nobles grew weaker, the Junker became increasingly ruthless, aggressive and self-seeking.[63] A new note of shrillness and frantic insistence entered into his clamourings for special attention. He put his own preservation as the first *raison d'etat*. Economic competition and the precariousness of his material existence caused him to turn away from his old feudal and patriarchal principles and to become more materialistic, even bourgeois in his point of view. The very transformation of society from a historic caste system into a society based on wealth in itself had forced him into free competition and a materialistic attitude.

Beset with the dangers of an inimical age of liberalism the Junkers welcomed romanticism not only as an escape from harsh realities but also because in many ways it sustained and promoted those feudal ideals from whence they drew their strength. But romanticism did not provide aid and refuge for long and the hard-pressed Junkers resorted, at first slowly but more rapidly after the rise of Bismarck, to the methods and practices of their rivals, the bourgeois capitalist and politician. Thru their willingness, however reluctant, to adapt themselves to the changes of the times and to modernize their aims and their activities they were able to rejuvenate their caste and give it strength to resist the alien forces assailing it. In fact we have cause to be astonished, not that the Junkers were losing ground in an age of liberalism but rather that they offered such stout resistance and that they were able in such a large measure to maintain their position and power.

The basic legal privileges of the landed nobility were taken away from them at the outset of the 19th century by the reforms both of vom Stein, who tried as he modernized the State to conserve as much

63. Preuss (109) p. 5.

as possible of Prussia's historical character, and of the doctrinaire liberal, von Hardenberg. The emancipation of the serfs in 1807 partly destroyed the Junker's patrimonial rights over his tenant-laborers. The freeing of landholding and manufacture from all class and residence restrictions, the recruiting of a citizen's army and the introduction of the principle of equal citizenship reduced him, in theory at least, to a position of legal equality. Furthermore, his administrative jurisdiction over the residents on his estate and in the neighboring village was whittled away during the 19th century. At first the Junkers were able to keep local self-government on a feudal basis and to perpeutate their supremacy as an Estate. Indeed, they were even able to gain control over the Provincial Diets which were reestablished in 1823. But the restored Diets which met in one chamber including bourgeois landowners, city property owners and peasants and which had jurisdiction only over strictly provincial affairs, limited the scope of the Junkers' political action. By mid-century they began to suffer a definite curtailment of their administrative power. In 1848 they lost the right of patrimonial justice over their estates and villages and by the Circle regulation (*Kreisordnung*) of 1872 they were forced to surrender the right to police their estates and villages and to appoint the village magistrates and oversee the general administration of the village or *Landgemeinde*.[64] The village regulation (*Landgemeindeordnung*) of 1891 went so far as to provide for the consolidation of village and estate under the administrative jurisdiction *of the village*—a complete reversal of the situation at the opening of the century. But the Junkers were able to make this law meaningless by inserting the provision that the vote to consolidate must take place in the Circle Assembly which they generally controlled themselves. Moreover, the Junkers were able for the most part to offset these inroads into their privileged legal and administrative position by their continued economic and social supremacy and power. Altho losing ground before the law they continued in practice to dominate their local sphere.[65] Their ability to command and rule and their self-confident assumption of authority were impaired little if at all by these changes.

64. Bornhak (52) v. 2, p. 187.
65. Preuss (109) p. 103.

Altho the economic position of the Junkers as large-scale farmers also deteriorated during the 19th century it nonetheless remained strong enough to sustain their local political influence and social supremacy. Furthermore, their economic decline did not set in until late in the century. It is not surprising that Hardenberg's agrarian reforms which were based on the principle of free economic enterprise had the effect of increasing the scope and strength of the Junkers' large-scale capitalistic farms at the expense of the peasants.[66] The "Regulation"[67] of peasant lands gave the noble landlord an opportunity to bring more land under his direct control or to assure himself of a cheap labor supply, or both. He could acquire one-third or one-half of the lands of the "regulated" peasants and then buy up the rest when as free peasant proprietors they got into economic straits. Thus Junker estates did not reach their full size and compactness until the 19th century.[68] The squire was able by these policies to reduce part of the peasant landholders to the status of landless day laborers. On the other hand he could refuse to turn over any land to the cotters and force them to continue to render labor service in return for their holdings. The Junker landlord was now freed from the prohibition against the annexation of peasant lands, introduced by Frederick II, and from his obligations to care for the health and well-being of his laborers. Altho many Junkers continued to show a patriarchal benevolence and solicitude for the families that lived on their lands some could not resist the temptation to take advantage of these new opportunities to add to their profits at the expense of their workers.[69] This·tendency grew as the century advanced and the competition became keener.

66. Franz Schnabel (117) *Deutsche Geschichte im Neunzehnten Jahrhundert,* v. 3, p. 277. ". . . so hatte doch die Stein-Hardenbergische Reform, so sehr sie die politische und soziale Vorherrschaft des Adels einschraenkte, diesem auf wirtschaftlichem Gebiete eine staerkere Bewegungsfreiheit verschafft als er sie vorher besessen hatte."

67. "Regulation" was the system devised for establishing the peasant's title of ownership to land held in customary usufructuary tenure at the cost to the peasant of one-third to one-half of that land. The land taken from the peasant was added to the landlord's estate.

68. Hintze (167) *Hist. Z.,* 1914, p. 499.

69. Ford (66) pp. 192-93, says, "The picture of conditions on the private estates east of the Elbe is that of an advancing, increasingly profitable, large scale capitalistic agriculture with an economically and socially declining agricultural laboring class."

The opening of rural land-ownership to the middle class and the eager adoption by the Junkers of free, rationalized, large-scale, capitalistic agriculture put them at the mercy of unrestricted competition and the hazards of world prices and liquid capital. Landed property passed with increasing frequency into the hands of bourgeois merchants and industrialists who craved to own country estates for social as well as economic reasons. The Junker, for his part, was often forced by his need for cash to mortgage or sell one or more of his estates. Gradually bourgeois landowners filtered into the Junkers' own domain until by the end of the century only one-third of the owners of knights' estates (*Rittergutsbesitzer*) in the six provinces east of the Elbe were still nobles.[70]

With the advance of modern capitalism and industrialism in eastern Prussia the Junker had a growing need for ready money to buy his supplies, introduce new crops, set up sugar refineries and other mills, etc. His wife and daughters also wanted cash so that they could dress and conduct their household more luxuriously in order that they might compete with the increasing opulence of the bourgeoisie and show by their manner of life as well as their title that they were socially superior. In his need for cash the noble landowner occasionally went so far as to marry his sons to bourgeois, sometimes even to Jewish, heiresses of industrial fortunes. His commercial and financial interests created bonds between him and wealthy middle class or ennobled manufacturers. In spite of his social scorn for the parvenu, the Junker responded to a growing political affinity for the industrial magnates, because of their common hatred and fear of the Social Democrats. The noble farmer's effort to reap benefits for himself from the industrial revolution by setting up distilleries, breweries and beet sugar refineries on his own estates strengthened this community of interests. Subtly the Junkers were being indoctrinated with bourgeois and materialistic attitudes but at the same time they were drawing some middle class families into the circle of Junker influence.

It was not until the collapse of the agricultural price structure in the late 1870's, however, that the Junkers' declining economic posi-

70. Johannes Conrad (127) "Die Latifundien im preussischen Osten," *Jb. f. Nationaloek. u. Stat.*, 1888, pp. 138-41.

tion became desperate. It was the disintegration of their economic security and the spectre of insolvency and the loss of all their lands which, in my opinion, brought forth or intensified the Junker's aggressiveness, his narrow selfishness and his materialism. Whether convinced that the survival of his caste was essential for the welfare of Prussia or simply humanly selfish and anxious to hold on to his favorable place in society, the Junker became determined to fight with any means to defend his position. He took to exploiting his labor more cruelly and relentlessly than heretofore. The old social bonds between landowner and agricultural worker disintegrated as the former became more and more interested in the cheapness and seasonal availability of his laborers and less and less in their physical and spiritual well-being. German workers moved to the west or to the cities where they hoped to find more freedom and more regard for human dignity,[71] but this drain on the agricultural labor supply did not concern the Junkers as greatly as it would have done in earlier times, for they were now willing and able to solve their perennial labor problem by the importation of cheap migratory workers from Russian Poland. These were available in inexhaustible numbers and did not require even that modicum of decent consideration which the landowners still felt obliged to show regular German workers. The scramble for profits, or even for solvency, and the introduction of foreign seasonal laborers hastened the dissolution of the social solidarity of the *Gutsherrschaft*. Altho some old-fashioned Junkers retained their traditional sense of responsibility for the welfare of their dependents and a warm-hearted fatherly interest in their affairs, for the most part the Junkers tended to lose or disregard their characteristic patriarchal solicitude and their sense of *noblesse oblige*. By encouraging the immigration of Polish workers they were even willing to put economic gain above their strong Prussianism.

The Junkers also made every effort to exploit their political power and influence in order to protect and rehabilitate their economic position, without which their political power could not long endure.[72]

71. Max Weber (155) "Der Nationalstaat und die Volkswirtschaftspolitik," *Gesammelte politische Schriften*, pp. 8-15.
72. Preuss (109) p. 7. "So schritt still und allmaehlich der wirtschaftliche Niedergang des Junkers fort; und in absehbarer Zeit faende von hier aus auch das politische Problem seine natuerliche Loesung, wenn nicht in der zwoelften Stunde

Instead of at least attempting to put their estates on a solvent basis by reforming their agricultural methods and reorganizing their estates they turned to their old patron, the King, and to political agitation for legislative aid to protect them at the expense of the rest of the nation.[73] They wanted to use their inherited influence and that unique strength which they still possessed as an anachronistic feudal class in order to protect their modern capitalistic agrarian economy.

The Junkers' political power and influence had survived the vicissitudes of a liberal age better than their legal or economic position. This was due in part to their willingness and ability to adjust their aims and methods to the advance of the century. The threat to their political supremacy inherent in the reforms of both Stein and Hardenberg did not fully materialize, for the victories of 1813-1815 made possible the general restoration of the principle of absolute monarchy and encouraged Frederick William III to resist political and constitutional reforms and to reaffirm the old partnership between the Crown and the landed nobility. Altho the King retained his absolutist convictions and authority and altho he treated the bureaucratic officials, some of whom like Motz and Maassen were liberals and bourgeois, as his royal servants, he felt the necessity of renewing the bonds with the Junkers because he, too, feared the rising bourgeois tide with its threat of revolution and freedom. He saw in the nobility, whose position was also threatened, the only class on which he could depend for the support of the monarchical principle. In return for support against bourgeois liberalism the King gave the Junkers preferment in the bureaucracy and in the Officers Corps and heeded their demands for greater influence in local affairs. Despite the pressure of the rapidly growing middle class the Junkers were able to restore their position in the Officers Corps from a bare majority in 1819 to one of predominance by 1848.[74] In the bureaucracy sons from Junker families or from the newer service nobility served the Crown conscientiously and selflessly but with pride in their office. The Junker

---

das Junkerthum den Versuch unternommen haette, seine noch behauptete politische Position zur Wiederaufrichtung seiner wirtschaftlichen Stellung auszunuetzen."

73. Eckart Kehr (87) *Schlachtflottenbau und Parteipolitik, 1894-1901,* pp. 247-77, *passim.*

74. Demeter (59) pp. 17-20.

element fused the two services and gave a military coloring to all departments of State activity.[75]

The preservation of the old alliance between the Crown and the landed nobility perpetuated and intensified the Junkers' loyalty and devotion to the throne until they claimed to be "monarchical to the marrow of their bones." But the relationship was not nor had it ever been entirely harmonious and the Junkers still maintained an independent and obstructive attitude as well. They objected to Frederick William III's use of the bureaucracy as a tool of absolutism.[76] Even if its personnel included a large aristocratic element, a bureaucracy loyally serving an absolute monarch was the enemy of the old feudal, patriarchal and particularistic regime of which the Junkers still dreamed. They took up the battle against both a rationalistic bureaucracy and a liberal democracy. Their loyalty was neither to these nor to any form of modern national and constitutional State but to their romantic ideal of a Christian-Germanic State with a patriarchal and feudal monarchy. They combined the Legitimism of political Romanticism with a pietistic and authoritarian Protestantism.

The Junkers had always been ardently Protestant.[77] Most of them had adopted the Lutheran belief early in the Reformation period. Some few such as the Dohnas became Calvinists and these were delighted when the Elector Johann Sigismund was converted from the Lutheran to the Reformed Church in 1613. The union of these two churches in a State-ruled Evangelical Church (*Evangelische Kirche Altpreussischer Union*) by Frederick William III in 1817 antagonized the pious and tradition-bound old Lutheran nobles, particularly in Pomerania.[78] Frederick William IV's cloudy romanticism and mysticism was much more congenial to their pietism and their patriarchal feelings of authority and social responsibility. Gradually

---

75. Schnabel (117) v. 2, pp. 303-04.
76. *Ibid.*, p. 34; Schweinitz (39) v. 1, p. 7; Walter Schmidt (115) *Die Partei Bethmann-Hollweg . . .*, pp. 29-30.
77. See Tante Adelheid's outburst against the Catholics in Theodor Fontane (65) *Der Stechlin*, p. 98; also Elard von Oldenburg-Januschau (37) *Erinnerungen*, p. 28. F. von Schulte (150) "Adel im deutschen Offizier- und Beamtenstand." *Deutsche Revue*, 1896, states that there were scarcely 300 Catholic officers in the Prussian army in 1895.
78. Schnabel (117) v. 4, pp. 346-47.

most of them came over to loyal and devoted support of the Evangelical Church and they frequently held office in its Consistories or administrative bodies. Their great piety made them faithful churchgoers. Furthermore, the rise of the liberal movement with its threat of revolution brought forth an alliance between Church and large landholders whereby each used its influence to strengthen the worldly position and authority of the other.[79]

The experience of the Revolution of 1848 served to strengthen the Junkers in their old Prussian corporate, Evangelical convictions and to tie them more closely to the dynasty in their role of sole supporters and protectors of the Crown. While the political situation was confused and fluctuating the Junkers took the initiative, met in the famous *Junkerparlament* and offered their advice and services to the King in defense of the monarchy. They formed a Conservative political organization later known as the *Kreuzzeitungspartei*. For the first time country squires from the farthest corners of Pomerania and the Mark felt obliged to play an active role in politics to protect their King and their political ideals and social and economic institutions.[80] Henceforth they resorted more and more to the wiles, the calculating shrewdness and the aggressive insistence of the politician.

Frederick William's grant of a written constitution providing for a representative assembly, the Prussian Diet, with an elected lower house and a property franchise increased the Junkers' need for political organization and action. Manifestly the introduction of modern limitations on the power of the King and a franchise based on qualifications of wealth was a serious blow to the political power of the feudal landed gentry and they were forced to resort to modern political tactics to defend themselves. They could measure their immediate success by the fact that the three-class electoral law of 1849 assured them a large representation in the House of Deputies (*Abgeordnetenhaus*) whereas the final composition of the *Herrenhaus*, or upper

---

79. Erich Jordan (85) *Die Entstehung der konservativen Partei* . . . , pp. 187-88; H. Rauh (147) "Die Landarbeiterfrage und die evangelische Geistlichkeit in Ostelbien." *Soziale Praxis*, 1895, pp. 1008-09.

80. Schmidt (115) pp. 25-26. That they entered politics unwillingly is implied by Gerhard Ritter (112) *Die preussischen Konservativen* . . . , p. 366, when he speaks of the "junkerliche und pietistische Abneigung gegen die politische Taetigkeit ueberhaupt."

house, provided for a large bloc of Life Members elected by the old landed gentry of eastern Prussia, i.e. by themselves.[81]

The decade of 1850 to 1860 when the Gerlach camarilla controlled King and Ministry was the Indian summer of the old Junker imbued with feudal, pietistic and patriarchal ideals. After 1862 Otto von Bismarck, who himself came from this Junker circle, was to carry the Junkers forward into a new age of realism and power politics where reasons of State would replace ideals of monarchical legitimism and universal conservatism. A few doctrinaire reactionaries remained irreconcilable but these fell by the wayside.[82] The greater part of the Junkers were won over by Bismarck to a political philosophy of calculating realism and nationalism. Some joined the new Free Conservative party, founded in 1866, which supported Bismarck *sans phrase*. Most of them did not go so far as Bismarck in extending their patriotism beyond Prussia to the German Empire. They supported the Empire because of Prussia's primacy in it and they were jealous of any increase in Germany's strength at the expense of Prussia. These Junkers remained with the Conservative or *Kreuzzeitungspartei* but they transformed it, particularly under such men as von Helldorf-Bedra who was a close collaborator with Bismarck, into a modern agrarian party dedicated to the protection of agriculture and the promotion of Prussian greatness thru the Empire.[83]

The Junkers' way to support of Bismarck and the Empire was made easier for them by the fact that Bismarck's victories, particularly his great military victories, were also a triumph for the Junkers. It was an army led in large measure by Junker officers which defeated the Austrians and the French. Altho the old Prussian element in the Officers Corps had been diluted because the supply of Junker candidates no longer met the need after the army increase in 1860 and because of the incorporation of other provinces in 1866[84] the old Junker feudal spirit still prevailed. The victories of 1866 and 1871 served to foster and strengthen the military character of the Junker caste. Moreover, they drove the military spirit deep into bourgeois

81. Hermann Crueger (56) *Chronik des preussischen Herrenhauses*, p. 18.
82. The Austro-Prussian War dealt the last blow to Ludwig von Gerlach's political influence. See Ritter (112) p. 190.
83. *Ibid.*, p. 377; Heinrich Heffter (74) *Die Kreuzzeitungspartei* . . . , pp. 3-5.
84. Demeter (59) p. 23 ff.

circles.[85] In fact, both Bismarck's encouragement of militarism in Prussia and his conservative solution of the German problem helped the Junkers to extend their attitudes and principles down into the middle class and to draw large numbers of the bourgeoisie over to their own political and social point of view. This process of "feudalizing" the bourgeoisie proved to be the most effective way of meeting middle class competition and preserving the Junker character.

The Junkers also retained their tradition of service and their favorable position in the civil administration under Bismarck. He had inherited the old Conservative noble officials appointed by Manteuffel and Westphalen. Altho he often disapproved of their reactionary attitude he kept them in office[86] because he recognized that their devotion to the Crown, their energy and their incomparable knowledge of government acquired thru years of service made them indispensable. Few Junkers, however, were appointed to the newer branches of the administration, such as the social agencies, which were added by Bismarck himself.

It was the collapse of agricultural prices in the 1870's and the deterioration of Prussian political life after the dismissal of Bismarck in 1890 which made the Junkers as a group thoroughly self-centered and materialistic in their political aims. Fearing economic extinction, they clamoured and pressed for the special protection of agrarian interests during the last decade of Bismarck's rule and were able to get favorable tariff rates on agricultural products. In the years immediately following Bismarck's dismissal it seemed as if the New Course, Caprivi's liberal commercial policy and the Christian Socialist element in the Conservative party would crowd the Junker agrarians out of power. But Caprivi's tariff and commercial treaties so angered and frightened the agrarians that they roused them to desperate and aggressive measures. In 1893 the large landholders formed the *Bund der Landwirte* or Agrarian League. Its purpose was to unite all their agricultural interests, draw small farmers and peasants into their orbit and act as a pressure group in the Reichstag. Indeed, the Junkers in the Agrarian League did not shrink from the most blatant demagogic practices in order to win votes while at the same time damning the

85. F. Toennies (180) "Deutscher Adel im 19. Jahrhundert," *Neue Rundschau,* 1912, p. 1058.
86. Ritter (112) p. 73.

Social Democrats for rabble-rousing. The hard pressed agrarians were soon able to dominate the Conservative party thru the Agrarian League and they resorted to every kind of political manoeuvre on the floor or in the lobby of both Reichstag and Prussian Diet to promote their own political program. It was now apparent that the Junkers had been, by force of circumstance, slowly and subtly infected by the elective and parliamentary system. They had found themselves obliged to act along party lines and think in terms of parliamentary majorities in spite of their continued vehement denouncements of the parliamentary system, their personal aversion to a parliamentary career and their insistence upon a personal regime in which, of course, they would be the favored advisers of the King and Emperor.[87] Thus the party of principle under Gerlach had become a party of interests under Heydebrand and the Agrarian League. Even the realistic devotion to *Staatsraison* which had been inculcated by Bismarck had given way in many instances to purely selfish motives. Of course, not all Junkers were equally ruthless in their calculating exploitation of the political situation to their own particular advantage. Some Junkers were aggressive, militant, ambitious for themselves and their class. These men, along with a group of bourgeois landowners and journalists, formed the leadership of the Conservative party and were the conspicuous objects of attack by the liberal and socialist spokesmen. The old-fashioned rustic squire was for the most part passive in political life and still idealistic in political motives. In addition to his instinct for self-preservation he was filled with a naive devotion to his sovereign and an equally naive conviction that the continued existence of his class of old landed, military and farming aristocrats was absolutely essential to the welfare of the Prussian State. Hence he was a Conservative and could be depended upon to support the Conservatives whenever he was called upon to act. Otherwise he stayed at home and awaited instructions from the party's district leader. He directed the cultivation of his estate, hunted, attended his

87. These sentiments are best expressed by von Oldenburg-Januschau (37) pp. 60, 65, who says, "Wir stehen zu einer starken koeniglichen Regierung und verzichten bereitwilligst auf eine Parlamentsherrschaft mit ihren wechselnden Anschauungen. Damit haben wir eine sichere Basis im Leben und im Sterben"; "Holt Euch endlich einen anderen Schafskopf, der Frau und Kinder, Haus und Wirtschaft verlaesst, um leeres Stroh zu dreschen. Ich passe gar nicht in das Parlament. Wie viel Ferkel eine Sau in Januschau bekommt, interessiert mich mehr als die geistreichste Rede des Abgeordneten Richter."

parish church and sent his sons into the Officers Corps and the administrative service much as his forefathers had done.

SUMMARY OF JUNKER CHARACTERISTICS

All of the foregoing historical developments and many more of lesser importance had made their contribution to the character of the Junker as he appeared under the last of the Hohenzollerns. To recapitulate briefly, the old, original Junkers belonged to the lesser nobility as distinguished from the great nobles and Princes of Prussia. They were the landed gentry of Prussia's eastern provinces. Of these Pomerania with its remote stretches of rural country was the homeland of the genuine, old-fashioned Junker. Brandenburg, the Altmark and West Prussia were only slightly less favored. Silesia altho not annexed until 1742 and inhabited by many *grands seigneurs* and industrial magnates had a large number of small, poor, socially self-conscious and politically active Junkers whereas the East Prussian nobles were traditionally unco-operative and liberally inclined, at least down to 1848.[88]

In general the Junkers owned only small estates; they were not great landed magnates and did not possess the latifundia. Their small landholdings together with their frequently antiquated and unprogressive agricultural methods produced only moderate incomes which were often insufficient for the support of their large families.

88. In Theodor Fontane (65) *Der Stechlin,* pp. 188-89, Tante Adelheid characterizes the various Prussian provinces as follows: "Schon unsere Provinzen sind so verschieden. . . . Was ich Adel nenne, das gibt es nur noch in unsrer Mark und in unsrer alten Nachbar- und Schwesterprovinz [Pomerania], ja, da vielleicht noch reiner als bei uns. . . . Da sind zum Beispiel die rheinischen jungen Damen, also die von Koeln und Aachen; nun ja, die moegen ganz gut sein, aber sie sind katholisch, und wenn sie nicht katholisch sind, dann sind sie was anders, wo der Vater erst geadelt wurde. Neben den rheinischen haben wir dann die westfaelischen. Ueber die liesse sich reden. Aber Schlesien. Die schlesischen Herrschaften, die sich mitunter auch Magnaten nennen, sind alle so gut wie polnisch und leben vom Jeu und haben die huebschesten Erzieherinnen; immer ganz jung, da macht es sich am leichtesten. Und dann sind da noch weiterhin die preussischen, das heisst die ost-preussischen, wo schon alles aufhoert. Nun die kenn ich, die sind ganz wie ihre Litauer Fuellen und schlagen aus und beknabbern alles. Und je reicher sie sind, desto schlimmer. . . . warum ich . . . so sehr fuer unsre Mark bin, ja speziell fuer unsre Mittelmark. . . . Und dann haben wir hie noch zweierlei: in unserer Bevoelkerung die reine Lehre und in unserm Adel das reine Blut. . . . Einige meinen freilich, das, was sie das 'Geistige' nennen, das litte darunter. Das ist aber alles Torheit. Und wenn es litte (es leidet aber nicht) so schadet das gar nichts. Wenn das Herz gesund ist, ist der Kopf nie ganz schlecht."

Frugality was a common characteristic of the landed gentry, who, however, had no need to bolster their social position by lavish expenditures. Von Schweinitz once said, perhaps bitterly, that "Noblemen, that is to say poor officers' sons, are accustomed to privations from their childhood on."[89]

The Junkers were strongly conscious of their hereditary privileged social position and it was their most fundamental principle to fight to conserve in all its aspects a social order of which they were the chief beneficiaries. They drew from their deep Protestant faith the conviction that the existing order was God-ordained and that the priority of the oldest was according to God's law.

Because of their strong pride in their position Junkers were careful to marry neither above their class nor below it unless driven by ulterior considerations. They also took care to enter only those professions which they had come to consider as worthy of their estate, that is to say, agriculture, the army and the administration. Of the two services the military was preferred because of the knightly tradition, the historic military glories of Prussia, the social prestige of the military caste and other reasons which will be discussed later. The Junkers were definitely a military as well as a farming aristocracy.

The work of directing their farms, combined with meagre incomes, kept the Junkers on their estates. Hence they remained a rural, sometimes even a rustic nobility. They had little opportunity or inclination to travel but they went to one or another estate in the neighborhood and visited among themselves.[90] This sociability resulted quite naturally in frequent intermarriages between the Junker families of each district and province. The Junker's rusticity may account in part for his intellectual backwardness and his lack of cultural interests. Altho intelligent and quick at native repartee the Junkers had no time or interest for arts and letters or for cosmopolitan social amenities. With a few conspicuous exceptions, they were not interested in education except for the military or bureaucratic careers. For the most part they were prosaic and practical, suspicious of innovations

89. Quoted by Demeter (59) p. 21.
90. Erich Marcks (96) *Bismarcks Jugend, 1815-1848,* pp. 185-86, describes the social life of the Junkers in the 1840's: ". . . sie kamen in den Staedten, wie Plathe oder Greifenberg, in den Badeorten, wie Polzin, den kleinen Seebaedern, den groesseren Garnisonen zusammen, da gab es Kraenzchen, Baelle, Quadrillen, Auffuehrungen. Vor allem man traf sich auf den Guetern selbst. . . ."

and of intellectual abstractions or aesthetic pleasures.[91] Living apart
from the world's great social centres, they lacked the urbanity and
cosmopolitan sophistication of the higher aristocracy.

By his continued active participation in the direction of his estate
and by his combination of modern, large-scale commercial agriculture
with a feudalistic social order the Junker was able to preserve his
feeling of authority, mastery and self-assurance within his immediate
sphere. He thoroughly enjoyed the dominion over his laborers and
tenants which custom and economic power still left in his hands.
In the past this tradition to command had generally carried with
it a sense of responsibility for those living under the jurisdiction of
the *Gutsherrschaft*, but by the end of the 19th century the Junkers,
with the exception of a few old-fashioned patriarchs, had surrendered
their sense of obligation to their lust for profits or their eagerness
to survive at all. There was no longer any economic necessity for
them to protect the health and strength of their workers now that
they were landless wage earners and seasonal laborers.

The old habit of ruling and the sense of command essential to the
Junker was also kept alive by his retention of a controlling influence
over the self-government of his Circle and province. Here he could
still keep his feeling of independence and of a feudal share in the
sovereignty. Moreover, by taking up political activities, thru force
of necessity, and by entering into party politics he was again able
to exert great influence at the centre of the State as well. He was
often able to win his election from his home district to the Prussian
Diet, particularly if he was the local *Landrat*. The Junker, with his
landed estate, his rustic sociability, his wide administrative and
judicial authority within his district, should he be *Landrat*, and his
seat in the Prussian Diet is strikingly like the English country squire
of the 18th century who was appointed Justice of the Peace by the
Crown and sent up to Parliament at the County elections. Of
course, the English squire and Justice of the Peace had a broader
and more progressive social and political viewpoint. He had aban-
doned his feudal concepts to a much greater degree than the Junker
even of the 20th century. Nonetheless there remains a close historical
parallel between the character and background of the English squire
and the Prussian Junker and between the frequent election of one

91. Theodor Fontane (64) *Briefe an seine Familie,* p. 211.

to the English Parliament and of the other to the Prussian Diet.

The Junker felt independent and self-sufficient in his own district and in the Diet and he did not hesitate to offer vigorous and stubborn opposition to the Government wherever his principles and his interests were involved.[92] On the other hand, his long schooling in the army and the bureaucracy[93] had made him a loyal and devoted supporter of the monarchy. Because of this fundamental characteristic of loyalty to the Crown the Junker and his Conservative party could never go over permanently to the parliamentary Opposition.

Within the soul of each genuine Junker there was ever present a sense of tension between a feeling of loyal and pious obedience to the monarch and a spirit of independence which put loyalty to ideals and honor above the commands of the monarch[94] and which inspired Bismarck to say with satisfaction that he could always retire "behind the cannons of Schoenhausen."[95] Sometimes one and then the other feeling would gain ascendency within a single man, causing contradictory actions. Sometimes he would be increasingly motivated by one tendency alone. But the Junker was always concerned, consciously or unconsciously, with the resolution of this inner conflict between his independent nature and his monarchical loyalties.

These various qualities were characteristic of the Junker prototype, the central stock of the Prussian lower nobility. But within the whole group of nobles, known as Junkers, who conformed to the same general sociological pattern and who were motivated by the same political, economic and social aspirations there were many variations from the pure original Junker type. During the course of centuries a great many noble families of different origins had been assimilated into the Junker class as the consequence either of an unconscious affinity or of conscious imitation. Indeed in the 19th century a good many bourgeois families had adopted the Junker outlook and Junker

---

92. Theodor Fontane, who was a faithful observer of Junker life, writes (65) *Der Stechlin,* p. 243, "Und der alte Dubslav, nun, der hat dafuer das im Leibe, was die richtigen Junker alle haben: ein Stueck Sozialdemokratie. Wenn sie gereizt werden bekennen sie sich selber dazu."

93. It is also clear that positions of authority in both of these services also gave the Junker opportunity to express his propensity to command and dispose.

94. Fontane (65) p. 122, has old Dubslav say that the real aristocrats, "die gehorchen nicht einem Machthaber sondern dem Gefuehl ihrer Pflicht."

95. From a letter of Bismarck to his sister, November 12, 1858, *Bismarckbriefe, 1836-1872* (21), p. 167.

ideals and attached themselves to the fringe of the Junker group, partly thru personal ambition, partly as a result of the "feudalization" of the middle class by the Junkers. At the same time the Junker group had lost families both to the higher nobility and to the middle class.

The greatest addition to the ranks of the landed gentry came from the nobility of service. Many of the original Junkers themselves had been royal ministers who had received grants of land. From the earliest settlements in the Mark right down to the fall of the Hohenzollerns large numbers of royal officials received patents of nobility, acquired estates in the eastern provinces and sometimes retired from active service to devote themselves to farming. They married into neighboring Junker families and sent their sons back into the Officers Corps or the civil administration. The custom acquired by the old Junkers in the 18th century of sending their sons into government service contributed to the rapid assimilation of the new service nobility by the old landed gentry. Even families of officials ennobled as late as the 1880's identified themselves rapidly with the Junker group.

The acquisition by Prussia of new territory in the east, particularly of Silesia, brought great additions to the ranks of the Junkers. Old Silesian noble families of Protestant faith and with small landholdings who rapidly found positions in the Prussian army and administration and whose sons brought home wives from Brandenburg or Pomerania are surely to be considered as members of the Junker group.[96] The annexation of West Prussia and Posen created the problem of the assimilation of the Polish landed nobility in these areas. Some Polish nobles of Catholic faith and strong national sentiment remained the enemies of Prussia and the Junkers but others, particularly the Protestants, entered the Prussian service and the Conservative party and acquired a real Junker outlook.

There was always an influx into the Junker group from single families or branches of families who moved in from the west or from

---

96. Johannes Ziekursch (124) *Hundert Jahre schlesischer Agrargeschichte*, p. 389, described the sociological complexion of Silesia at the end of the 19th century as follows: "Der Kleinadel beherrscht also noch immer den groessten Teil der fruchtbaren Oderebene; laengs des Gebirges und in Polnischschlesien ueberwiegen dagegen . . . die buergerliche Elemente. Ueber ihnen stehen aber in jenen Gegenden die alten Familien mit dem ausgedehnten Latifundienbesitz."

Mecklenburg, Denmark and Sweden and took up land in the East Elbian provinces.

At the same time the Junkers were losing members to other social groups. Some by the acquisition of wealth and property had become *grands seigneurs* and moved into the circle of the affluent, independent and cosmopolitan higher nobility. Some members of the old Alvensleben and Schulenburg families, for instance, typical old Junker stock who had plagued the Great Elector and Frederick William I, had added to their holdings and become great magnates. On the other hand some Junkers had, in outlook and living habits at least, sunk into the bourgeoisie. The poor country squire by his unreserved acceptance of a capitalistic competitive economy and his daily struggle for his livelihood had gradually acquired certain bourgeois characteristics. Also the bureaucratic official and, somewhat less so, the poor army officer who had inherited no property and lost touch with the land and who had devoted his life exclusively to his government career had drawn away from the landed gentry toward a bureaucratic and a colorless or even a bourgeois social outlook.[97]

It is therefore clear that there are wide variations within the larger social group comprising all those with Junker characteristics and ideology. In order to estimate the full significance of the Junker caste as a unique sociological group and as a power in Prussian politics it is necessary to take into account not only members of pure old Junker origin but also all those who have been early or more recently absorbed into the Junker tradition and who in crucial social and political questions could be expected to act as if they were Junkers. Since the purpose is to estimate the extent of the Junker's potential political influence in the administration and to do this in part quantitatively by reckoning the proportion of Junkers in the various departments of the Prussian administration between 1888 and 1914 it seemed the right procedure to include among those

97. Max Weber (157) "Wahlrecht und Demokratie im Deutschland," *Gesammelte politische Schriften,* p. 309, insists that the families of the poorly paid officials, whether aristocratic or not, are "oekonomisch und sozial ebenso wie nach ihrem Horizont ein buergerlicher Mittelstand." Ernst Kohn-Bramstedt (90) *Aristocracy and the Middle Classes in Germany,* p. 23, who recognizes the many differentiations within the aristocracy says that the widest gap is between the noble who could live on the income from his landed property and the noble who was obliged to live on a professional income.

counted as Junker officials these accretions to the central stock. In all, 668 families have been counted as Junker for the purposes of this study and these have been divided into several classifications. The families of original Junker stock include all those who were ennobled and held property in the seven eastern provinces before the beginning of the 18th century. The next group is composed of those who were absorbed into the Junker tradition before the 19th century. This includes all the Silesian nobles reckoned as Junkers and many others who were ennobled or moved into the East Elbian area before 1815 and acquired estates there. The third large category consists of those who attached themselves to the Junker stock during the 19th century. These are mostly members of the service nobility, some of whom acquired estates in the east, others of whom became Junker-like thru faithful service to the Prussian State. Two smaller groups are composed of those families who were originally Junkers but had grown above their class and those Polish nobles who had become assimilated with the Junkers. In these last groups there are a number of borderline cases. In many instances a family's Junker qualities were almost evenly balanced by non-Junker characteristics and the decision whether to include or exclude the family was extremely difficult and in the end arbitrary. The test criteria used were: ennoblement by 1888, property in the seven eastern provinces but no great wealth, Protestant faith, no close relationship with the western German, Saxon or Mecklenburg aristocracy,[98] custom of service in the Prussian army and administration and no middle class occupations, marriage into old Junker families, membership in the Conservative party. Care was taken to be as generous as possible in the inclusion of families in these groups so that all those nobles who could possibly be expected to react as Junkers in administrative and political questions would be included in the computation of totals and ratios. The 668 Junker families connected with the administration in our period present, therefore, a wide range of Junker types. It is the officials from these families who have been examined, compared and counted in the following pages.

98. I have not included the von Buelow family among the Junkers because they originated in Mecklenburg and in our period by far the greater part of the family was resident either in Mecklenburg or in Schleswig-Holstein. Moreover, they seemed to be too cosmopolitan to be classed as Junkers. There is also the fact that some branches of the family had become Catholic.

II

TYPES OF CAREERS OF JUNKER OFFICIALS

THE Junker, with his affiliated groups, emerges from his historical background as a distinct social type, one often and explicitly recognized by his contemporaries in the period from 1888 to the outbreak of the war. His close association with the Prussian administration, which originated in the 18th century and had become a strong tradition as well as a useful political expedient in the post-Bismarckian era was, as we have seen, one of his important characteristics and one which contributed much to the importance of the Junker as a social factor in German politics. It is well, therefore, to consider in detail the relationship between the Junker, with his peculiar social background and habits, and officeholding on the basis of the case histories of all the Junkers who served between 1888 and 1914. Similarities in the background and careers of individual officials corroborate the general concept of the characteristic Junker bureaucrat. On the other hand, such analyses of individual cases reveal wide variations among the Junker officials who range from a landed proprietor of ancient lineage who serves as *Ritterschaftsrat* in the Uckermark to a poor, landless and conscientious *Regierungsrat* poring over his files in the government offices of Cassel or Muenster. Altho the group of Junker officials is homogeneous it is not uniform. Aside from individual differences there is a diversity between the several distinct groups into which Junker officials seem naturally to fall. In some instances the characteristics of these groups seem to indicate that certain types of administrative careers modified the outlook and way of life of Junker officials and to suggest the lines diverging from the old central Junker type along which the modern Junker was tending to move,. The professional and landless hereditary bureaucrat, for example, seems to be approaching the bourgeois social pattern and the aggressive political official to be moving toward the unprincipled political boss. At any

41

rate the multiplicity of variations within the group of Junker officials indicates that it was not a static but a fluid social body and that, as is so often the case, the norm was an assumed pattern rather than a reality.

The careers of a total of 1500 Junker officials have been studied as the basis for the following generalizations and ratios. These include a wide variety of officeholders. Of first importance are the members of the regular bureaucracy, the so-called higher officials ranging from the *Regierungs-Assessoren* at the bottom to the *Regierungs-* and *Ober-Praesidenten,* the Ministerial Directors and the Ministers at the top. All Junkers in these positions in any of the seven test years chosen, i.e., 1888, 1890, 1895, 1900, 1905, 1910 and 1914, have been studied. Among them are those Junkers who served as higher officials in the *Staatsministerium* or any one of the Prussian Ministries exclusive of its *Ressorts* or subsidiary departments, as well as all such Junker officials serving in the *Ober-Praesidia* of the 12 provinces and the *Regierungen* of the 34 governmental districts (*Regierungs-Bezirke*). All Junker *Landraete* in the 34 *Regierungen* have been given special attention. Foreign envoys have been included among the higher officials of the Foreign Office. Court officials of top rank both in the Royal Household and the Military Retinue of the Emperor and King form a small but important section of the total group of Junker officials.

In the provincial governments the *Landeshauptmaenner* or *Landes-Direktoren* and all members or deputy members of the Provincial Executive Committees (*Provinzial-Ausschuesse*) and Provincial Diets (*Provinzial-Landtage*), the Provincial Councils (*Provinzial-Raete*) and the District Committees (*Bezirks-Ausschuesse*) in the seven years selected have also been studied. In addition all directors and counsellors (*Raete*) of the provincial *Landschaften* or land credit institutions have been observed. Wherever the director of the provincial fire department was a Junker the fact has been noted. Because of the close relationship between the Junkers and the Evangelical Church the national Evangelical Supreme Church Council (*Evangelischer Ober-Kirchenrat*) and its provincial consistories and synodical directories were included in this analysis. Also included were members of the *Oberlandesgerichte* or Provincial Supreme Courts in order to discover how many or how few Junkers sought a career in the higher judicial offices. Lastly the Junker members of the Prussian Diet, both the *Herrenhaus* and the House of Deputies, in the seven test years were counted and studied in order to note the extent of the formal relationship between the Junkers and Prussian politics and to find instances where a political career was combined with a bureaucratic profession.

It was the Junker's habit to keep to the general administrative and political offices rather than to enter fields of technical specialization,[1] but within the general field there was a variety of acceptable and attractive careers open to him. He might be appointed to a Court office or the diplomatic service or he might enter the Prussian State administration and work toward a bureaucratic career or a *Landratsamt*. Or he might prefer honorary provincial offices. Sometimes he followed in the footsteps of his father and grandfather. He was free to combine two or more provincial or Court offices or to switch in mid-career from the Prussian State administration to provincial work, as we shall see below. But in general the Junker official spent the best part of his life and made his real contribution to the Prussian administration within the one particular branch of the government service which he had selected.

Court Offices

Perhaps the easiest way to become acquainted with the Junker officials in their various positions is to glance thru a number of careers in the several main administrative branches of the Prussian State. Some of these examples will illustrate the normal or the average career; others are brought in to give evidence of interesting contrasts or significant trends. First we shall consider some Junkers in Court offices, which, altho not a part of the government in the ordinary sense, were important for the Junkers and put them in

1. Because of the technical and highly specialized nature of their work and because, doubtless for this reason, almost no Junkers entered these fields of the administration, the following departments of the provincial governments have been omitted: Medizinal-Kollegium; Universitaeten und Hochschulen; Berg-Behoerden, Aichungs-inspektion; Eisenbahn-Behoerden; Eisenbahnrat; Post-Direktion; Telegraphen-Direktion; Direktion der Rentenbanke; Invaliditaets- und Alters-Versicherungsanstalten; Aertze- und Handelskammern; Wasserstrassenverwaltung; Provinzial-Feuersozietaeten.

positions of political responsibility and influence and often required a considerable amount of administrative detail as well. Junkers looked on Court appointments, either to the Royal Household or the Military Retinue, as their natural right because of their long tradition of personal service to the King and their position as the staunchest supporters of the Prussian monarchy. For the most part they filled these offices, often of great responsibility and delicacy, with the ease and dignity of those born to the rank of courtiers. They were generally chosen from old, renowned and well-established aristocratic families. Members of the Royal Household, once appointed to their court office, usually continued in that or a higher office until old age, poor health or royal disfavor forced them to resign, whereas members of the Military Retinue might return after a few years to a regular military command.

The most influential and one of the most statesmanlike courtiers of the reign of William II was Count August zu Eulenburg (1838-1921). He belonged to the famous old Eulenberg family of the original Saxon nobility which had early settled in East Prussia. He was the son of Botho, High Steward (*Landhofmeister*) in Prussia, the brother of Botho Wend who was twice Minister of the Interior and President of the Prussian Ministry from 1892 to 1894, and the cousin of Prince Philipp zu Eulenburg, the notorious personal friend of the Kaiser. Together with his relatives August was able to win great power and renown for the Eulenberg family, which became one of the leading houses under William II. Neither he nor Botho Wend held property, but their younger brother, Karl, had inherited the family estate of Wicken (2390 acres) in Kreis Friedland, East Prussia. By 1888 August was already *Ober-Zeremoniemeister,* Court Marshal, Chairman of the Office of Heraldry, and Colonel à la suite in the Prussian Army. By 1895 he had been raised to the posts of *Ober-Hof- und Hausmarschall,* to succeed Wilhelm von Liebenau, and had become a Major General. In 1907 he was made Head of the Royal Household (*Hausminister*) which office he held until his death in 1921. After the Kaiser's flight to Holland Eulenburg served as his plenipotentiary in Berlin.[2]

2. He had married Hedda von Witzleben from Mecklenburg in 1864 and was the father of one son and two daughters. The son, Count Viktor, entered the diplomatic service.

Because of Eulenburg's position of great responsibility and his constant personal association with the Kaiser he was able to exert a great deal of influence in political affairs.[3] He was a Conservative and an agrarian and often tried to improve relations between the Conservative party and the Kaiser.[4] In the autumn of 1894, during the Caprivi crisis, he came out definitely on the side of the agrarian Conservatives and against the Chancellor. On October 20, 1894, for example, he joined Count Louis von der Groeben-Arenstein at the head of a delegation from the East Prussian branch of the Agrarian League which came to urge the Kaiser to fight for "religion, morals and order." This demonstration was given further weight by the presence at the delegation's reception by the Kaiser of the Junker Minister of Agriculture, Wilhelm von Heyden-Cadow, and August's brother, Botho zu Eulenburg.[5] In fact, the whole Eulenburg clan, which was so close to the Kaiser during these years, had considerable influence on the course of the Caprivi crisis.[6] That August zu Eulenburg's influence was based not only on propinquity and convictions but also on high principles, ability and statesmanship is attested in the accounts of his contemporaries.[7]

Some Court officials, like August zu Eulenburg, confined their activities to their Court duties and exerted a political influence only informally and indirectly. Others combined Court duties with political and provincial offices. Typical of these is Werner von Veltheim. A member of the original Saxon nobility, of Lutheran faith and son of Werner and Isadore, née von Krosigk, he had inherited the

3. Rudolf von Valentini (40) *Kaiser und Kabinettschef*, p. 49, says that he was ". . . der einflussreichste Vertraute der koeniglichen Familie." Bogdan, Graf von Hutten-Czapski (34) *Sechzig Jahre Politik und Gesellschaft*, v. 1, p. 407, writes, "Die markanteste Persoenlichkeit am Hofe war Graf August zu Eulenburg, zunaechst Oberhofmarschall, dann Hausminister. Ich habe es fuer ein Unglueck gehalten, dass dieser bedeutende Mann kein verantwortungsvolles politisches Amt erhielt. . . . Immerhin hat er auch politisches Einfluss ausgeuebt und ihn waehrend der Kanzlerschaft Buelows in dessen Interesse verwandt. In manche Regierungskrise hat er ausgleichend eingegriffen."
4. Graf Kuno Westarp (43) *Konservative Politik . . .* , v. 1, p. 350.
5. Egmont Zechlin (122) *Staatsstreichplaene . . .* , pp. 131-32.
6. Zechlin, *ibid.*, p. 138, stresses the fact that there were four Eulenburgs with the Kaiser at the royal hunting party at Liebenburg during the height of the Caprivi crisis.
7. Prince Bernhard von Buelow (24) *Memoirs*, v. 1, p. 72; Count Robert von Zedlitz-Truetzschler (46) *Twelve Years at the Imperial German Court*, pp. 44-45; Graf Alexander von Hohenlohe (32) *Aus meinem Leben*, pp. 368-69; Baron Hugo von Reischach (38) *Under Three Emperors*, p. 61; Valentini (40) p. 49.

fideicommissum of Schoenfliess (8000 acres) in Kreis Niederbarnim, just outside Berlin. He also owned the estates of Stolpe and Glienecke.[8] During the year 1887 he was made a Master of Ceremonies and Governor (*Schlosshauptmann*) of Castle Freienwalde, both of which offices he held until 1905. In 1910 and 1914 we find him acting as Governor of Castle Koenigswusterhausen. During this whole period he was also a Conservative member of the Prussian Diet, a deputy in the Lower House from 1887 to 1908 and after that a life member of the *Herrenhaus* for the district of Barnim. He was as well a member of the Brandenburg Provincial Diet and in 1900 he served as counsellor of the provincial *Landschaft* for the Mittelmark. It is quite likely that von Veltheim's inheritance of the estate of Schoenfliess was the basis of his selection for his several posts.

Hans von Boehn may serve as an example of a Junker army officer who was assigned to service in the Kaiser's Military Retinue. He was a member of the original Pomeranian nobility, his ancestors having already settled in Kreis Stolp by 1279. He himself was the son of Julius, a Lieutenant General without landed property, and he decided to follow in his father's footsteps and enter on a military career. In 1895 he appears to have been a Major in the Kaiser Alexander Grenadier Guards Regiment #1 in Berlin. By 1897 he had been appointed aide-de-camp to the Kaiser. He accompanied William II on several of his North Cape cruises. In 1905 he was still serving as aide-de-camp and, as a Colonel, was Commander of the 1st Cavalry Guards Brigade in Berlin. By 1910 he had become a Major General à la suite of the Kaiser and King and was Commandant of Berlin. In 1914 he was a Cavalry General on the reserve list (*z.D.*).[9] Like Hans von Boehn most of the Junkers—and, indeed, most of all the officers—in the Military Retinue were regular army officers who served in this capacity for a short period only and then returned to regular army positions. Most of them resembled him also in that they did not own any landed property.

8. He had married Auguste von Gadenstedt in 1868 and was the father of four sons and three daughters.

9. He had married Virginie, Baroness von Beaulieu in 1903 and was the father of two children.

DIPLOMATIC SERVICE

Junkers did not tend to enter the diplomatic service as much as other fields of government. Because of their small incomes, their narrow, rural environment and their blunt, forthright natures they generally did not find the smooth, sophisticated ways of diplomats congenial nor did they make such good material for the delicate, complicated and socially exacting missions of the German Foreign Office as did the somewhat more cosmopolitan higher nobility or the more versatile aristocrats of south and west Germany.[10] There were nonetheless some few Junker envoys and no less than three Junkers—Hans Lothar von Schweinitz, Bernhard von Werder and Johann, Count von Alvensleben—held the post of Ambassador to Moscow during the reign of William II. This is no coincidence, for the Junkers felt stronger political ties with Russia than with any other country and admired its government and its reigning house above all others outside of Prussia. Hence some of them were *personae gratissimae* with the Tsar and the obvious choice of a conservative Prussian government for this important diplomatic post.

Another Junker with a somewhat less distinguished diplomatic career was Gustav von Below, the descendant of an original Pomeranian noble family and the owner of four large estates in Kreis Putzig, West Prussia, with a total area of 7500 acres.[11] From 1905 he was a life member of the *Herrenhaus*. Von Below entered the diplomatic service in 1886 as Legation Secretary in the Embassy at Athens. During the next decade he served in the same capacity in Copenhagen and Lisbon and at the Vatican. He was raised to the rank of Legation Counsellor in 1894 and in 1900 he became Consul General in Sofia. Three years later he was made Minister to Saxe-

---

10. That such nice considerations were not always operative in the selection of diplomatic envoys is illustrated by the story of Hermann von Eckardstein's appointment by Bismarck. Von Eckardstein, who was, it must be said, a talkative and not too reliable source of information, writes (27) *Lebenserinnerungen* . . . , v. 1, p. 88, that while a Lieutenant in the Brandenburg Curassiers he attracted the attention of Bismarck, who invited him to dinner. Soon thereafter he was transferred to the Foreign Office and Herbert Bismarck said that his father gave the following reasons for Eckardstein's appointment: "Er [Bismarck] sagte, der Kerl ist ueber sechs Fuss gross, kann saufen, bleibt dabei immer nuechtern, und da er sich auch sonst zu eignen scheint, wollen wir den Kerl in den diplomatischen Dienst nehmen."

11. He married Henny von Quistorp in 1887 and was the father of three daughters.

Weimar and in 1908 he was sent to Stuttgart as Prussian Minister to Wuerttemberg where he was still serving in 1914.

REGULAR BUREAUCRATIC SERVICE.
TREND TOWARD BOURGEOISIE

The regular bureaucratic service under the Ministry of the Interior or within the other Ministries was a field for which the Junker was much better suited by tradition and inclination and one where he had a much greater opportunity to satisfy his personal ambitions for political influence and executive authority by rising to the top offices of Minister, Ministerial Director and *Ober-* or *Regierungs-Praesident.* At the least it offered him a chance to make a living in a socially respected profession where he was ensured security of tenure, even in the lower brackets of the service, and a pension upon retirement. It is, therefore, not surprising that of the total of 1500 Junker officials and of a total of 812 holding salaried offices about 365 were in the regular bureaucratic service, exclusive of the *Landratsamt.* In addition there were some who filled the post of *Landrat* for only a brief period as one step in a bureaucratic career.[12]

It was usual for a Junker bureaucrat to start out as a *Regierungs-Assessor* at about the age of thirty and to move up in the service until he was made an *Ober-Regierungsrat* or, if more fortunate, a *Regierungs-Praesident* by the time he was fifty or fifty-five. The history of Ruediger von Haugwitz may serve as an example of a typical bureaucratic career. Ruediger came from a very old Meissen noble family which moved to Silesia where its members entered widely into the Prussian service and married into old Silesian families. Ruediger himself was the third son of Gotthard von Haugwitz of Rosenthal and Marie, Baroness von Glaubitz.[13] In 1888, at the age of thirty, Ruediger became a *Regierungs-Assessor* attached to the *Regierung* of Breslau. By 1895 he had become a *Regierungsrat* in the same governmental district and by 1900 he had been transferred to the *Ober-Praesidium* of Silesia. In 1905 we find him promoted to the rank of *Ober-Regierungsrat* and serving in Magdeburg,

---

12. See below.

13. He married a von Kleist in 1891 and was the father of six sons and one daughter.

and by 1910 he had been raised to the post of *Ober-Praesidialrat* in Westphalia where he was still serving in 1914.

Friedrich von Rohr, scion of an ancient noble family of the Mark, had a similar but somewhat less genteel career. Friedrich was the son of Eduard von Rohr, a Lieutenant Colonel without landed property, and Anna von Schmidt.[14] In 1886 von Rohr was a *Regierungs-Referendar* and in 1888, at the age of thirty-six, a *Regierungs-Assessor* in Bromberg in the province of Posen. By 1890 he became a *Regierungsrat* in the same governmental district. In 1895 and 1900 we find him serving as *Regierungsrat* in the governmental district of Muenster in Westphalia but by 1905 he had become a *Vortragender Rat*[15] in the Ministry of Public Works in Berlin and a member of the commission for narrow gauge railways. He still held this post in 1914, but by 1910 he had been raised to the rank of *Ober-Regierungsrat.*

The cases of Kurt von Schmeling and Detlof, Count Schwerin which follow may be cited as examples of somewhat more successful but still typical bureaucratic careers. Kurt von Schmeling was descended from the ancient Pomeranian nobility. His father was Bogislav Oswald von Schmeling, a Lieutenant Colonel without landed property, and his mother, Anna von Rohr.[16] In 1890, at the age of thirty, Kurt was a *Regierungs-Assessor* in Danzig. Five years later we find him a *Landrat* in Kreis Stuhm in the governmental district of Marienwerder and in 1900 and 1905 he was *Landrat* of Kreis Stolp in Pomerania. By 1910 he had become a *Geheimer Regierungsrat* and a *Vortragender Rat* in the Ministry of Agriculture and had been elected to the Prussian House of Deputies and by 1914, at the age of fifty-four, he had been appointed *Regierungs-Praesident* of Stettin where he was still serving in 1916.

Dr.jur. Detlof, Count von Schwerin also rose in the service to the rank of *Regierungs-Praesident.* He came from a famous old Pomeranian noble family, which was raised to the rank of Prussian Counts in 1740, and was the son of Helmuth, Count Schwerin and

14. Friedrich von Rohr himself married a commoner, Hedwig Ponet, and was the father of three sons and a daughter.

15. *Vortragende Raete* were Ministry officials who made regular weekly reports to their Minister on the work of the various subdivisions of the Ministry.

16. Kurt married Karla von Burgsdorff and was the father of two sons.

Antonie von Bornstedt.[17] Unlike the three preceding officials Detlof owned landed property, the estate of Ziethen (1875 acres) in Kreis Greifswald. Furthermore, he was a Cavalry Captain in the Reserves and a member of a student corps, the Guestphalia of Heidelberg. Hence he had all of the prerequisites for a successful bureaucratic career.[18] In 1882, at the age of twenty-nine, Count Schwerin was already a judicial aid in the Supreme Court in Berlin (*Kammergerichts-Assessor*) and an assistant in the Ministry of the Interior and two years later, at the age of thirty-one, he became *Landrat* of Kreis Usedom-Wollin in Pomerania and director of shipping in Swinemuende. Here he remained until about 1900 when he was made Police President in the governmental district of Hannover. Within the next five years he was appointed *Regierungs-Praesident* of Koeslin in his home province of Pomerania and he still held this office in 1914.

Other Junkers attract our attention because of the unusual ease and rapidity with which they rose to top offices.[19] Georg, Baron von Tschammer-Quaritz and Rudolf von der Schulenburg, for example, had been made *Regierungs-Praesidenten* by the time they were forty-five. Georg von Tschammer-Quaritz came from an ancient Silesian noble family of Evangelical faith. He was a younger son of Arthur, the owner of a fideicommissum and several other estates in Silesia, and of Johanna von Lieres und Wilkau, member of another prominent Junker family in Silesia. Georg himself owned no property and he never married. He was both a Lieutenant in the Reserves and a member of an aristocratic student corps, the Hasso-Borussen of Bonn. In 1896, he was a *Gerichts-Referendar* and in 1898, at the age of twenty-nine, a *Regierungs-Assessor*. By 1901 he had been made *Landrat* of Kreis Luebben where he remained for several years but by 1910 he had become a Privy Finance Counsellor (*Geheimer Finanz-Rat*) and *Vortragender Rat* in the Finance Ministry. As early as 1914 he was *Regierungs-Praesident* of the governmental district of Breslau.

17. He married a member of another ancient Pomeranian Junker family, Anna von Puttkamer, and was the father of three sons and one daughter.

18. See below, Chap. III, p. 104.

19. As the purpose of these paragraphs is merely to illustrate the various types of careers preferred by the Junkers I will leave a consideration of the causes for rapid advancement, other than genuine ability, until a later time.

The career of Rudolf von der Schulenburg of the renowned old Schulenburg family in the Altmark was equally rapid and even more successful. Rudolf was the son of Werner, from whom he inherited the estate of Ramstedt (2250 acres) in Kreis Wolmirstedt, and of Amalie, Baroness von Maltzahn.[20] Rudolf did not belong to the Officers Corps but as a student he joined the elite Saxonia student corps of Goettingen. Schulenburg was slow in starting his career. In 1891 he was only a *Regierungs-Assessor* and he did not become a *Landrat* until 1896 or 1897 when he was already thirty-six or thirty-seven. But by 1905, at the age of forty-five he had already been made *Regierungs-President* in Potsdam and by 1915 he had been raised to the distinguished office of *Ober-Praesident* of the Province of Brandenburg.

Another Junker who not only rose to the highest offices in the administration but also played an active and important role in politics was Friedrich Wilhelm von Loebell. Altho he came from an ancient Silesian noble family his small estate of Benken (968 acres of which 515 were woods) was situated in Kreis Zauch-Belzig in the Mark.[21] In 1885, at the early age of thirty, he was already *Landrat* in Kreis Neuhaus in Stade, Hannover. He later took over the *Landratsamt* of West-Havelland where he was made an honorary member of the cities of Friesack and Pritzerbe and from whence he was elected to the Provincial Diet and to the Prussian House of Deputies and the Reichstag for short terms. As *Landrat* and a member of the Conservative fraction of the Diet von Loebell attracted the attention of the leader of the Conservatives in the House of Deputies, Ernst von Heydebrand und der Lasa. He soon became one of Heydebrand's close collaborators[22] and a power in the Conservative party. From 1906 to 1909 he was an Under-Secretary and Chief of the Imperial Chancellory. It was he who first suggested the dissolution of the Reichstag in 1906 as the Government's answer to the opposition of the Centre Party.[23] He was a close worker with Buelow and an enthusiastic supporter of the Block, much to the

20. He had married Marie von Gerlach-Rohrbeck and was the father of four children.
21. He was the son of Robert and Lilla von Thuemen. He married Margarete von Flottwell and was the father of six sons.
22. Westarp (43) v. 1, pp. 63, 369.
23. Theodor Eschenburg (63) *Das Kaiserreich am Scheideweg*, p. 42.

disgust of von Heydebrand[24] but Buelow looked on him as an "old and devoted colleague" and proposed him for the post of *Ober-Praesident* in Brandenburg,[25] an office which he assumed in 1909 but left in the following year.[26] In 1914 von Loebell accepted the post of Minister of the Interior on the condition that he should not be asked to introduce or sponsor a bill for electoral reform in Prussia.[27]

While some Junker officials in the regular administration stood out above the average because of the ease with which they reached high offices others are noticeable because, due to lack of ambition or ability, they did not make the usual progress and jogged along for years as a *Regierungsrat,* an *Ober-Regierungsrat* or a *Forstrat.* For example, Gebhard von Alvensleben-Kalbe, son of Udo and Agnes, née von Pritzelwitz, and owner of the estate Schollene (3015 acres) in Kreis Jerichow II, served from 1905 to 1919 or 1920 as *Regierungsrat* in the governmental district of Potsdam. That he did not advance further is the more striking because he belonged to a famous Junker family and was also a member of an aristocratic student corps, the Saxonia of Goettingen. Another perennial *Regierungsrat* was Siegfried von Holtzendorff, descendant of an ancient noble family of the Uckermark and son of the retired Colonel, Friedrich von Holtzendorff and Klara, née von Goertzke. Neither father nor son owned any estates.[28] In 1895 we find Siegfried as *Gerichts-Assessor* and *Justitiar*[29] in the governmental district of Stralsund in Pomerania and deputy member of the District Committee by government appointment. By 1905 he had risen to the rank of

24. Westarp (43) v. 1, p. 369; Adolf Wermuth (42) *Ein Beamtenleben,* p. 257.
25. Buelow (24) v. 3, p. 75. Hutten-Czapski (34) v. 1, p. 399, calls von Loebell "ein Muster altpreussischen, konservativen Beamtentums!" and claims that he was indispensable to von Buelow in the handling of domestic affairs.
26. As retired *Ober-Praesident* von Loebell was one of the editors of *Deutschland unter Kaiser Wilhelm II* (3 vols., Berlin, 1914), a composite work prepared by a group of leading Conservatives in honor of the 25th anniversary of the reign of William II and the 100th anniversary of the battle of Leipzig.
27. Wilhelm Otto Vollrath (121) *Der parlamentarische Kampf um das preussische Dreiklassenwahlrecht,* p. 56.
28. Siegfried married Ida von Schweder but had no children.
29. A *Justitiar* is an administrative official with functions of a judicial nature and who therefore is trained as a *Gerichts-Assessor* rather than as a *Regierungs-Assessor.*

Regierungsrat and was serving in the governmental district of Koeslin. He was later transferred to Cassel where he remained until 1914, still as *Regierungsrat*.

Another bureaucrat, Ludwig von Bornstedt, descendant of one of the oldest families of the Mark, grandson of Ludwig, lord of Ehrenberg and only son of Karl, *Landrat* of Kreis Friedeberg in Neumark spent twenty years as director of a district administrative court (*Verwaltungsgericht*).

Top posts in the forestry service, which went alongside the regular administration, were attractive to the Junkers because, altho they offered little opportunity for advancement to high government positions or for political activities, they made it possible for the sons of country gentlemen to remain in their congenial rural atmosphere. As foresters they held offices worthy of their rank and their duties, with which they were often already familiar thru the supervision of the forests on their own or their fathers' estates, were pleasant and far from onerous. They could associate freely with their cousins and friends who lived on neighboring estates and take an important part in the many hunting parties given in the district, for the Junkers were passionate hunters. They looked forward eagerly to the special hunts which came with each season of the year and each lord of a manor entertained the neighborhood at one or more hunt banquets in the course of a year. These were the most important social functions in the remote rural districts of Pomerania or Silesia and here the Junker host showed to the full his hearty and bountiful hospitality.[30] It is therefore quite in keeping with Junker conventions and tastes for Hans von Waldow, third son of August von Waldow of Dannenwalde and other estates totaling 10,000 acres (4000 hectares), and younger brother of the prominent Wilhelm von Waldow, the *Regierungs-* and later *Ober-Praesident,* to be a simple Top Forester (*Oberfoerster*)[31] and Forest Inspector (*Forstmeister*). We find him in 1888 as *Forst-Assessor* in the Ministry of Agriculture and in 1901 as Top Forester in Himmelpfort, in the governmental district of Potsdam. He was as well a Captain of the Reserves in a

---

30. See, *inter alia*, Ulrich von Wilamowitz-Moellendorf (44) *Erinnerungen, 1848-1914,* p. 18; Hellmuth von Gerlach (31) *Von Rechts nach Links,* pp. 35-36.
31. A rank equal to that of a *Regierungsrat*.

Light Infantry (*Jaeger*) Battalion. By 1910, at the age of forty-nine, he was Forest Inspector in Hohenbrueck, Pomerania, and a retired Captain.

Another scion of an old noble family who chose a forester's career was Carl Albert von Platen of the Pomeranian Platens on the island of Ruegen (since 1255). He was the first son of Bertram, a retired Major without landed property, and Adele von Buelow. In 1903, at the age of thirty-seven, he was a Top Forester and from 1910 to 1914 he was a *Regierungs-* and *Forstrat* in the governmental district of Magdeburg and a retired Captain in the Light Infantry Corps of the Militia.[32]

As some of the foregoing examples of bureaucratic careers indicate, the Junker administrative official held office not only in his homeland, the seven eastern provinces, but also in western Prussia. It is, of course, to be expected that members of a bureaucracy, as impersonal agents of the State, would be sent about to those places where they could render the greatest service without regard for their individual wishes or private affairs. Nonetheless it is true that proportionately fewer Junker officials were sent into the western part of Prussia than into the eastern provinces.[33] This is undoubtedly due in part to the survival of old customs such as the *Indigenatsrecht*[34] and to the traditional connection between landholding and office-holding. But it may also be attributed to the fact that the efforts of the Ministry of the Interior to spread the Junker "feudalizing" influence over the more liberal and bourgeois west by sending Junker agrarian Conservative officials into this area proved double-edged in its effect. It is no doubt true that some Junker officials in the western part of Prussia converted some middle class men to their own feudal point of view and drew them into their Junker sphere. But on the other hand it appears certain that the experience of serving in western Prussia also had the opposite effect of bureaucratizing the Junker official and effacing his feudal characteristics. For the placement of a Junker younger son in the Rhineland or Westphalia separated him from his family and its estates and from the natural environment

---

32. He married Elisabeth Johansen in 1897 and was the father of two sons and one daughter.
33. For a fuller discussion see Chapter V.
34. The rights of natives.

of the Junker social group. He was able to see the varied problems of government from the point of view of the State as a whole. He began to project himself into the apparatus of the State and to act with the broader vision of one seeking the welfare of the nation as a whole rather than that of one particular section or social class. In other words, he came to be a non-partisan bureaucrat. And the more he approached the bureaucratic type the less of a Junker and the more of a bourgeois he became. Thus we already find evidence that the Junkers' ability to increase their influence and numbers by "feudalizing" the bourgeoisie was offset by the tendency of some Junker officials to move away from the central Junker stock because of the bureaucratizing effect of administrative service.

We may count Bernhard von Tieschowitz among the Junker officials who seem to have moved toward the bourgeoisie because of their years of service in the west of Prussia. Bernhard came from an old Upper Silesian family and was the second son of Theodor, a *Regierungsrat* without real estate, and Anna Elsner von Gronow. For twelve years from 1876 to 1888 he served as *Landrat* in Kreis Wetzlar, Coblenz, and in 1890 we find him as an *Ober-Regierungsrat* in Cologne. Between 1890 and 1895 he was sent to the east of Prussia and made *Regierungs-Praesident* of the governmental district of Koenigsberg where he remained until his death in 1909. Altho himself a member of the Evangelical Church von Tieschowitz married Helene Buhlers, a Catholic from Erfurt, in 1869 and his four children were all Catholics.[35]

A similar example is Moritz von Wedel-Parlow of a distinguished old family established in Pomerania since 1240, son of Moritz, lord of Parlow and Friedingen (2518 acres), and Karoline Bauer. In 1895 and 1900 Moritz was a *Regierungs-Assessor* in the governmental district of Koeslin in Pomerania, by 1905 he had been appointed *Regierungsrat* in Cassel and in 1914 he was serving, still as a *Regierungsrat,* in the governmental district of Wiesbaden. His wife was Ottonie Malcolm from Baden.[36] Both of these men, von Tieschowitz and von Wedel-Parlow, who were without estates of

---

35. He was a retired Captain in the militia guards and a member of the Saxo-Borussia student corps of Heidelberg.
36. He was a 1st Lieutenant of the Reserves in a regiment of Dragoons.

their own, who held bureaucratic offices all over Prussia and who married commoners—the von Wedels even in the second generation and von Tieschowitz even a Catholic—seem to be drifting away from the true Junker type.

A family custom of service in the bureaucracy for two or more generations tended to have the same effect of eroding Junker attributes, especially where both father and son had lost all direct connection with the land. Some of these officials came to be hereditary bureaucrats and to lose the character of the landed gentry; others may have kept a connection with the land thru their relatives or by marrying back into landed Junker families. We find that three generations of Counts von der Goltz, a famous old family from the original nobility of the Neumark, served in the Prussian administration and were without landed property. Gustav, the grandfather, remained a *Landrat*. He married Cecile le Chevenix de Beville and their eldest son entered the regular bureaucracy. He served from 1863 to 1880 as *Landrat* of Kreis Zuellichau-Schwiebus, Frankfurt a.O. and then became a member of the Central Audit Chamber (*Ober-Rechnungskammer*). In 1895 he was made Vice President of the same, which office he held until his retirement in 1906. He and his first wife, Caecelie von Perbandt, had a son, Guenther, Count von der Goltz, born 1869, who followed his father and grandfather into the administration. In 1905 he had become a *Regierungs-Assessor* in the Government of Aix la Chapelle and by 1910 he was a *Regierungsrat* in Frankfurt a.O. in Brandenburg, which post he still held in 1914. He was a retired Lieutenant and a bachelor.

The von Pommer-Esche family has a similar record. Of old Ruegen stock, it was ennobled by Sweden in 1813. Altho it never held any estates it devoted itself to the Prussian public service. The grandfather, Adolf, rose to the rank of *Ober-Praesident*. He and his bourgeois wife, Julie Picht, had a son, Albert (1837-1903), who served first as *Landrat* of Kreis Moers in Duesseldorf from 1868 to 1884 and then as *Regierungs-Praesident* in Stralsund and Trier. By 1895 he had been made *Ober-Praesident* of the province of Saxony where he remained until his death in 1903. He was not a Reserve Officer but he belonged to the student corps of Saxo-Borussia in Heidelberg. He had married Mathilde Berend in 1865 and was the father of four sons and three daughters. His third son,

Rudolf, took up his father's career and appears in 1905 as *Regierungs-Assessor* in the governmental district of Breslau. In 1910 he was still a *Regierungs-Assessor,* now in Bromberg, and by 1914 he was *Landrat* in Kreis Graetz in Posen. He was a Captain in the Field Artillery of the Militia Guards and a member of the Saxonia student corps of Goettingen. He married Anna Robert-Tornow, making three generations of bourgeois marriages.

There are many more instances of a family tradition of administrative service. Of particular interest is the case of Adolf von Perbandt. He was descended from the oldest known noble family of the Samland in East Prussia, which claimed to be of Pruzzen origin. Yet his father, who owned no real estate, had entered the judicial profession, a branch of the government not popular with the Junkers, and Adolf was a mere government surveyor or *Baurat* in the governmental district of Duesseldorf. It was very unusual and unworthy of a Junker to hold a position as a technician or technical adviser. In addition, Adolf von Perbandt had married a middle-class girl from the Rhineland, Rosa Mengelberg, and thereby made himself even more bourgeois and *déclassé* in the eyes of the old-fashioned Junkers.

Another Junker who appears to have sunk into the middle class was Emil von Schenckendorff, from an old noble family of Lower Lusatia which had settled in Brandenburg by 1313. His father, Moritz, owned no real estate but lived on his income. His mother was from the middle class. In 1888 and 1890 Emil held the post of Counsellor to the Telegraph Direction in Goerlitz. During the same period and, after his retirement, right down into the war period he was elected to the House of Deputies from Lauban-Goerlitz. Moreover, he was a member of the National Liberal fraction, very unusual for anyone of Junker heritage.

Equally interesting is Kurt, Count von der Schulenburg-Angern. Altho one of the famous Schulenburgs and second son of Edo, a distinguished member of the *Herrenhaus* and lord of the fideicommissum Angern (3750 acres), which had been in the family since 1448, Kurt seemed to drift toward the middle class. He had chosen the profession of forester and for thirty-one years, from 1890 until his death in 1921, he served as *Regierungs-* and *Forstrat* in the governmental district of Cassel. Moreover, he married a commoner,

Luise Raab. Schulenburg seems to have been drawn away from his family tradition and Junker environment by his long residence in Hessen-Nassau.

The foregoing case histories give weight to the assumption that years or even generations of bureaucratic service together with the uprooting of the Junker from his natural environment by his transfer from one part of Prussia to the other and his loss of direct land ownership had a tendency to wear away his most prominent Junker characteristics and to turn the Junker bureaucrat into a bourgeois. These individual careers seem to justify Max Weber's statement that administrative officials were really bourgeois, whether nobles or not.[37] Otto Hintze in his article, *Der Beamtenstand,*[38] claims that the combination of old Junker officials with the influx of the bourgeoisie since the mid-nineteenth century had created a "noble-bourgeois aristocracy of service" and points out, as has been illustrated above, "It is in fact so that a very large part of the official class in its several branches produces its own successors."[39] We may fairly conclude, therefore, that the movement between the Junkers and the middle class was in two directions—from the "feudalized" bourgeoisie toward the Junker aristocracy and also from the Junker stock thru bureaucratic service and probably thru other channels as well, toward the bourgeoisie.

LANDRATSAMT

The *Landratsamt,* altho it was an office in the regular administrative organization, must be given separate consideration because of its unique characteristics and its outstanding importance. Its most significant distinction is that it united the functions of the Prussian State administration in the Circle with the local, self-governing affairs of the same Circle in the person of one single official, the *Landrat.* Or to put it another way, the *Landrat* stood with one foot in the Prussian State administration and the other in the local self-government. Bismarck—to change the metaphor—calls him a "Janus."[40] He was both the impersonal bureaucratic agent of the

37. See Chapter I, p. 39, note 97.
38. (132) *Gehe-Stiftung zu Dresden: Vortraege,* v. 3, pp. 95-175.
39. *Ibid.,* p. 138.
40. In *Gedanken und Erinnerungen* (22) v. 1, p. 28, Bismarck writes of the

Ministry of the Interior in charge of police, direct taxes and military affairs[41] and the head of the communal activities of his Circle, Chairman of the Circle Assembly (*Kreistag*) and of the Executive Committee (*Kreisausschuss*) and in constant personal contact with the local inhabitants. It was this communal, self-governing phase of the work which gave the greatest satisfaction to many Junkers.[42]

If the *Landrat* owned one or more estates in his Circle, he had a direct personal concern in the affairs which he administered. If he were a Junker, he was sure to feel a strong corporate community of interest with his fellow Junker landlords. In fact the most important aspect of the *Landratsamt* was its traditional but still very organic half-feudal character.

Within the one office of *Landrat* there were variations in the types of careers. The fact that some of the above illustrations of typical bureaucratic careers include some years of service as a *Landrat* is an indication that the office was often merely a stage in the progress of such officials toward the top. These illustrations may serve as examples of the *Landrat* who was moved up after a brief period in this office. The reader will no doubt have noticed that in every one of these cases where a *Landrat* was promoted he soon reached the office of *Regierungs-Praesident* at least, and sometimes that of *Ober-Praesident* and Minister. In other words, if the *Landrat* did not remain a *Landrat,* then he was almost invariably sent on to high and important offices.[43]

Not all *Landraete* could be promoted, of course, but neither did they all wish to move on. For the *Landratsamt* was also looked on as an office of prestige and importance in itself and many Junkers had no other aspiration than to hold the office of *Landrat* for life or until they wished to retire from active service. There is a story current

---

Landrat, "der einen Januskopf trage, ein Gesicht in der Buerokratie, eins im Lande habe."

41. Conrad Bornhak (52) *Preussisches Staatsrecht,* v. 2, pp. 296-97.

42. For example, Rudolf von Valentini writes (40) p. 39, "Zweifellos hat der Landrat wichtige staatliche Aufgaben zu erfuellen; aber die Taetigkeit in diesen Geschaeften, die wie Steuerveranlagung, Heeres-Rekrutierung, Polizei im wesentlichen eine bueromaessige Erledigung erfordern, tritt doch sehr zurueck gegen die Beschaeftigung mit den Aufgaben, die ihm in der Kommunalverwaltung des Kreises als Vorsitzendem des Kreisausschusses und Kreistages erwachsen. Hier kann er selbstaendig wirken und Positives schaffen."

43. For a further discussion of this point see Chapter V, p. 180f.

in the family of Wilhelm von Rauchhaupt, leader of the Conservatives in the Prussian Diet and *Landrat* in Kreis Delitzsch from 1855 to 1892, that when Bismarck offered him a higher post he replied, "It is my highest ambition to be and to remain *Landrat* of Kreis Delitzsch."[44]

When we come to examine the Junkers who spent years in the *Landratsamt* we find that they fall into two general categories: those who served as *Landrat* only, without further participation in the communal activity of the province, and those who combined the *Landratsamt* with a great variety of provincial activity. The former are of two general types—those who held property within the Circle and those who had no property and/or came in from outside. As an example of the propertied *Landrat* who confined his public activities to this office we have Erich, Baron von Knesebeck-Milendonk who served for seventeen years until his death in 1907 as *Landrat* of Kreis Ruppin where he owned the large estate of Karwe (3250 acres). He was a descendant of an original noble family of the Altmark and older brother of Waldemar, lord of Tylsen and other estates in Kreis Salzwedel, who was Master of Ceremonies in the Neue Palais.[45] Erich was a retired Cavalry Captain and a member of the Vandalia student corps in Heidelberg. He held no civil office other than that of *Landrat*.[46]

In decided contrast is Maximilian, Baron Lauer von Muenchhofen who neither owned landed property nor held office in his home province. He was descended from a family raised to the Imperial nobility in 1790 and to the Prussian baronage six years thereafter that had settled in the vicinity of Frankfort a.O. His father, Eugen, owned no estates and his mother was a commoner, Elisabeth Pusch.[47] In 1895 Maximilian appears as a *Regierungs-Assessor* assisting the

---

44. H. von Arnim and G. von Below (49) *Deutscher Aufstieg,* p. 251. The two opposing views of the *Landratsamt* as a stage in a bureaucratic career and as a career in itself are further developed under the discussion of the *Landratsamt,* Chapter V, p. 178f.

45. He married Helene von Ohlen und Adlerskron and was the father of five sons and three daughters.

46. That he was a founder and subscriber to the *Familiengeschichtlichen Blaetter* (see v. 2, p. 20) is an indication of his interest in genealogy and lineage.

47. Maximilian married Charlotte von Tiedemann, daughter of Christoph, the *Regierungs-Praesident* in Bromberg.

Landrat of Kreis Stolp in the governmental district of Koeslin and as a Lieutenant of the Reserves in the 2nd Foot Guards Regiment. From 1900 to 1915 he served as *Landrat* in the western part of Prussia, first in Kreis Ottweiler in the Rhineland and later in Kreis Hanau in Hessen-Nassau. He retired from the army after reaching the rank of Captain in the Reserves.

The career of Friedrich, Count Finck von Finckenstein of the Brandenburg branch of that original old East Prussian family offers a similar example. Friedrich was the second son of Rudolf, lord of Reitwein (1935 acres) and younger brother of Guenther who inherited the estate. For thirty-three years, from 1885 to his death in 1918, Friedrich served as *Landrat* in the distant Silesian Circle of Habelschwerdt.[48]

On the other hand, Dr.jur. Ewald von Massow, scion of one of the oldest and most distinguished families of Pomerania, served for years in his native province altho he owned no estates. He was the eldest son of Anton, a General in the Infantry but without landed property, and Countess Innhausen. In 1895 he appears as a *Regierungs-Assessor* in Posen, but from 1900 to 1918 he held the post of *Landrat* in Kreis Kammin, Pomerania.[49]

Ludolf von Bismarck gives us a fine example of the other type of *Landrat* who was active in various provincial affairs. He comes from the original old Bismarck family of the Altmark and owned the fideicommissum of Briest and the estate of Welle (3510 acres) in Kreis Stendal.[50] For thirty years, from 1865 to 1895 Ludolf served as *Landrat* in his home Circle, Stendal. During all of the period from 1888 to 1914 he acted as *Landeshauptmann* of the Altmark[51] and chairman of its communal society for the old feudal Estates (*Kommunalstaendischer Verband*). From 1900 to 1910 he

48. He was a member of the Hasso-Borussen in Bonn and a Lieutenant in the cavalry militia. He had married Elisabeth von Zastrow in 1880 and was the father of three children.
49. He was a 1st Lieutenant in the Reserves. He married into the famous Schulenburg family but had no children.
50. He married Elisabeth Woldeck von Arneburg and was the father of four sons and four daughters.
51. The *Landeshauptmann* of the Altmark was merely head of a local communal organization which had survived since feudal times but had little or no administrative importance. He is not to be confused with the *Landeshauptmann* of the Province of Brandenburg.

was an elected member of the Provincial Council of the Province of Saxony and in 1914 he was a deputy member of the Provincial Executive Committee. In the same year he served as a deputy director of the Provincial Fire Department. In 1900 and 1914 he was a member of the Provincial Diet. From 1900 to 1914 he was as well a member of the Executive Committee of the Agricultural Chamber of Saxony. In 1922, at the age of 88, he was still *Landeshauptmann* of the Altmark. For him the *Landratsamt* may have been just another local job.

Before we leave the *Landratsamt* let us, because of its key position and variety of duties, examine the proportion of *Landraete* in each of the several categories described. Of a total of 328 *Landraete* 66 or 20.12% held the office for a brief period as a step to higher posts. The remaining 262 or 79.88% did not go beyond the *Landratsamt*. Of these some dropped out after a few years; others made a career of the office and many of these combined it with a variety of provincial administrative activities. In fact, only 73 or 22.25% held the office of *Landrat* alone whereas 126 or 38.41% combined it with membership in one or more provincial organizations.[52] Altho this percentage is not large it should be borne in mind that Junkers serving in any other administrative post, e.g. as *Regierungs-* or *Ober-Regierungsrat,* almost never held any office in the provincial self-government. This was peculiar to the *Landrat* because of his dual character. Finally, 41 or 12.50% were members of the House of Deputies at the same time that they were serving as *Landraete* whereas of the others who held career offices (regular bureaucratic or Court officials) only 11 or 2.24% were in the House of Deputies. Of the 41 *Landraete* 38 were German Conservatives and three[53] were Free Conservatives. There were 13 *Landraete* in the *Herrenhaus.*

PROVINCIAL SELF-GOVERNMENT

Of the total number of 1500 Junkers in office between 1888 and 1914 as many as 698 or approximately one-half served in the pro-

---

52. Sixty of the 126 combined the *Landratsamt* only with membership in the Provincial Diet altho at least 127 *Landraete* were at one time members of the Provincial Diets; 66 were active in a number of provincial bodies while they were *Landraete*.

53. Wilhelm von Kardorff, his son, Siegfried, and Joachim von Bonin.

vincial self-government only. This means that only slightly more than one-half of the Junker officials were in the service of the Prussian State. All offices in the provincial self-government, with the important exception of that of *Landeshauptmann* or chief of all the self-governing institutions of the province, were honorary and their Junker incumbents were almost without exception owners of knights' estates in the area. Sometimes Junkers might, as in the above cases, combine the *Landratsamt* with provincial offices, often as in the case of these 698 they served only in a local capacity. Some were chosen for a number of important provincial offices, others held only a modest position as a member of a District Committee or of the Agricultural Chamber. In all of these cases officeholding was only incidental to the Junker's real profession as large-scale farmer, retired army officer or retired bureaucrat.

A splendid example of an outstanding provincial administrator is to be found in Ruediger, Baron von der Goltz (1837-1910)[54] who combined local activities and a political career with a successful vocation as a progressive farmer. He was descended from the original Neumark noble family of von der Goltz and was the only son of Karl von der Goltz, formerly *Landrat* and *Landesdirektor* of the Neumark. His mother was a von Arnim. He had inherited four fine estates in Pomerania with a total area of 9695 acres (3878 hectares) and his main occupation after the death of his father in 1865 was the farming of these estates. He could not perform any military service because of his health but he entered the civil administration after receiving the degree of Doctor Juris. From 1865 (the year when he took over his father's estates) until 1871 he served as *Landrat* for Kreis Schivelbein. Ten years later he was made *Landesdirektor* or administrative head of the provincial self-government of Pomerania, which post he held for twelve years, until 1893. From 1893 until his death in 1910 he held the office of Chairman of the Pomeranian Provincial Executive Committee. From 1900 to 1910 he was also a member of the Provincial Council of Pomerania. After 1881 von der Goltz' main public interest was in the welfare of his home province. He had many progressive ideas

54. Ruediger, Frhr. von der Goltz (164) "Ruediger von der Goltz," *Pommersche Lebensbilder*, v. 1, pp. 279-87.

and was anxious to introduce improvements particularly in the administration of social insurance and the extension of electrification to this backward region.[55]

Von der Goltz also played a role in politics. He entered the Prussian Diet in 1870 and the Reichstag in 1871 and was at first a member of the Conservative fraction but when it broke with Bismarck he went over to the *Reichspartei*. This brought down on him the wrath of his old conservative friends in Pomerania such as Moritz von Blanckenburg. Goltz was a staunch monarchist but with true Junker independence and self-assertion he freely criticized the administration policies. He was opposed to Miquel's tax reforms as confiscatory and to the Caprivi tariffs, believing that tariff protection for agriculture was necessary for the preservation of the peasant and the large landowning class (!). In 1898 von der Goltz entered the *Herrenhaus* as a life member.

In spite of his interest and enthusiasm for provincial and national affairs Goltz' chief occupation was the direction of his four estates. He had by travelling in England and by study acquainted himself with the latest agricultural and forestry technics and he endeavored to apply them to his own farms. He made many scientific improvements in the administration of his forests and was a pioneer in the mechanizing of farm work, the use of artificial fertilizers and the construction of narrow gauge field railways in Pomerania. His innovations excited resentment and antagonism among his old-fashioned Junker neighbors, as did his individualistic but profound religious views which did not conform to the ruling Evangelical orthodoxy. Goltz took a paternal interest in his peasants and laborers and made provision for their education and their care in sickness or want, altho his son says that he made no display of his charities.[56]

Ruediger and his wife, Marie von Bassewitz, had two sons. The elder, also Ruediger, followed in his father's footsteps, studied law and entered the civil administration. Until his father's death he served as *Landrat* in Kreis Kolberg-Koerlin in Pomerania. He became a Reserve Officer in the Curassier Guards Regiment. After inheriting his father's four estates he held office only in the District Committee

55. *Op. cit.*, pp. 286-87.
56. *Ibid.*, p. 282.

of the Koeslin *Regierung* and in the Provincial Executive Committee
of Pomerania. Magnus, the younger son, entered upon a military
career and became a Cavalry Captain.

In direct contrast to Dr. Ruediger von der Goltz with his variety
of offices is Kurt, Baron von Schlichting, descendant of an old
Lutheran family of Silesia and owner of the fideicommissum of
Wierzbiczany in Kreis Hohensalza, Bromberg. For twenty years, from
1894 to 1914, he held the modest post of member of the Bromberg
District Committee and this post only. He was, however, a chamber-
lain (*Kammerherr*) and a retired Cavalry Captain. A similar case
is that of Rudolf von Kannewurff of an old Thuringian family that
had long since settled in East Prussia. He had inherited the family
estate of Baitkowen (2812 acres) in Kreis Lyck. His only public
office was that of deputy member of the East Prussian Provincial
Executive Committee which he filled from 1888 until his death in
1900. His younger brother, Ernst, who had no property, entered
the regular bureaucracy and became Police President in Koenigsberg
in 1900.

Another field of provincial activity favored by the Junkers was
that of the *Landschaften* or provincial land credit institutes. Because
of their aristocratic origins in the 18th century when rural landholding was restricted almost entirely to nobles they were still largely
in the hands of Junker landlords. To hold the honorary post of
Landschaft Counsellor or Director was both natural and distinguished
for the Junker. Some combined *Landschaft* offices with other provincial or political activities, other men or even families seemed to
concentrate on this provincial institution alone. Thus two of the
three brothers, Barons von Czettritz und Neuhaus, an original
Silesian noble family, served in the Silesian *Landschaft* (Bernhard,
lord of Kolbnitz, 1295 acres, as Director of the Schweidnitz-Jauer
Landschaft and Werner, lord of Seitendorf, 675 acres, as Counsellor
in the same). In the ancient Silesian family of von Prittwitz und
Gaffron eight out of the fifteen members holding office between
1888 and 1914 were in the Silesian *Landschaft* and seven of these
served in that capacity only, the eighth being also a deputy to the
Provincial Diet. On the other hand, Friedrich, Baron von Steinaecker,
from the old noble family of that name in Pomerania, combined top

offices in the Pomeranian *Landschaft* with other provincial activities and a legislative career in the Prussian Diet. He was the son of Karl, also a *Landschaft* Counsellor and a member of the Diet, and of Euphemie, née von Eickstedt-Peterswaldt. His father left him the estate of Rosenfelde (2150 acres) in Kreis Greifenhagen. From 1900 to 1910 Friedrich served as General *Landschaft* Counsellor representing Further Pomerania and in 1914 he was a General *Landschaft* Director for Pomerania and a member of the Central Prussian *Landschaft* in the Ministry of the Interior. During these same years von Steinaecker was a member of the Pomeranian Provincial Executive Committee and of the Provincial Council. He also represented his home electoral district of Randow-Greifenhagen in the House of Deputies after 1903.[57]

The notorious Jordan von Kroecher combined high offices in the Brandenburg *Landschaft* with an outstanding political career. He was descended from an ancient Magdeburg family which appeared in Kreis Wolmirstedt as early as 1184 and was himself the modern counterpart of the rough, self-assertive, egotistical, rebellious Junker knight. Hellmuth von Gerlach says of the family, "The Kroechers are the real *Krautjunker* of the Mark. They are so pious that the oldest son is always named Jordan and must always be baptized with water from the Jordan."[58] He accuses Jordan of betraying his friend, Wilhelm von Hammerstein, editor of the *Kreuzzeitung*. Even von Buelow, with his friendly feelings toward Junkers describes von Kroecher in these words. "He had all the faults attributed often unjustly to the Junkers but not the great qualities which they really possess." He was "coarse but without humour" and had a "peasant's shrewdness but no real insight." And again, he was "assiduously interested in the welfare of his party and his class but he was without due consideration for the state as a whole."[59]

Von Kroecher owned the two fideicommissa of Vinzelberg (6250 acres) in the Altmark and Joachimsdorf-Vogtsbruegge (3125 acres)

---

57. He was a member of the *Gesellschaft fuer Pommersche Geschichte und Altertumskunde* and a retired 1st Lieutenant. He married a Countess Schlieffen and was the father of one son.

58. Gerlach (31) p. 136.

59. Buelow (24) v. 1, p. 513.

in the Priegnitz.[60] He had retired from the army as a Cavalry Captain. Kroecher played a leading role in the Brandenburg *Landschaft*. In 1888 he was already *Ritterschaft* Director and from 1889 to 1914 he was a Chief *Rittershaft* Director for Brandenburg as well as member of the Central Prussian *Landschaft*. His most important work, however, was in the Prussian House of Deputies which he entered in 1879 as the representative for the Altmark district of Salzwedel and where he held the high office of President of the House from 1898 to 1912. He was re-elected in 1913 but not to the Presidency. Von Kroecher was an arch reactionary and his tactics as presiding officer were partly responsible for the famous defeat of the Canal Bill in 1899.[61]

Altho the Junkers might combine a political career or even the hybrid office of *Landrat* with various political activities they almost never passed over from a purely bureaucratic career to the field of provincial self-government. Service in the Prussian State administration was looked on as a life career and the *Regierungsrat* devoted his time and energies toward advancement in this line rather than spending them on local affairs. If a member of the Prussian State administration did pass over to the provincial administration it was generally a *Landrat* who, because of the dual nature of his office, had already taken part in the local self-government. In this connection it is interesting to note briefly the unusual career of Hugo, Baron von Wilamowitz-Moellendorf, who twice switched back and forth between the Prussian State administration and offices of the provincial self-government. Hugo belonged to the distinguished Wilamowitz family which had moved from Brandenburg to Posen early in the 19th century and acquired extensive properties there, including Markowitz with Moellendorf (2650 acres). He was the older brother of the renowned classicist, Ulrich von Wilamowitz-Moellendorf who gives unity to Hugo's varied career by his comment that Hugo devoted his life to the service of Posen.[62] Hugo started out as a *Landrat* in Kreis Inrowrazlawo, Posen (1867-1876). In 1874 he took over

60. He was the son of Wilhelm and Bertha von Gerlach and the husband of Luise von Krosigk.
61. See, *inter alia*, Hans Herzfeld (76) *Johannes von Miquel*, v. 2, p. 603.
62. Wilamowitz-Moellendorf (44) p. 11.

the administration of his father's estates and in 1888 and 1890 he
appears only as a member of the Provincial Executive Committee.
He was appointed to the *Herrenhaus* in 1888. In 1891 he again held
a post in the Prussian State administration and the one which was
most closely related to provincial affairs, the distinguished office of
Ober-Praesident of Posen. He was retired from that office in 1899,
probably because of the opposition of the Eastern Marches Association (*Ostmarkenverein*) which denounced his lack of zeal for the
German national cause in Posen and the half-hearted way in which
he carried out the policy of German colonization on Polish estates.
As a genuine conservative he could not promote what seemed to him
an infringement of property rights.[63] On leaving the post of *Ober-
Praesident,* Hugo went back again to provincial activities and acted as
Marshal of the Posen Provincial Diet until his death in 1905.

Even more singular is the career of Friedrich von Berg from the
original Uckermark noble family of that name, who owned the
estate of Markienen (1250 acres) in Kreis Friedland, East Prussia.
He entered the administrative service and by 1905 he had become
Landrat of Kreis Goldap in the governmental district of Gumbinnen.
He was a Captain of the Reserves in the aristocratic 1st Foot Guards
Regiment and a member of the elite Hasso-Borussia student corps
of Bonn. In 1906 Berg left his native soil and went to Berlin to hold
the administrative post of *Vortragender Rat* in the Civil Cabinet.
Then, after two years here, he was appointed by his home province
of East Prussia as *Landeshauptmann,* which office he still held in 1914.
In 1918 Berg went back to Berlin as Chief of the Civil Cabinet but
he apparently resigned within a few months.

CHURCH AND JUDICIAL OFFICES

Because of their close affiliation with the Evangelical Church
and their strong and fervent orthodoxy Junkers often played a role
as lay[64] members in the direction of the state church. Offices on

63. Richard W. Tims (119) *The Prussianization of German Poland,* p. 70;
Wilhelm von Massow (97) *Die deutsche innere Politik unter Kaiser Wilhelm II,*
p. 185.
64. Altho Hans von Kleist-Retzow claimed that the Prussian nobles were "die
geborenen General Superintendenten und kirchlichen Leiter" and altho he urged
them to turn more and more to theological training (see Hermann von Petersdorff

the provincial synodical committee or in the Evangelical Supreme Church Council were honorable and distinguished and they gave the Junker layman an opportunity to express his pious and missionary impulses.[65] For some Junkers membership on the provincial church board was one more phase of their public activities in their home territory, for others it ran parallel with a political career and these were able at the same time to fulfill their sense of duty to their God and to their State or political estate.

Hans von Kleist-Retzow, that grand old patriarchal figure of a Junker, found the inspiration for his political actions in his religious faith and he combined a distinguished parliamentary career with offices on his own provincial and the Prussian Church Council. Imbued with the spirit of Pomeranian pietism and for some time associated with its leader, Ludwig von Gerlach, Kleist-Retzow based his political policies upon his positive religious convictions. He hammered away at his program of Tory socialism, unswerving in his belief that he was doing God's will and must be adamant. His home life was filled with the same spirit of conscientious pietism. His most recent biographer, A. O. Meyer, says of him, "He was a very biblical head of the family."[66] He read prayers morning and evening for his family and servants; his wife always spoke of him as "Mein Herr." Kleist-Retzow's stubborn and missionary conservatism made him unacceptable as a state official in the New Era after 1858 and he was dismissed as *Ober-Praesident* of the Rhineland. But in the same year, 1858, he was appointed a member of the *Herrenhaus* to represent the von Kleist family and in 1877 he was elected to the Reichstag where for years he was a dynamic exponent of Christian Conservatism. He work for a return to the old *Staendestaat* and his ideal was a union of "Christianity, German nationalism and nobility." He became a powerful protagonist of these principles within the Conservative Party, so powerful that at times he was able to have a deci-

(106) *Hans von Kleist-Retzow*, p. 535) the fact remains that I found no Junkers in clerical offices.

65. Junkers were also occasionally appointed canons of cathedral chapters (*Domstifter*). These offices, too, were honorable and distinguished and, according to Eugen von Jagemann (35) *Fuenfundsiebzig Jahre des Erlebens und Erfahrens*, p. 149, they often served as good berths for used-up Generals and statesmen.

66. A. O. Meyer (172) "Hans von Kleist-Retzow," *Pommersche Lebensbilder*, v. 2, p. 127.

sive influence over party councils and party policy.[67] Meyer points to Kleist-Retzow's Junker character when he writes. "In Kleist Christian humility was combined with an aristocratic feeling of authority."[68] Kleist-Retzow was a lay member of the provincial synodical committee from its origin in 1881 until his death in 1892. He also served as a lay member of the Evangelical Supreme Church Council from 1880 to 1892.[69]

Leopold, first Count von der Osten-Jannewitz and descendant of an old Saxon family which had established itself in Pomerania by the 14th century, played a more modest role than Kleist-Retzow in the Evangelical Church. He owned large properties (totalling 14,410 acres) in Kreis Lauenburg in Pomerania, the most important of which was the fideicommissum Gross Jannewitz. He was a retired Major, a life member of the *Herrenhaus* since 1897, in which year he had been raised to the rank of Count, and a Circle delegate (*Kreisdeputierter*). His wife, Helene von Barby, bore him three sons and two daughters. From 1895 down to the war Count Leopold was a member of the synodical committee of Pomerania. This with his membership in the *Herrenhaus* was his only public service. He was too wealthy to seek any remunerative post and evidently had no interest in general provincial activities.

Altho training for an administrative and a judicial career was identical up to the final stage and altho the courts had many distinguished and highly paid positions to offer, the judicial department of the government was never popular with the Junkers. The first explanation of this is probably custom, for judicial work was repugnant to the proud Junkers of the countryside from early times

67. Wilhelm von Kardorff writes in the *Deutsches Wochenblatt* (135) 1892, p. 246, "Der Kampf des Herrn von Helldorf gegen seine Widersacher in der eigenen Fraktion haette schwerlich die unguenstige Wendung fuer ihn genommen, wenn Herr von Kleist-Retzow nicht das Schwergewicht seines Namens gegen ihn in die Wagschaale geworfen haette, und selbst die Haltung der konservativen Partei des Abgeordnetenhauses bei der Berathung des Schulgesetzes einschliesslich der Haltung des Grafen von Zedlitz-Truetzschler als Kultusminister, wurde vielfach auf die persoenlichen Einwirkungen des Herrn von Kleist-Retzow auf manche Parteimitglieder zurueckgefuehrt, vielleicht ohne Berechtigung, aber jedenfalls bezeichnend fuer die Schaetzung der Autoritaet desselben seitens der uebrigen Parteien."

68. A. O. Meyer (172) p. 141.

69. For an account of Kleist-Retzow's activities as a layman on Church boards see Petersdorff (106) p. 533.

when Roman law was first introduced into Brandenburg. Lawyers were household servants of the prince, often commoners and without land and dependent upon the royal will, altho they might later be granted estates from the royal domains, whereas the Junkers were proud and independent nobles, entrenched in their local estates. Furthermore, judicial offices required from the beginning a high degree of technical training and such training was always distasteful to the Junker. Not until the 19th century was the course prescribed for prospective *Regierungs-Assessoren* as rigorous and theoretical as that for *Gerichts-Assessoren*. Moreover, judicial offices did not offer as much social prestige as administrative posts. They were looked on as bourgeois.[70] Neither did they offer the same freedom of movement. The independence of the judiciary meant that judges as individuals were to be free from material and political influences in the formulation of their judgments. But this also meant that they were expected to hold themselves aloof from the political arena and not to engage in any political campaigns or intrigues, altho they sometimes did enter politics as in the 1860's. A policy of exclusion from politics would have been a great restriction on the Junker. An added and a fundamental reason why judicial service fell below administrative service in the estimation of the Junker was the fact that the highest judge, with all his national distinction and professional prestige, had no governing powers whereas an administrative official had authority to govern and rule from the time that he entered the modest office of *Regierungs-Assessor*. Nor did the judicial service offer the same opportunity to rise to top positions in the State unless, of course, a judge moved over to the administrative side of judicial affairs and became Minister of Justice. Thus the early preference of the Junkers for administrative rather than judicial offices was fostered by these other factors until it had become more firmly fixed as a custom.

It is for these reasons that examples of Junkers in high judicial offices are rare. Of the 1500 officials studied only 15 or 1% held

70. Hellmuth von Gerlach (31) p. 76, in describing his experiences in the bureaucratic service says that he wanted to become a *Regierungs-Referendar* because it was inexpressably finer and socially superior to the office of *Gerichts-Referendar*. Alexander von Hohenlohe (32) p. 328, also refers to the higher social standing of the administrative official, ". . . auch die Verwaltung galt als vornehm, wohingegen man die Justiz den Buergerlichen ueberliess."

judicial posts. These ranged all the way from *Gerichts-Assessor* to President of a Provincial Supreme Court but not one Junker became Minister of Justice. The 1% shows us that occasionally sons of distinguished old Junker families did have a personal preference for a judicial career. Thus we find Karl von Wartenberg, scion of an ancient noble family of the Altmark, serving from 1895 to 1918 and after as a judge of the Supreme Court or *Kammergericht*[71] in Brandenburg. Prior to that he had been a magistrate (*Amtsrichter*) and judge of a local court (*Amtsgerichstrat*). He was the eldest son of Karl, a retired army Captain, and Marie Esmarsch. Neither father nor son owned any landed property. Karl also married commoners, Martha Kaestner and Elisabeth Esmarch. He held no other post except that in the *Kammergericht* and he performed no military service.

More distinguished is the career of Carl Ludwig von Plehwe of East Prussia. He was the second son of Carl von Plehwe, a retired Cavalry Captain and member of an old East Prussian family which had owned the estate of Dwarischken in Kreis Pillkallen for two hundred years. Carl Ludwig decided to prepare for government service and studied law at Berlin and Bonn. At the latter university he joined the Alemania Burschenschaft rather than one of the aristocratic student corps.[72] When he reached the crossroads in his state training he chose the judicial rather than the administrative path and became a public prosecutor (*Staatsanwalt*). Carl Ludwig went right up in the judicial service until in 1899 he appeared as President of the East Prussian Provincial Supreme Court in Koenigsberg, which high office he held until 1910. Thereafter he held the honorary post of Chancellor of Prussia.

Von Plehwe had inherited Dwarischken from his father and he hired a professional administrator to direct it until 1903 when he deeded it to his eldest son who had retired from the Officers Corps to study agriculture. As owner of Dwarischken Carl Ludwig was sent to the *Herrenhaus* as a representative of the East Prussian old and established landowners (*Verband des alten und befestigten*

71. The *Kammergericht* in Berlin served as Provincial Supreme Court for the province of Brandenburg and also had jurisdiction over all of Prussia in a few restricted appeal questions.
72. He married Sophie von Gossler, daughter of *Oberlandesgerichtspraesident* Gustav von Gossler and sister of the two Prussian Ministers, Gustav and Heinrich.

Grundbestizes) and as such he also took part in the 200th anniversary of the crowning of the King of Prussia in 1901. He also served his province as a member of the Provincial Executive Committee and of the synodical committee of East Prussia. He was a retired Captain of the militia.

PRUSSIAN DIET

While we are examining the various types of public careers followed by the Junkers and the many individual combinations of their varied activities it seems proper to study the background and extra-parliamentary activities of the Junker members of the Prussian Diet. For the relationship between administrative offices and political representation is of primary importance. Junker membership in the *Herrenhaus* was based for the most part on ownership of old and · established estates or membership in the society of Counts (*Grafen-verband*) or in one of the eleven to seventeen noble families especially endowed with the right to present a member for royal appointment to the *Herrenhaus*. As a result members were generally men of distinguished lineage or much property or both. Some held no other offices. Others were prominent in provincial affairs, sometimes *Landraete*. Still others, like Hans von Kleist-Retzow, combined an active Reichstag career with membership in the *Herrenhaus*.

Altho socially more respected, the *Herrenhaus* was politically overshadowed by the House of Deputies with its 433 (later 443) members elected by the three-class system. The Junker representation, which ranged from 59 to 79 over the 26 years, averaged 68 of whom 91% were Conservatives and 4.44% Free Conservatives. Since both the leading Conservative politicians in the Diet and the average Junker deputy represent a wide variety of activity ranging from a straight parliamentary career to a multitude of occupations in the bureaucracy and provincial government it is possible by an examination of the careers of the politicial leaders to get a true impression of the regular Junker representative as well.

Oskar von Normann, leader of the Conservative fraction in the Reichstag and Count Hans von Kanitz-Podangen, an agrarian leader prominent in the Agrarian League and famous for the Kanitz motion, confined their activities entirely to a parliamentary career. Four other

Conservative and Free Conservative leaders, Wilhelm von Rauch-haupt, Georg von Koeller-Kantreck, Ernst von Heydebrand und der Lasa and Wilhelm von Kardorff, filled the office of *Landrat* in their home Circle during some of the time that they sat in the House of Deputies. Three of these held provincial offices as well. Hans, Count Schwerin-Loewitz, Elard von Oldenburg-Januschau and Konrad von Wangenheim-Klein Spiegel, prominent Conservative leaders and aggressive agrarians, combined membership in the House of Deputies with a variety of provincial activities, particularly in agricultural organizations. Friedrich, Count Limburg-Stirum and Jordan von Kroecher held offices only in their provincial *Landschaften* in addition to their seats in the House of Deputies. More unusual are Kuno, Count Westarp and Octavio, Baron von Zedlitz-Neukirch, the prominent Free Conservative, who held regular administrative offices at the same time that they were in the Diet. The former was a judge in the Supreme Administrative Court (*Oberverwaltungsgericht*) in Berlin and the latter a *Vortragender Rat* in the Ministry of Public Works. It is significant not only that of the thirteen Conservative leaders here mentioned only these two were in the administration but also that these same two were the only ones out of the thirteen who did not own estates.

If we examine the whole group of Junker deputies we find that they do actually fall into the same general classifications as their leaders. A total of 202 Junkers held seats in the House of Deputies at some time between 1888 and 1914. One hundred and fifty-nine or 78.71% of these owned estates. Sixty-eight of the 202 or 33½% held no other offices except that of deputy whereas another 66 or 32½% played a role in provincial affairs as well and 19 Junker deputies were *Landraete* as well as provincial leaders. Twenty-two were *Landraete* only, making a total of 41 deputies or 20% who were also *Landraete*. No more than 6 held top bureaucratic offices (*Regierungs-Praesident* and over) and only 8 held other offices in the regular administration.

TENURE IN OFFICE

In our study of Junker officials we are interested not only in the actual offices held, their variety and combination but even more in the attitude of the Junkers toward these offices. An important key to an understanding of their attitude is the length of time which they spent in office. Did they look on an administrative career as a serious profession and a life work or merely as a pleasing interim occupation or avocation? In answering this we must discriminate between the several general types of offices. Clearly local estate owners serving in a provincial capacity as *Landschaft* Counsellors or members of the Provincial Executive Committee did not devote their life to their office but looked on it as incidental to their main occupation as large-scale farmers or rentiers. Since such provincial offices are honorary there were no economic motives for keeping them. Length of tenure in these offices depends rather on such imponderables as personal interest in local affairs and a willingness to take responsibility, feelings of prestige which come from officeholding, popularity with neighboring landowners, a family tradition of leadership in the province and the like. It is therefore not surprising to find the tenure in provincial offices varying from a brief period to 26 years, the maximum span under consideration.

In the field of salaried and career offices the situation is quite different. When we examine the lives of regular bureaucratic officials, *Landraete* and even courtiers and foreign envoys we find, as in the cases given above, that long terms of office are the rule. Thus of the 705 holding offices in the Prussian State administration including the *Landratsamt* between 1888 and 1914, 625 or 88.65% had entered the administrative service before 1888 or continued in it after 1914. Some held office for the whole 26 years or a large part thereof; some had already served many years prior to 1888 but retired before 1914; others were hardly launched as *Regierungs-Assessoren* by 1914 but we may presume from the habits of their older colleagues that they intended to devote many years to their chosen profession. The figure of 625 includes those who had entered office after 1888 but died before 1914. This leaves only 80 officials who acted contrary to the regular custom of administrative officials and voluntarily retired from office after only a few years.

Of the 102 Junker Court officials only 77.45% held office over the entire period or were in office before 1888 or after 1914 and 23 or 22.55% held a court office for a period within the 26 years. The explanation for this smaller percentage lies largely in the nature of the office and the economic background of the officeholder. Aides-de-camp, for example, might serve the monarch for only a brief period in a long military career. Or wealthy landowners might hold office in the Royal Household for a few years because of the social brilliance of the post or personal friendship with the Emperor and then retire. Some might be dropped because of royal disfavor. Yet in spite of these factors a brief tenure in office remained the exception.

To return to the Junker who entered the Prussian State administration, it is evident from the foregoing figures that he did so with the intention of making it his life work and of carving out a career for himself within this profession. He hoped no doubt to rise to the top. But he knew that once established he could without disgrace spend the rest of his life simply as a *Landrat* or *Regierungsrat*. He expected to devote his full time and attention to his job and was ready to be sent to any part of the Prussian kingdom altho, if he was a *Landrat* with landed property, he hoped and expected to hold that office in his own Circle. For such *Landraete* with nearby country seats the office may have been less the centre of their activity, less vital to their livelihood and more incidental to other interests than was the case with the landless regular bureaucrat. It is likely, also, that such men felt more independent and more free to challenge the higher authorities.

More interesting than the Junker who followed the normal pattern and spent the twenty-five to thirty best years of his life in administrative work are the eighty exceptions—those who left the service while still *Regierungs-Assessoren* or even as *Regierungs-Referendare* and those who rose higher and yet left office in a short time. Thirty-six of these were *Landraete* (10.98% of all the *Landraete*). We know that at least twenty of the eighty left office when they inherited their father's estates and we presume that another ten left for the same reason. Some of these, like Konstantin von Boehn, had not passed the stage of *Referendare* or, like Hasso, Count Yorck von Wartenberg, of *Assessoren*. Others had reached the rank of *Regierungrat* or Police President as had Paul von Somnitz and Bernhard von Puttkamer respectively. These 20 or 30 men may not have expected to inherit estates, or at least not for a considerable number of years, or it may have been that they had a real predilection for legal training and bureaucratic work and preferred to spend their early years in this occupation with the knowledge that they would soon have to retire to their ancestral estates. However, we may safely assume that this transient attitude was exceptional in the administrative service and that the choice of a bureaucratic office as a temporary occupation was due rather to ill health which prevented military service or the desire to become eligible to hold the local *Landratsamt* at some future time.

Another 6 out of the 80 short-term officeholders neither rose beyond the rank of *Regierungs-Assessor* nor inherited property. Of these we know only that Hellmuth von Gerlach left the service for a journalistic career. It is possible that the others lacked the capacity to go on to higher office. Either this or ill health may explain why Bolko von Uechtritz und Steinkirch spent 10 years as a *Regierungs-Assessor* and then retired. He died 6 years after he left office. As to the grounds for early retirement of the remaining 44 officials I cannot hazard an explanation.

The custom of Junker career officials of devoting their entire lives to their profession grows in interest when compared with the quite different custom of Junker army officers. Of these latter a majority[73] spent only a few years in active service and then retired to their estates with the rank of 1st Lieutenant, Captain or, if especially capable, even of Major. It seems apparent that whereas a Junker son often looked on army service only as a stop-gap—a congenial occupation with a salary that went part way toward meeting his expenses and one which would fill in the years from the end of his schooling to the time when he should take up the cultivation of his estate—he approached the bureaucratic career with the serious intent of devoting his whole life to it. The practice of long tenure in administrative office was assuredly an important factor in the transformation of some Junker officials into bureaucratic and even bourgeois types.

73. The analysis of the army service of the officers in the thirteen typical families described in Chapter IV shows that 60% of these retired within a few years.

III

THE ECONOMIC AND SOCIAL BACKGROUND AND THE QUALIFICATIONS FOR OFFICE OF THE JUNKER OFFICIAL

AS IN every social group there is with the Junkers a close relationship between their occupation or profession and their economic status. In the case of the Junker official, economic and social position determined in part not only the type of career which he would make but also the effect of officeholding on his attitudes and, conversely, the influence of his attitudes and position on the character of the office. We already know from the Junkers' early history that not only tradition, social custom and the royal will but also, and perhaps primarily, economic considerations prompted the Junker to seek public office. We also know, conversely, that the Junker officeholder had an economic reserve thru his own possession or the ownership in his family of landed property. In earlier times the Junker official's economic range lay between the landless younger son, living on his salary but without fear of destitution because of the landed wealth of his brothers and cousins, and the large landowner who lived in ease on his estates and could afford to hold honorary and unremunerative provincial posts. By 1888 some Junkers were so far removed from the land that they could no longer draw sustenance from it in case of need. Hence the Junker official's economic situation was now dependent upon two major factors—his or his family's landed property and his salary from the government.

LAND-OWNERSHIP

Since the relationship between landholding and officeholding is traditionally so significant in Prussia it is clearly important to examine the extent to which Junker officials in the years from 1888 to 1914, or their relatives, owned estates and the relationship between the size of these estates and the type of office held. Finally, we should try

78

to ascertain if there is any indication of a gradual dissolution of the bond between officeholding and landholding.

Of the total of 1500 Junker officeholders, 764 or 50.93% owned estates themselves. Another 311 or 20.73% were the sons of Junkers who owned property.[1] Of the 764 officials who owned estates themselves I have been able to ascertain the size of the properties of only 523. These range all the way from 225 to 22,250 acres (90 to 8900 hectares) but these figures represent two unusual extremes and the size most frequent with Junker officials was 2500 to 5000 acres, as the following table indicates:

Number of hectares	*Number of acres*	*Number of Junker officials holding estates of this size*	*Percentage of 523*
0- 500	0- 1250	67	12.81
500-1000	1250- 2500	134	25.62
1000-2000	2500- 5000	189	36.13
2000-5000	5000-12,500	96	18.35
over 5000	over 12,500	37	7.07

It is important to note that only 7.07% of those who have been considered as Junkers owned property amounting to more than 12,500 acres. This coincides with the fact that Junkers were not large landholders but of the poorer lesser nobility, for estates up to 12,500 acres were not exceptionally large according to the standards in the seven eastern provinces. Johannes Conrad in defining a latifundium in eastern Prussia in 1888 sets 12,500 acres as a minimum area and implies that estates of smaller size are not exceptional or such as to give the owner conspicuous superiority over his neighbors.[2]

We can now take each of these arbitrarily selected acreage categories and find out what office was most frequently held in each category or what relationship existed between the size of the estate and the nature of the office. If we take the three offices which appear most frequently in each acreage range we get the following results:

---

1. Some of the remaining 28% may have been the brothers of landowners.
2. Johannes Conrad (127) "Die Latifundien im preussischen Osten," *Jb. f. Nationaloek. u. Stat.*, 1888, pp. 128-29. In this same essay (pp. 140-41) Conrad makes some interesting observations regarding the distribution of estates between the aristocracy and the middle class. He points out that of the 9115 who owned estates of from 250 to 2500 acres 71.91% were bourgeois and only 25.80% nobles whereas of those who owned estates over 2500 acres 68.40% were nobles.

```
    0-  1250  acres .....................Total Junker officials—  67
              Landschaft officials        —21 or 31.34%
              Landraete                   —17 or 25.37%
              Hon. Prov. officials        —10 or 14.91%
 1250-  2500  acres .....................Total Junker officials—134
              Landschaft officials        —38 or 28.35%
              Hon. Prov. officials        —27 or 20.15%
              Landraete                   —26 or 19.40%
 2500-  5000  acres .....................Total Junker officials—189
              Landschaft officials        —43 or 22.75%
              Hon. Prov. officials        —38 or 20.10%
              Landraete                   —34 or 17.98%
 5000-12,500  acres .....................Total Junker officials—  96
              House of Dep. Members       —20 or 20.83%
              Hon. Prov. officials        —19 or 19.79%
              Herrenhaus members          —16 or 16.66%
over  12,500  acres .....................Total Junker officials—  37
              Court officials          ⎫
              Hon. Prov. officials     ⎬ —9 or 24.32% each
              Herrenhaus members       ⎫
              House of Dep. Members    ⎭ —4 or 10.81% each
```

It is interesting to note that until we reach the large estates of 5000 acres and above three types of officials—*Landschaft* officials, other honorary provincial officials and *Landraete*—constantly hold the top three places. Even in the last two categories honorary provincial officials keep their place among the top three while *Landraete* and *Landschaft* officials have dropped to fourth place in the 5000-12,500 group and to third and fourth place respectively in the group over 12,500.

If we turn the figures about and approach the size of the estate from the direction of the type of office we get the following results. Let us consider seven different varieties of offices—courtiers, regular administrative officials, *Landraete*, honorary provincial officials, *Landschaft* officials, members of the *Herrenhaus* and members of the House of Deputies. In five of these categories (*Landschaft* and honorary provincial officials, *Landraete*, bureaucratic officials and members of the *Herrenhaus*) the largest percentage of landowners in that category falls in the range of 2500-5000 acres. This is, as we have seen above, the range in which the largest percentage of the total estates fall. The two exceptions are Court officials, of whom 9 out of 19 or 47% held estates of over 12,500 acres, and members of the House of Deputies, of whom 20 out of 66 or 30% owned estates ranging between 5000 and 12,500 acres.

In the above computations we have been considering only those Junkers in each type of office who owned property and the relationship between the type of office and the size of the estate. But we know that 736 officeholders or 49.07% of all the Junker officials held no property whatsoever. So we must now consider the relation between officeholding in general and landholding and the tendency of certain types of officials more than others to own property. Our figures illustrating the preponderance of certain types of officials in the different acreage ranges together with our general observations regarding provincial officials show that Junker provincial officials, either in the main institutions of provincial self-government or in the *Landschaften* almost always owned estates. The honorary and unremunerative character of these offices would also lead us to expect that their Junker incumbents lived from the land. Therefore in this discussion of the relationship between the types of office and the extent of landholding we are concerned primarily with salaried offices and we shall limit our consideration to these.

Of the total Junker officials, 705 held salaried administrative offices and an additional 102 held Court offices with salaries attached, making in all 807 salaried officials or 53.80% of all Junker officials. Of these 807 salaried officials, 466 administrative officials and 67 Court officials or 66.04% of all salaried officials owned no landed property.[3] Moreover, the fathers of 222 out of the total of 533 landless administrative and Court officials also owned no real estate. Thus 27.50% or over a quarter of those holding salaried positions were at least two generations removed from the land and were apparently entirely dependent upon their professional incomes.[4] This

3. The remaining 203 Junkers without property consist of members of the Diet, army officers serving for a short time in the War Ministry, officials whose immediate background could not be identified and the few Junkers without property in provincial offices.

4. Only a very few of these could be from the most recently created service nobility who held titles without lands because I did not include such men in the Junker group. It should be pointed out here that since propertyholding was used as one of the main criteria for the inclusion of a noble as a Junker there is some contradiction in turning about and computing the number of Junkers who held property. But this would have the effect of weighting the numbers on the side of landholding.

would seem to indicate that there was a considerable tendency for Junker officials to become detached from the land, the cornerstone of the Junker's peculiar sociological character, and to move toward the professional middle class or at least toward the "noble-bourgeois aristocracy of office" of which Hintze speaks.[5]

Of the 222 fathers who owned no land the greater number (95 or 42.79%) were, however, not officials themselves but active or retired army officers. Sixty-seven or 30% of the fathers had been in the civil service but half of these held judicial and only one-half held administrative posts.

If we subdivide the salaried offices into their several types and examine each of these we find some wide variations in the proportion of property owners. Of the 102 Court officials 33 or 32.35% owned estates but 25 of these were members of the Royal Household and only 8 were from the Military Retinue. This would seem to indicate that the aides-de-camp and generals in attendance were for the most part younger sons making a life profession of army service whereas about half of the Junkers in the Royal Household, altho they might spend years in their high office, were still landowners. Since the estates of Court officials were considerably above the average in size we may presume that appointment to high Court offices was often contingent upon the ownership of extensive lands.

The situation in the diplomatic service is similar to that in the Royal Household and here again property was undoubtedly an important factor in the selection of candidates since the office of Ambassador or Minister required a private income as well as the prestige and aristocratic background which come from large landholding. And so we find that of forty-one Junker diplomats fourteen owned estates themselves, six were the sons and two the brothers of landowners. Thus about 50% of these envoys had a close connection with the land.

If we turn to the regular administrative service, exclusive of *Landraete*, we find an entirely different picture. Of 336 bureaucratic officials only 49 or 14.58% owned any landed property. This is considerably below the general percentage (33.95%) for all salaried

5. Otto Hintze (132) "Der Beamtenstand," *Gehe-Stiftung zu Dresden, Vortraege*, v. 3, p. 137.

officials with land. If we exclude from the number of regular officials all who rose to the rank of *Regierungs-Praesident* and above, the figure drops still further—to a flat 10%. This of course indicates that top ranking officials were more frequently landowners than those in lower brackets and indeed we find that of 57 *Regierungs-* and *Ober-Praesidenten* 21 or 36.84% owned estates. This leads one to the conclusion that ownership of landed property was a real asset in making an administrative career. For apparently, so far as economic and social considerations were concerned, certain Junkers were preferred for the posts of *Regierungs-* and *Ober-Praesident* not because they had need of larger salaries but, on the contrary, because their ownership of estates gave them an economic stability and a social distinction which made them more acceptable for these high posts.

When we consider the *Landraete* in this connection we find that here again they show exceptional and significant characteristics. In the first place we find that of the 387 *Landraete* as many as 127 or 41.76% owned estates. Hence this category of salaried Junker officials was more closely related to landholding than any other with the exception, possibly, of the diplomats. This is not at all surprising considering what we know of the origin and character of the *Landratsamt*. Because originally it was almost invariably held by a local squire and because it always kept its communal self-governing functions it was by nature more closely related to the local rural scene than any other office in the Prussian State administration.

This close bond with the land undoubtedly had certain important effects upon the attitude of the *Landrat* toward the State. If, as was likely, he owned an estate within the Circle which he was administering and if, moreover, he lived on and from that estate he could conduct the affairs of his office as a side issue, as an activity incidental to his status as a landlord. And indeed his functions as *Landrat* brought him into association with the same men whom he met as neighbors at all the local hunting parties or, if peasants, as fellow farmers at the meetings of the local agricultural society. The coincidence of *Landrat* with local landowner meshed the office firmly into the fabric of the local scene. It gave the *Landrat* an almost paternalistic, even a proprietary attitude toward his office and in some cases the same *Landratsamt* actually passed from father to son. In eight cases[6] a *Landrat* with a local estate handed on his office to a younger son who did not inherit the property and in three others the son inherited both the property and the office.[7] All this gave the *Landrat* a sense of security and of independence toward the central government and made him feel free to give vent to his Junker impulses of self-assertion and arrogance and even to challenge the administration of which he himself was an agent.

The *Landratsamt* was, in fact, the administrative office most congenial to the Junker. It is significant that of all the 700 Junkers holding office in the Prussian State administration (including 41 diplomatic envoys) 328 or almost half were in the one office of *Landrat*. If we review briefly the various peculiarities of this hybrid office we shall see that they all have some connection with the unique character of the Junker. The dual, half-feudal nature of the office which combined bureaucratic with local communal functions reflected the traditional twin interests of the Junker official and put him, as *Landrat*, in a position to influence both central and local affairs. The multiplicity of provincial offices held by the *Landrat* in contrast with the official in the regular administration is a direct result of the dual character of the office. The less rigorous entrance requirements for the *Landratsamt* and their local communal nature[8] are to the advantage of the Junker above all others. The close connection between the office and land-ownership, which is both cause and result of the preceding characteristics and which is also the occasion of the Junker's traditional association with the office, means that the Junker in the seven eastern provinces was the favored candidate for the *Landratsamt* there.

We have already had occasion to refer to a special form of land-holding, known as the fideicommissum or entailed estate, in our description of the background and careers of various types of Junker

6. Bernard and Ernst von Bismarck; Richard and Leo von Busse; Otto and Heinrich von Gottberg; Ludwig and Hans Peter von Kotze; Leo and Friedrich von Loesch; Hans and Philipp von Lucke; Bernhard and Heinrich von der Marwitz; Adolf and Fritz von Richter.

7. Carl Felix and Carl Friedrich, Grafen von Behr; Leuthold and Michael von Meyer-Arnswalde; Ulrich and Joachim von Winterfeldt. Dr. Warner von Saldern followed in the footsteps of his father-in-law, Bernd von Gerlach, as *Landrat* in Kreis Koenigsberg in N/M.

8. See below, p. 102f.

officials and it would seem well to pause here to examine the relation between the ownership of fidecommissa and officeholding, so far as the families of Junker officials are concerned. The fideicommissum consisted of certain property or properties, generally land, which had been set up in trust by law and which could not be reduced in size or in any way encumbered by debt so that the property would be handed down intact from generation to generation. The purpose of this institution was, of course, to ensure to a family in perpetuity the land and wealth necessary to preserve its social prestige and elegance. As such it was particularly attractive to the noble who had not only his position but a title which he must worthily represent. The fideicommissum was, however, severely criticized by economists and sociologists on several scores.[9] It had the effect of keeping large blocks of land in the hands of a few, often incapable landlords, thus reducing the area open to cultivation by small peasants. Moreover, it seldom produced an income sufficient to farm it properly and since it could not be mortgaged there was no way of procuring the necessary funds to improve it and make it solvent. Hence economic progress was excluded from large tracts of land in eastern Prussia. Sociologists complained, in addition, that the insufficient income for the main-tenance of the estate had the effect of reducing the birthrate among owners of fideicommissa until these families died out, thus defeating the purpose of the institution. One vehement opponent makes the further statement, which is particularly pertinent to our study, that the concentration of property in a few families thru the instrument of the fideicommissum led to the concentration of army and administra-tive offices among the younger sons of the same families.[10] It would

9. The institution was severely attacked during the Revolution of 1848 and the Prussian Constitution of 1850 abolished it, but it was restored by a special law in 1852 and the number of fideicommissa grew rapidly during the second half of the century, particularly between 1871 and 1890. In 1903 there was another effort to restrict the fideicommissa but it failed to have any real effect. By 1907, one-fifteenth of the total area of Prussia was in the dead grip of fideicommissa. Silesia had as high as 15.9% of its area under entail, Brandenburg, 8.1% and Pomerania and Westphalia, 7.8%. See Johannes Conrad (126) "Der Grossgrundbesitz in Ost Preussen," *Jb. f. Nationaloek. u. Stat.,* 1891, pp. 836-39; Lujo Brentano (53) *Familienfideikommisse,* pp. 15-22.

10. Brentano (53) p. 25. "Zu der Konzentration des Grundeigentums in wenigen Haenden kommt als weitere Folge die Konzentration der Beamten- und Offizier-stellen in den Haenden der nachgeborenen Soehne."

be worthwhile to test these claims by an examination of the life histories of the sons of all the fideicommissaries in Prussia. I can simply pass on my observations regarding the families of fideicommissaries who were Junkers and Prussian officials.

Of the 764 Junker officials who owned estates only 197 or 23.42% were proprietors of fideicommissa. It was not apparent that this status had any effect whatsoever on the size of the families of these men. The range was as wide as in other Junker families. Of the sons of these fideicommissaries sixty-one held some public office between 1888 and 1914. Thirty-five inherited the fideicommissum and of these thirteen held honorary provincial offices and ten entered the *Herrenhaus*.[11] Three were diplomatists, three were *Landraete*, four or five followed a regular bureaucratic career until they inherited their property. Of the twenty-six who were left without property sixteen entered the regular administration, seven becoming *Landraete*. Five entered the army and three the diplomatic service. Inheritance or non-inheritance of a fideicommissum apparently only accentuated the tendency of property owners to hold local offices and of younger sons to seek a career in the administration.

In the preceding discussion of the connection between officeholding and landholding we have had occasion to point out the relationship between the various types of salaried offices and the ownership of landed property. We know, to recapitulate briefly, that of 1500 Junker officials 807 or 53.80% at one time or another held salaried offices. We found also that regular administrative officials, particularly in the lower bracket, rarely owned property and hence were dependent for their livelihood upon their official salaries or other sources of income. Junkers in high posts, however, often owned estates so that, altho they received larger salaries they had less need for them. Likewise *Landraete*, over 40% of whom owned estates, were as a group less dependent on their salaries.

SALARIES

We come now to an examination of the various types of offices from the point of view of the salaries involved together with the

---

11. Sometimes appointment to the *Herrenhaus* was made contingent upon inheritance of the family fideicommissum.

Junker habits regarding these offices. If the Junker official's direct or more remote connection with the land was the most vital factor in his economic situation and in determining the type of office which he would enter, the question of his salary was hardly less important. For the bureaucrat's or the army officer's salary offered the only socially acceptable solution to the economic dilemma of the landless younger son or the sons of a younger son. Or it might be that the salary of a *Landrat* coming to a small Junker landowner would tip the scales for him from bankruptcy to solvency.[12]

The central administration offered the Junker not only the posts of greatest prestige and influence but also the greatest economic inducements with salaries rising to a total of 54,000 marks for the President and Vice-President of the Prussian Ministry (36,000 marks regular salary and an additional 18,000 marks for official expenses).[13] Regular Ministers received 36,000 marks salary plus 14,000 marks for official expenses or a free residence. *Ober-Praesidenten* were the next highest paid officials with 21,000 marks yearly and a free residence, but the President of the Evangelical Supreme Church Council received the same salary. The scale of salaries for other administrative officials is as follows:[14]

Yearly salary in marks

20,000	— Undersecretaries of State in Ministries — President of the *Kammergericht*[15] in Berlin — Chief of the Civil Cabinet (raised from 15,000 in 1889) plus free residence
15,000	— Presidents of Provincial Supreme Courts plus free official residence to 3000 marks

12. Of course, it might also make it possible for an inefficient and careless landlord to continue with his slovenly agricultural methods when the spectre of bankruptcy might have forced him to reform his ways.

13. The figures given for the salaries of administrative officials were taken from the *Staatshaushalts-Etat* of Prussia, 1889/1890, 1899/1900 and 1914/1915, and from the "Erlass vom 26 Mai, 1909" *Gesetzsammlung fuer die Koeniglich preussischen Staaten,* 1909, Anlage 6. The ordinance of 1909 made some slight increases in the general salary scale but these were only to offset the rise in living costs and hence have no real political or sociological significance.

14. Salaries of judges and certain other State officials are included for purposes of comparison. Figures for these were taken from the same sources as the salaries of administrative officials.

15. See p. 72, note 71.

14,000-17,000	— Department Directors in Ministries — *Oberlandstallmeister*
13,000	— *Regierungs-Praesidenten,* plus 1000-3000 for official expenses
11,500-13,000	— Presidents of Prov. Evangelical Consistories
7,000-11,500	— *Vortragende Raete* in Ministries — *Ober-Praesidial-Raete* — Judges of Supreme Administrative Court — Counsellors of Evangelical Supreme Church Council — Senate Presidents of Prov. Supreme Courts — Presidents of Prov. District Courts (*Landgerichte*)
6,500	— Full professors at University of Berlin and Technische Hochschule plus additional allowance of 1000 marks
6,000- 9,000	— Police Presidents or Directors
6,000- 7,200	— Judges of Provincial Supreme Courts
4,200- 7,200	— *Ober-Regierungsraete* representing *Regierungs-Praesident,* plus 2100 marks additional compensation — *Ober-Regierungsraete,* heads of depts., plus 1200 marks additional compensation — *Regierungsraete* — *Forstraete* — Directors of District Administrative Courts — Top Forest Inspectors
3,600- 7,200	— *Landraete*—some had free residence and salaried side offices
3,600- 6,600	— Directors of chief stud farms
3,000- 7,200	— Top Forester — Public prosecutors attached to Prov. Supreme and District Courts
3,000- 6,000	— *Oberlehrer*
2,700- 4,800	— *Landrat's* assistants (post held by *Regierungs-Assessoren*)
2,400- 4,800	— Regular seminary teachers

The office of *Regierungs-Assessor* as such was not represented in the budget because it did not have budgetary status but whenever a *Regierungs-Assessor* held a post, such as assistant to a *Landrat,* which appeared in the budget, or served as a substitute in some other office, then he received the salary appropriated for that office. Where a minimum and a maximum salary was provided the official in question received automatic increases according to his length of tenure, that is to say at the end of each requisite term of years in the same office. This meant that altho the salary attached to an office might be low to start with the official was assured of considerable increases *if* he remained in office for a long period of years and *even if* he remained in the same office. Such an arrangement would tend to encourage an official to continue in office until he had reached the retiring age when he could be sure of a life pension.

Furthermore, officials became eligible for pensions only after ten years of service. Any administrative official paid by the Prussian State who was forced to retire because of any physical or mental incapacity after he had completed his tenth but before the end of his eleventh year in the service was entitled to a life pension amounting to 15/60 of his last salary. If he remained in office beyond 10 years then the pension for which he was eligible increased each year by 1/60 of the yearly salary which he had received between his tenth and twelfth year in the service, up to a maximum of 45/60. In other words, the longer a man remained in the service, the larger his life pension when he was retired. After he had passed his 65th birthday he could of his own accord retire on a life pension.[16]

I have not been able to ascertain the salaries received by members of the Royal Household—Masters of Ceremony, Court Marshals and the like. Members of the Military Retinue who had been transferred for a period of years from the regular army received their pay as army officers. Aides-de-camp to His Majesty, who might range in rank from the lowest ranking staff officer to a General, received salaries from 6552 to 13,980 marks annually. The Chief of the Military Cabinet received an additional 4500 marks for expenses and the Commander of Headquarters an additional 900 marks.[17]

16. Gustav Herrfurth (75) *Das gesamte preussische Etats-, Kassen- und Rech-nungswesen,* v. 5, pp. 1-4, 17-18, 108.
17. "Etat fuer Kgl. preuss. Reichs-Militaer-Kontingent," Reichstag, *Der Reichs-haushalts-Etat,* 1907.

Salaries of diplomatic envoys were scaled according to the importance and social standards of the capitals to which they were sent. The German minister to Bangkok received only 35,000 marks annually whereas the ambassadors to Paris, Rome, Vienna and Constantinople received 120,000 marks and a free residence and the ambassadors in London and St. Petersburg were given 150,000 marks and free residence. Embassy and Legation secretaries received 6,600-17,400 marks in London, 6,000-15,000 marks in Rome and only 4800 marks in Stuttgart.[18]

When we turn to the offices of the provincial self-government we find that the salaried offices were generally of a technical nature or were held by the classes of lesser or lower officials whereas the offices held by Junkers were usually honorary posts. The one great exception to this was the *Landeshauptmann* or *Landesdirektor.* He was the one big and important official in the whole provincial self-government because as chief executive for all communal institutions and activities he held in his hands the direction of all local affairs. He was one of the three ranking officials of the province, along with the Commanding General and the *Ober-Praesident.* As he held a position which required his full time and attention as well as training and practical experience it is to be expected that he would receive a considerable salary. In East Prussia in 1905 the *Landeshauptmann* received 15,000 marks with an additional 3000 marks for a residence;[19] in West Prussia, 15,000 marks and free residence.[20] The *Landeshauptmann* of Pomerania received 15,000 marks in 1903 and 18,000 marks in 1915.[21] Altho this salary of around 18,000 marks falls below that of the *Ober-Praesident* the *Landeshauptmann* was a relatively highly paid official and he held a post particularly attractive to the Junkers because of its independence and its influence over local affairs. Moreover, he might be appointed to the office of *Ober-Praesident* as was Hugo von Wilamowitz-Moellendorf or even a Minister as was Arthur, Count Posadowsky-Wehner.

18. Reichstag, *Der Reichshaushalts-Etat,* 1900.
19. "Provinzialhaushaltsplan," East Prussia, Provinzial Landtag, *Verhandlungen,* 1905.
20. West Prussia, Provinzial Landtag, *Verhandlungen,* 1905, Vorlage #3.
21. "Bericht des Provinzial Ausschusses ueber die Verwaltung der Angelegenheiten des Provinzialverbandes von Pommern," Pomerania, Provinzial Landtag, *Verhandlungen,* 1903; 1915.

Junkers in all other provincial offices, e.g., members of the Provincial Diet or Executive Committee or of the Provincial Council, received no salary whatsoever, only travelling expenses and daily allowances for the days which they spent at the sessions of the Diet,[22] the Provincial Council, etc.[23] Local officers of the *Landschaften* or Provincial Land Credit Institutes also received no salaries and even the General Directors rarely received more than a recompense for expenses incurred.[24] Yet we know that in spite of their unremunerative character large numbers of Junkers gave their time and energy to these offices. In fact about 45% of the Junkers holding office during our period served in honorary offices. This is a proof that the economic factor was not the chief consideration for the Junker. Often he was able, as a country gentleman, to give his time and attention to the affairs of his community in a spirit of *noblesse oblige,* asking only to be compensated for his actual expenses. We must not forget, however, that these voluntary services which the Junker performed coincided with his own sphere of interests. It was distinctly to his advantage to keep the organs of provincial self-government and of the local credit institution in the control of his own group even at the cost of some time and effort. The Junkers possessed this advantage both easily and naturally because as the leisured and relatively well-to-do rural class they could best afford to hold honorary provincial offices.

The *Landrat,* we find, was not a very highly paid official, for his maximum salary was only 600 marks a month, and yet the *Landratsamt* was considered a good career office. These two apparently contradictory facts may be explained in part by the third fact that 41% of the Junker *Landraete* owned estates, i.e., they lived on a combined income from farming and officeholding. Many others were the sons

22. Deputies to the House of Deputies received train or ship fares and 15 marks a day while the Diet was in session. See Herrfurth (75) v. 4, p. 109.

23. See Provinzial Landtag, *Verhandlungen,* of each province for the provincial budget.

24. Von Bitter says, (51) *Handwoerterbuch der preussischen Verwaltung,* v. 2, pp. 49-50, "Die hoeheren Beamten [der Landschaften] werden gewaehlt und vom Koenige oder dem Minister bestaetigt, die mittleren und unteren Beamten werden von der Direktion ernannt. Vollbesoldete Beamte sind der Regel nach nur die Syndici und die mittleren und unteren Beamten. Die Generallandschaftsdirektoren und Raete beziehen gewoehnlich nur maessige Bezuege als Entschaedigung fuer Zeitverlust und Repraesentation." It is, however, possible that in exceptional cases a General *Landschaft* Director did receive a regular salary.

and younger brothers of local landlords. Besides, 600 marks a month went far in a small country town.

Judicial offices, which were unpopular with the Junkers, carried approximately the same salaries as administrative offices of the same rank. For example, the President of a Provincial Supreme Court, who held the highest provincial office in the judicial branch of the service, received 15,000 marks and free residence or somewhat more than a *Regierungs-Praesident* but less than an *Ober-Praesident*, who was the administrative head of the province for the Prussian State. Regular Provincial Supreme Court judges had a higher minimum and an equal maximum salary with *Regierungsraete* whereas public prosecutors had a maximum equal to *Landraete*. If the economic factor were a prime consideration with the Junkers we would expect to find as many Junker Provincial Supreme Court judges and public prosecutors as we do *Regierungsraete* and *Landraete* whereas actually, as we know, only a very few chose to enter the judicial profession. We must, perforce, conclude that the Junker's aversion to judicial work was strong indeed and that the matter of salary was not crucial enough to cause him to overcome his prejudice.

It is very important but also very difficult to compare administrative salaries with salaries in the Officers Corps, the other profession favored by the Junkers. For certain fundamental differences between the two services prevent any exact parallels. In the first place, it is difficult to find ranks which coincide. A Commanding General, who was the highest paid officer, receiving in all about 34,400 marks,[25] is hard to discuss at all in conjunction with administrative officials. He was, of course, under the War Minister both in rank and salary, but he also possessed more importance, independence and salary than the administrative official immediately beneath the Minister of the Interior, i.e., the *Ober-Praesident*. We might reasonably compare a Lieutenant General with a *Regierungs-Praesident* and we find that the maximum official income for the former, including official allowances, appropriations for clerical expenses, etc., was 19,250 marks as against a maximum of 16,000 marks for the latter. We may also safely compare a Major with a *Regierungsrat* or an *Ober-Regierungs-*

25. "Etat fuer Kgl. preuss. Reichs-Militaer-Kontingent," Reichstag, *Reichshaus-halts-Etat,* 1907.

rat, for they were both men about forty to forty-five, but here comparisons are hampered by the fact that the salaries of administrative officials vary within each rank according to the years of service. Thus a Major's salary of 6552 marks was about the same as that of a *Regierungsrat* or a *Landrat* who had filled this post for several years or of a newly appointed *Ober-Regierungsrat*. A Captain was paid 3402-4602 marks or approximately the salary of a newly appointed *Regierungsrat*, his civil equivalent in rank. But the latter could by long tenure in the same office arrive at a salary of 7200 marks whereas the Captain, if he were lucky, and became a Major, would get only 6552 marks. On the other hand, the Captain and the Major had been drawing salaries for many more years than the *Regierungsrat* or the *Landrat*. Altho their original salary as 2nd Lieutenants was only 1290 marks they had started to earn it at the age of twenty-one to twenty-three and had received several increases whereas the administrative official's first salary, which may have been 2700-4800 marks if he were assisting a Landrat, did not begin until he was at least twenty-nine or thirty.[26] Here again exact parallels are rendered impossible by variations between the services. Altho it is true that an army officer began earning his salary at a much earlier age and could live at officers' quarters at the army's expense, on the other hand, he incurred heavy expenses because he felt obliged to maintain a certain show of elegance and indifference in financial matters which drained his income and made him dependent upon his monthly allowances from home.[27] An administrative official could make his income go farther because he could live in a modest way, particularly if only a *Regierungsrat* or Forest Inspector, and still worthily represent his official position. Furthermore, an army officer had to be moved up in rank, with a corresponding increase in salary, after a certain number

26. It is interesting to compare the total sums received in salaries by a thirty-five-year-old 1st Lieutenant who had begun to earn a salary at 22 and a *Landrat* of the same age who had begun with 3000 marks a year when he was 30 and been made a *Landrat* at 33. As I figure it the Lieutenant would have received 22,400 marks by the time he was 35 and the *Landrat*, a total of 19,800. Moreover, the Lieutenant was spared the *Landrat's* arduous and expensive course of study.

27. The famous *Zulagen*. See the memorandum of the Prussian War Minister von Kameke, "Ueber den Luxus in der Armee und die damit verbundenen Gefahren," Berlin, February 26, 1876, in Karl Demeter (59) *Das deutsche Heer und seine Offiziere,* Anhang 23, p. 355 ff., especially p. 357.

of years or else be retired. If he did receive successive promotions then all was well and good.[28] But if he failed to qualify for a higher rank[29] then he was retired and he lost his salary and perhaps his economic security as well.[30] The administrative official, on the contrary, was sure of a salaried position in the service for as long as he wished—barring illness or malfeasance. He could even increase his income without a promotion, simply by years of service. We must conclude, therefore, that altho the army officer began earning a salary sooner, the administrative service offered more security and more promise of economic improvement. For those who were seeking to make a career the economic advantages lay with the administrative service. When we consider that, despite this fact, many more Junker sons entered the Officers Corps than the civil administration we must conclude that the Junker's preference for the Officers Corps was based on many other considerations besides economic advantage.

Altho the administrative profession offered economic security it certainly held out no promise of riches. In fact, its members had the reputation with the general public of being poorly paid.[31] It is difficult to compare the salaries of officials with the incomes of men in other professions or in business because figures on the latter were not published. We do know that according to the Prussian Class Tax in 1888[32] incomes of 2001-6000 marks were classed as moderate, of 6001-20,000 marks as medium and of 20,001-100,000 marks as large. According to this only Ministers, Commanding Generals and *Ober-Praesidenten* had large incomes. A good many officials might reach the group of medium incomes by the time they were fifty or

28. F. von Schulte (150) "Adel im deutschen Offizier- und Beamtenstand. Eine soziale Betrachtung," *Deutsche Revue*, 1896, p. 190, says that the staff officers from the rank of Colonel were better off than civil officials of the same age. In peace time they had less work and more leisure and were better paid.

29. The critical turning point in an army career was the famous "Majorsecke."

30. *Op. cit.*, p. 189. "Unleugbar hat kein Berufsstand eine gleiche rechtlich unsichere Stellung. Der Offizier kann stets entlassen werden, sogar ohne Anspruch auf Pension, wenn lezteres gewiss auch nur aus den wichtigsten Gruenden geschieht."

31. Schulte, *op. cit.*, p. 191, gives expression to this prevalent opinion when he says, "Den reichen Kaufmann reizt das Einkommen der Offiziere und Beamten nicht, es ist gegen das Einkommen eines Direktors einer grossen Aktiengesellschaft unbedeutend."

32. Adolf Soetbeer (151) "Volkseinkommen im preussischen Staate," *Jb. f. Nationaloek. u. Stat.*, 1889, p. 415.

fifty-five, even if they remained *Regierungsraete* or *Landraete* but a large majority—even *Regierungs-Praesidenten* and *Vortragende Raete* —must have received less than 6000 marks for the greater part of their lives. It was only by several promotions and/or years of service that officials were able to pass the lower limit of the medium income group. On the other hand, the Prussian census of 1900 lists only 155,761 taxable persons or 4.27% of the total taxable persons with incomes over 6000 marks and this means that when Junker officials did reach this income they were among the top 4¼% in the general income scale. But 6000 marks, altho a relatively high income, would support only a modest standard of living. Max Weber in complaining of the aristocratic pretensions of noble officials goes even further and says, "An income of 10,000 marks is sufficient today [1917] for a simple bourgeois existence in the manner of a lesser official, but not for a manner of living which is in any way 'aristocratic.' "[33] Count Waldersee gives us another hint when, in speaking of Hammerstein in 1895, he says that the latter received 24,000 marks as editor-in-chief of the *Kreuzzeitung,* and yet this was considered insufficient for the editor of a big Berlin newspaper.[34] We know, too, that University professors, altho also State officials, were able to earn incomes well in excess of the ordinary bureaucratic official's because in addition to their regular salaries they received large sums as course fees and from their outside lectures, writings, opinions as experts, medical practice, etc.[35] Since some prominent professors, especially those in the faculties of law and medicine, made as much as 10,000-20,000 marks in course fees alone it was not unusual for a professor to earn as much as 17,000 marks a year thru his university work, not to speak of outside activities. Yet professors were never considered to be affluent and we may presume that the really big incomes of 50,000-100,000 marks and over went to the banker, the merchant and the

33. Max Weber (153) "Deutschlands aeussere und Preussens innere Politik," *Gesammelte politische Schriften,* p. 104.
34. Graf Alfred von Waldersee (41) *Denkwuerdigkeiten,* v. 2, p. 358.
35. A full professor at the University of Berlin or the Technische Hochschule—institutions which paid the highest salaries of any Prussian University—received a flat salary of 6500 marks plus 1000 marks additional allowance and income from his course fees which varied according to the number of students enrolled in his classes. All course fees in excess of a total of 4500 marks had to be divided equally between the professor and the University.

industrialist. They surely did not flow into the hands of State officials. The latter, however, enjoyed a certain security which the businessman, the doctor and the lawyer lacked. For the official could expect permanent tenure and was assured of a pension upon retirement whereas the business and professional man had to bear wide fluctuations in income, the danger of losing his occupation altogether and the necessity of providing for himself in his declining years. Hence the official could not hope for affluence, unless he had an exceptional career, but he could expect security and a modest but respectable standard of living.

MARRIAGES AND CHILDREN

Both economic and social considerations influenced the Junker in his choice of a wife. The tradition of clannishness within the Junker group led some young men to seek wives within their own circle, or even their own families. Others married into neighboring families or into Junker families in other provinces where they were stationed as *Regierungs-Assessoren* or Lieutenants.[36] Therefore we find that 47.77% of the Junker officials who married before 1888 and as high as 46.50% of those who married between 1888 and 1914 chose daughters of Junkers for their wives. It is significant that the percentage fell off so little in the period before the war.

Other Junker officials married into noble German families outside the Junker group and still others married middle-class girls. It is these last who were the exception and need special examination. Why did some Junkers stoop to a lower social class in choosing a wife? The first and best answer is apparently personal predilection. Why else should Adalbert von Bredow-Briesen, of distinguished Junker lineage, owner of the fideicommissum Briesen (5690 acres) and canon of Brandenburg (*Domherr von Brandenburg*), marry Elise Kuehne in 1849? Or why should Louis von der Groeben, an arch-Junker and lord of Arenstein (2620 acres) in East Prussia, marry Bertha Linde in 1867? The fact that the proportion of Junker officials marrying commoners before 1888 (19.37%) was only slightly lower

36. For example, Juergen von Kleist-Retzow, son of the renowned Hans von Kleist-Retzow, met his wife, the daughter of Robert, Graf Zedlitz-Truetzschler, when he was assigned as a young *Assessor* to work for her father who was then *Regierungs-Praesident* of Oppeln.

than that (22.51%) after 1888 and after the full effect of the agricultural depression had been felt seems to give further evidence that personal wishes outweighed economic considerations in the choice of middle-class wives. There is, however, an indication in some few cases that economic considerations prompted hard-pressed Junker farmers and bureaucrats to marry industrial heiresses or Jewish bankers' daughters.[37]

The bureaucratizing effect of a family tradition of administrative service together with detachment from the soil, which narrowed the social gap between these Junkers and the bourgeoisie, undoubtedly explains some of the marriages between Junker officials and commoners but not as many of them as one might at first expect. For the number of those who married commoners is only slightly if at all more than the average for Junker officials as a whole. Moreover, it is true that, altho some Junker bureaucrats married into the middle class for two or three generations, the sons of other Junker officials and middle-class mothers who followed their fathers into the service sometimes went back and married into their own Junker class.

The size of the families which the Junker officials raised also has its social and economic significance and its implications for the position of the Junker as a whole. For the number of children in Junker families not only reflects their social habits and economic security but is also a direct indication of the Junkers' ability to perpetuate themselves as a social caste and to maintain their numerical position in the government service. It was the Junker's natural social and cultural inclination to raise a large family. The old-fashioned Junker landowner and head of a household felt himself to be a patriarch and his religion taught him that children were a blessing and an indication of God's grace. Children were also less of an economic responsibility

---

37. Altho it is practically impossible to determine the wealth of the middle-class bride, two or three cases suggest ulterior material motives. Tilo, Baron von Wilmowski, son of Kurt and *Landrat* of Kreis Merseburg in the province of Saxony married Barbara Krupp of Essen in 1907. Dr. Albert von Schwerin, third son of Albert Julius von Zieten-Schwerin and lord of Ober-Steinbach in Franconia, gentleman of the bedchamber and member of the Prussian diplomatic corps, married Enole von Mendelssohn-Bartholdy, a Jewess, in 1897 but there are no exceptional motives apparent here. Richard, Graf von Schmettow, from an old Silesian and Brandenburg family and at one time a Major in the Military Cabinet, married Gertrude Heine, presumably a Jewess, in 1894.

for Junkers than for other social groups. It was less expensive to bring up children on a large farm where many of the necessities of life could be produced directly. Furthermore, younger sons who could not share in the inheritance could be relatively sure of a living in the army or the administration and daughters who failed to marry could be sent to an ecclesiastical establishment for aristocratic ladies (*adliges Fraeuleinstift*). Hence we find that of the 526 Junkers who married before 1878, twenty-one had families of eight children, twelve had nine children and nine had ten children while one family each had eleven, thirteen, fourteen and sixteen children. For the 656 Junker officials who married after 1878 the number of large families is somewhat less—only six with eight children, only four with nine, only two with ten and none with eleven or more. The figures are still exceptionally high but the relative decline would seem to indicate that the economic pinch caused by the agrarian crisis, the desire for a higher living standard to rival rich industrialists and the trend of the times had a tendency to counteract the Junker's social and cultural attitudes with regard to children and to cut down the size of Junker families. These factors apparently also tended to reduce the number of children of Junker officials as a whole. We find that for the 526 Junker officials married prior to 1878, that is, prior to the agrarian collapse, the average family was 3.85 children whereas the average family for the 242 married between 1878 and 1888 was only 3.17 and those 414 who married between 1888 and 1914 had an average of only 2.85 children.[38] Thus the average family of a Junker official was one child or 25.9% less after 1888 than it was before 1878. Furthermore, the drop was over twice as great from the period before 1878 to 1878-88 than it was from 1878-88 to 1888-1914 (3.85 to 3.17 as compared with 3.17 to 2.85). This would seem to indicate that the economic hardship engendered by the crisis of the 70's and 80's had a direct bearing on the size of the families of Junker officials. If we consider the most frequent number of children per family for

38. The families of those who married between 1888 and 1914 include only those children born by 1914. It is quite probable that couples married during these years had children born to them after 1914 but since the war, the revolution and the economic crisis would have changed the general attitude toward child-raising in these families and they would not fit into the prewar pattern it seemed just as well to leave them out. We must recognize, however, that whatever the number of children born after 1914 they would tend to raise the average for 1888-1914 above 2.85.

the same three periods we find a similar trend. Before 1878 the most frequent number of children was four (17.11% of the 526 families) and the next most frequent number was three (16.16% of 526). Between 1878 and 1888 the most frequent number of children had dropped to three (22.72% of 242) and from 1888 to 1914 the most frequent number was again three (23.18% of 414). This is in keeping with the general trend toward smaller families. Even families of five fell off from 14¼% before 1878 to 9½% between 1888 and 1914.

That the tendency of the average family of Junker officials to decline was representative of a general trend is borne out by the marriage and birth statistics for Prussia as a whole. The number of births per marriage in Prussia for the period from 1871 to 1888[39] was 4.77 whereas the ratio for the period from 1888 to 1914 was only 4.37, showing a drop of .40 children per family.[40]

39. Prussia, Statistisches Bureau (6) *Jahrbuch fuer die amtliche Statistik des preussischen Staates,* v. 4-5; Germany, Statistisches Amt (2) *Statistisches Jahrbuch fuer das deutsche Reich,* 1880-. Figures for both total marriages and total births were published only after 1871. These birth rates or productivity rates have been reached by the crude means of adding up the total marriages and the total births in each group of years and dividing the latter by the former.
40. F. Savorgnan in his important article, (176) "Das Aussterben der adeligen Geschlechter," *Jb. f. Soziologie,* 1925, pp. 320-40, gives figures showing that sovereign houses and families in the higher nobility had a higher birth rate than the Junker officials—3.22 for the sovereign and 3.19 for the mediatized houses in the period between 1890 and 1923. These figures represent the productivity, i.e., the number of children per total number of marriages, inclusive of barren marriages, of those married between 1890 and 1909 but producing children for 15 years thereafter, until 1923. Savorgnan also gives the following figures for purposes of comparison:

Social group	Years of Marriage	Productivity (children per marriage)
Swedish nobility	1895	3.10
Finnish nobility	1903	3.12
Swedish professors		2.43
Upper classes in Kopenhagen		3.44
Wealthy classes in Rotterdam & Dordrecht	1877-1881	4.18
Budapest	1904	3.65
French Officials	1907	2.37
French workingmen	1907	3.07
Well-to-do-Americans	1923	2.80
Well-to-do Americans	1887-1901	2.10

Savorgnan uses these figures as evidence in support of his thesis that aristocratic families were not threatened with extinction by biological causes and that consanguineous marriages did not cause biological sterility or even reduce the power of productivity.

Altho the productivity of Junker officials shows a marked tendency to decline this was, as we have indicated, not exceptional but common to Prussia as a whole. Moreover, these Junkers show by the size of their families, even after 1888, that they were still quite capable of maintaining and even of increasing the size of their social and professional group.[41] It is, of course, true that their increase was not enough to keep pace with the rapid multiplication of administrative offices during our period. Nor were they able to compete numerically with the supply of bourgeois candidates. Nonetheless it is quite evident that the Junkers in the administrative service, to say nothing of all those not connected with it, were producing a reservoir of potential Junker officials more than sufficient to replace those in office. Altho we must not overlook the increasing demand for officials we may yet be sure that conservative Prussian Ministers still had a constant pool of the preferred Junker material from which to make administrative appointments.

QUALIFICATIONS FOR OFFICE

The mere fact that one was a Junker was, of course, in itself not sufficient ground for appointment to an administrative office. Altho it is indubitable that the Junker's relative chances of being appointed and promoted were greater than for the bourgeois candidate, he, too, had to go thru the regular course of training and pass the prescribed State examinations in order to satisfy the official qualifications for entrance into the Prussian State administration. He, too, had to spend years of hard work and thousands of marks before he could receive an appointment. Preparation for the higher administrative service was long, arduous and expensive. After passing his *Abiturienten* examination at the age of eighteen or nineteen, the prospective administrator had to spend at least three years with the legal faculty of one or more universities and then to pass the *Referendar* or first big State examination. After that he had to spend four years as an apprentice in government departments. The first year he spent as assistant in a judicial office (*Gerichtsbehoerde*) after which the

41. Their average family being at least 2.85 or almost 3 children to a couple. This rate was definitely higher than that for French officials or well-to-do Americans of the same period. See above, p. 99, note 40.

apprentice had to choose between a judicial and an administrative career. If he selected the latter he became a *Regierungs-Referendar* and spent the next three years assisting in administrative departments. Twelve months of this time had to be spent with a *Landrat*. At the end of the four years he was admitted to the second great State examination, the *Assessor* exam. If he passed this he became a *Regierungs-Assessor* and was eligible for any post in the higher administrative service but he still did not automatically hold a specific post with budgetary status until he was made a *Landrat* or *Regierungs-rat*.[42] Three or four years at the university, one year military service and four years apprenticeship make a total of eight or nine years spent in preparation for the administration.[43] Not only was the prospective official not earning during all of these years; he or his parents were also paying large sums for his education. These have been estimated at between 15,000 and 25,000 marks. Even if the parents lived in a university town these expenses could not be reduced below 9000-12,000 marks.[44] It would seem reasonable to conclude that a Junker would not lightly enter upon this long and expensive training unless he had some expectation of holding office for years to reap the benefit from his extensive and costly period of study.

In the matter of the training of officials the *Landratsamt* again requires special consideration and for two important reasons. In the first place it is the one department expressly selected for the training of apprentices. Each candidate had to spend at least one year with a *Landrat* no matter where else he prepared. This is because, being at the base of the administrative hierarchy and concerned in the local sphere with every branch of administrative work, it gave the apprentice an opportunity to study the workings of all phases of government on a sufficiently intimate and comprehensible scale. It also permitted him to become acquainted with the structure of local self-government. The selection of the *Landratsamt* as the special training

42. Information on the training of officials taken from the Prussian Law of 10 August, 1906, as given by Clemens von Delbrueck (58) *Die Ausbildung fuer den hoeheren Verwaltungsdienst in Preussen*, pp. 18-25.

43. Delbrueck, *loc. cit.*, reckons that *Referendare* were generally thirty before they became *Regierungs-Assessoren* and that these were usually about thirty-five before they were appointed *Landraete*.

44. Schulte (150) pp. 186-87.

ground for officials is but another evidence of its unique character
as the backbone of the Prussian administrative structure.

The *Landratsamt* was also peculiar in that the prerequisites for
holding office differed from those for any other higher administrative
office. In spite of a lively effort to abolish them these exceptions to
the regular course still remained in 1914.[45] They had the effect of
making preparation for the *Landratsamt* less rigorous than for other
higher offices and hence more easily fulfilled by the local Junker
landlords. According to the law of March 19, 1881,[46] persons suitable
for the office of *Landrat* were of two kinds: (1) those who had passed
the requirements for the higher administrative or judicial service, i.e.,
those who had passed their *Regierungs-* or *Gerichts-Assessor* examinations, and (2) those who had belonged to the Circle for at least a year
by ownership of property or residence therein *and also* had for a
period of at least four years served either (*a*) as *Referendare* serving
their apprenticeship (*im Vorbereitungsdienst*) in judicial and administrative offices or (*b*) *in the offices of self-government* in the Circle,
district or Province in question—with the exception of the offices of
alternates or members of Circle commissions.[47] According to (2) (*b*)
a Junker landowner could live on his estate, serve for four years as
a delegate for his Circle or as a member of the Circle, district or
provincial executive committee and at the end of that time be eligible
for the office of *Landrat*. That is to say, he might dispense with both
the *Referendar* and the *Assessor* and even with the *Abiturienten*
examination. And the *Landratsamt* not only had great intrinsic importance but anyone filling that post was eligible for all higher offices
in the administrative service.[48] Students of the training system claimed
that this exception was of little practical importance, however, because *Landratsaemter* were almost always filled by applicants who

---

45. Delbrueck (58) p. 9.
46. Prussia, *Gesetzsammlung fuer die Koeniglich preussischen Staaten,* 1881.
47. Under (2) (*b*) service in a higher administrative office for a period of two
years may be counted in reckoning the four years of service required.
48. Hintze writes, (132) *Gehe-Stiftung zu Dresden, Vortraege,* v. 3, p. 140,
"Allerdings gibt es auch in Preussen Wege, die von der Selbstverwaltung ueber
das Landratsamt zur Minister- und Ober-Praesidentenstellung fuehren, ohne juri-
stisches Studium und selbst ohne Abiturientenexamen; aber das sind doch seltene
Ausnahmen, in der Regel ist auch der Landrat ein ausgebildeter Jurist."

possessed the qualifications for the higher administrative service. My findings corroborate this conclusion since out of a total of 328 Junker *Landraete* only ten or twelve can be suspected of being appointed without having trained in the usual way. These few examples are extremely interesting, however, since they show that a Junker landowner could live in his manor house, take part in the direction of local self-government and thereupon receive appointment to the key administrative and communal office in his Circle—all really just because he was a Junker landlord and as such entered naturally into local affairs. They reveal a vestige not only of the customs but of the actual power of the feudal lord. It is, of course, true that a commoner might follow the same procedure but probably only if he had become a "feudalized" bourgeois.

Let us briefly consider the careers of two men who appear to have stepped into the *Landratsamt* by way of local offices. Karl von Elern, from the East Prussian branch of an old Brunswick family and owner of the estate of Bandels, first entered upon a military career. In 1853 he switched from the Gymnasium to the cadet corps, which he left as a *Faehnrich* or ensign in 1858, at the age of seventeen. By 1859 he was a 2nd Lieutenant, by 1870, a Captain and by 1875 (age thirty-four) a Major in the Military Cabinet. While still in the army von Elern served as a member of the East Prussian Provincial Diet (1893-1896) and as a Circle delegate. In 1896 he retired from the army as a Colonel and in the same year he was appointed *Landrat* in Kreis Preussisch Eylau, East Prussia, which post he held until 1901. In 1903 he was elected to the Reichstag and joined the German Conservative fraction. Thru the ownership of property and a short period of membership in local institutions von Elern was able to pass directly from a long military career into a *Landratsamt*.[49]

Reinhold, Count Finck von Finckenstein, lord of Matschdorf (3050 acres) which he inherited in 1875, first served as a *Regierungs-Referendar* from 1890 to 1900.[50] During this period he also served for five or more years as deputy member of the district committee of

49. See *Wer Ist's* (19) 1905, p. 190.
50. He may have been merely a retired *Referendar* after 1893; the account is ambiguous.

Frankfurt a.O. In 1900 he was made acting and in 1901 permanent *Landrat* in Kreis West-Sternberg in Brandenburg, which office he still held in 1914. He was a retired 2nd Lieutenant. Count Finck von Finckenstein probably qualified for office by his years as a *Referendar* since it is clear that he never passed on to the rank of *Regierungs-Assessor*.[51]

Once the Junker had trained for the civil administration his chances of admission to the service were greater than those of other aspirants because he was more likely to possess the tacit, extra-official qualifications one or more of which were extremely useful, if not essential for entrance into the higher administrative service, namely: a title; membership in one of the aristocratic student corps; the rank of a commissioned officer, either retired or in the Reserves; marriage connections and loyalty to conservative principles and interests. These personal factors came into play after a candidate had passed his *Referendar* examination and while he was awaiting appointment as a *Regierungs-Referendar*. Such appointment depended upon the pleasure of the *Regierungs-Praesidenten,* for it was they who picked out certain *Regierungs-Referendare* and called them to the *Regierungen* to continue their apprenticeship.[52] Manifestly personal relations could have a decisive influence in such an arrangement. Only those who passed their examinations with the highest grades could be sure of an appointment regardless of station or connections. The rest had slim hopes for appointment by a *Regierungs-Praesident* unless they were nobles, members of a "feudal" student corps, Reserve Officers in an

---

51. Others who may be suspected of receiving appointment to the *Landratsamt* without passing thru the regular course of training are: Siegfried, Frhr. von Richthofen, Oskar, Frhr. von Wackerbarth, Hans von Portatius, Dr. Werner von Saldern, Wilhelm, Frhr. von Zedlitz-Neukirch, Sigismund von Treskow, Paul von Chappuis, Heinrich von Below-Seehof.

52. Hellmuth von Gerlach (31) *Von Rechts nach Links,* p. 76, says, "Die Entscheidung ueber die Annahme lag in der Hand der Regierungs-Praesidenten." Hintze (132) *Gehe-Stiftung zu Dresden, Vortraege,* v. 3, p. 140, emphasizes the implications of this procedure when he writes, "In Preussen und aehnlich auch wohl anderswo werden die Aspiranten fuer den hoeheren Verwaltungsdienst von den Regierungs-Praesidenten nach freiem Ermessen angenommen so wie beim Militaer der Avantageur von dem Regimentskommandeur; es kommt dabei nicht bloss auf das Referendarexamen, sondern auch auf die persoenlichen Eigenschaften, die Herkunft und den Bedarf der Behoerde an. Dass dabei politische und soziale Erwaegungen oder Vorurteile eine Rolle spielen koennen, ist klar."

aristocratic regiment or related to men in high places—and conservatives as well.[53]

Membership in a "feudal" student corps provided a prospective administrative official with very useful connections when it came time for him to seek appointment as a *Regierungs-Referendar*. It might well be that one or more *Regierungs-Praesidenten* or an *Ober-Praesident* or even the Minister of the Interior himself was an "alter Herr" (alumnus) in the candidate's own corps and would take a comradely interest in him—even allow him to use the familiar form of address. Furthermore, connection with such student corps was supposed in itself to imbue the candidate with the proper social virtues and political attitudes.[54]

Altho much more essential for the bourgeois Herr Schmidt than for a von Stuelpnagel or von Zitzewitz who belonged to the preferred class of lesser nobles, these connections could be useful to the Junker, too, and were indeed acquired by him to some extent. We find that of the total of 1500 Junker officials 439 or 29% belonged to a student corps. The three most aristocratic and "feudal" corps, and also the most expensive, were the Hasso-Borussen in Bonn, the Saxo-Borussen in Heidelberg and, to a lesser degree, the Saxonia corps in Goettingen. Of these the Saxo-Borussia was the favorite with 148 out of the 439 Junker officials; the Hasso-Borussia was second with 105.[55]

53. Alexander von Hohenlohe writes (32) *Aus meinem Leben*, p. 328, "Haette ein junger Mann diese beiden Stadien, Korps und Garde durchgemacht, dann konnte er auf einige Protektion rechnen, die er leicht bei seinen ehemaligen Korpsbrudern, die schon in dem warmen Nest einer diplomatischen Stellung oder in der Verwaltung sassen, fand." See also the remark of von Gerlach (31) p. 76, "Regierungs-Referendar zu werden hatte man begruendete Aussicht, wenn man dreierlei zugleich war: adelig, alter Herr eines Korps und Reserveoffizier."

54. Max Weber (157) "Wahlrecht und Demokratie in Deutschland," *Gesammelte Politische Schriften*, p. 309, speaks of the importance of student "Couleurbeziehungen" in getting an administrative appointment and says, "Das studentische Couleurwesen ist bekanntlich die typische soziale Erziehungsform des Nachwuchses fuer die nicht militaerischen Aemter. . . ." Eckart Kehr (170) "Zur Genesis des Kgl. preussischen Reserveoffiziers," *Die Gesellschaft*, 1928, p. 495, describes the effect of this customary connection by saying, "Und zwar vollzog sich dieser Prozess der Auslese und die Pflege zuverlaessiger Gesinnung in den akademischen Korps welche nach und nach die kuenftigen Beamten stellten."

55. All figures on student corps were gathered from the *Koesener-Korpslisten, 1798 bis 1904* (16).

The distribution of all of the officials who were members of corps was as follows:

Saxo-Borussen	148
Hasso-Borussen	105
Goettingen-Saxonia	58
Heidelberg-Vandalia	24
Halle-Marchia	12
Heidelberg-Guestphalia	10
Bonn-Palatia	10
Tuebingen-Suevia	8
Bonn-Hansea	8
Bonn-Neo-Borussen	5
Greifswald-Pomerania	4
Freiburg-Hasso-Borussen	4
Halle-Guestphalia	4
Leipzig-Saxonia	3
Others with 2 or 1	34

It is also interesting to consider what types of offices attracted the largest numbers of corps students and also which offices had the most members from the three most aristocratic corps. The regular administration, exclusive of *Landraete,* diplomatic envoys and Court officials, shows the highest proportion of corps members, 148 out of a total of 336 or 44%. But the figures here also show that the proportion in the "feudal" corps was smaller than for any other type of office and that as many as 40% of the 148 belonged to more obscure and bourgeois corps. This would seem to indicate three things: that membership in a "feudal" corps was not such an important prerequisite for admission into the administrative service if other qualifications were present, that the ordinary Junker official did not feel at home in the most elegant and expensive corps and that those with more aristocratic backgrounds tended to gravitate toward the more "feudal" and aristocratic offices. Thus we find that 43.90% of the Junker diplomatic envoys belonged to student corps and of these as many as 90% belonged to the three "feudal" corps, but it is, of course, true that the aspirant for a diplomatic post had the greatest need for good connections. Among the *Landraete* only 37% were corps members but 75% of these were in the same three corps. Of those in honorary provincial offices or in the Prussian Diet 20½%

had joined corps and 74% of these were in the Hasso-Borussia, Saxo-Borussia or Goettingen-Saxonia corps. Among the courtiers and Royal Adjutants only 9 or 8.82% were corps members, probably because so many were army officers or had not been educated at a university. All of these 9 or 100% belonged to the above-named aristocratic corps.

The clear-cut conclusions flowing from these figures are blurred, however, by the fact that when we study the individual cases we find certain inconsistencies. Occasionally sons of aristocratic old Junker families such as von Arnim or von Bonin joined the more obscure corps and then became *Landraete* whereas the son of a recently ennobled family might join the Hasso-Borussen and later become merely a surveyor or a *Regierungsrat*. It was also possible for a recent noble to join an obscure corps and acquire a prominent place in the administrative service in spite of it. In general, however, the "feudal" corps were preferred by sons from the most distinguished and elegant Junker families and these generally went into the most socially desirable administrative positions.

A more popular and a more customary precondition to appointment was connection with the Officers Corps either thru one or more years of active service or thru an office in the Reserves or both. Here again certain regiments were more aristocratic and "feudal" than others and hence of greater value in making a career. The most exclusive and elegant regiments were the Garde du Corps and the 1st Foot Guards. After them came the other Cavalry Guards, the other Foot Guards, all other Cavalry regiments and then all the Infantry regiments, again with certain distinctions among them. Artillery and Engineers corps were less distinguished and more bourgeois. The Guards and Cavalry regiments were most popular with the Junkers who tried to keep them exclusively for their own group.[56] The findings on the 1500 Junker officials serving between 1888 and 1914, altho not complete, tend to substantiate these generalizations. One thousand forty-seven or 69.8% of all the Junkers examined are given a military rank in the Gotha handbooks. Unfortunately these Gotha handbooks are not always reliable with regard to the previous army

56. Demeter (59) p. 36. Gerlach (31) p. 70, says that the Light Infantry were much more elegant than the Infantry and not so expensive as the Cavalry.

service of the men. Sometimes if a man goes on to high positions in other fields the title of army officer is dropped from the record. Hence I have not been able to determine if all of the remaining 453 men actually had no connection with the Officers Corps. This omission in the Gotha accounts is even more regrettable in the case of those Junkers who served in regular bureaucratic posts. After a very careful check I have been able to determine with certainty that of the 705 regular administrative officials (inclusive of diplomats and *Landraete*) 363 or 51.49% were at one time army officers. One hundred and three were not officers, according to definite proof in the Gotha handbooks or other biographical sources. This leaves as many as 239 about whom there is no definite assurance one way or the other. In order to make a tentative correction of the figure of 51.49%, which is surely somewhat lower than the actual figure would be if we could get full information, I propose the following procedure. The ratio of known careers is approximately 360 officers to 100 without service in the Officers Corps or 18 : 5. If we divide the 239 of whom we have no knowledge one way or the other on the basis of this ratio we get 187 officers to 52 without military service. If we then add these figures to those about whom we do have information we get the following results: 363 plus 187 or 550 officers and 103 plus 52 or 155 without service. This procedure gives us a final, if tentative, percentage of 78.01% for those in the bureaucracy who at one time served in the Officers Corps.

A third personal advantage for prospective administrators was family connections with officials in important offices. It is clear that a combination of intermarriage between Junkers and the presence of a large number of Junkers in administrative posts would lead to the use of family influence in securing appointments and promotions. Indeed, personal connections in high places may often have been a motive in the selection of a wife. It is impossible at this distance from the archives to determine the exact relationship between family connections and the actual appointments or promotions made but we have one reliable and typical example, at least, in Hellmuth von Gerlach. In his memoirs von Gerlach speaks quite frankly of his resort to family connections in order to get an appointment as a *Regierungs-Referendar.* "What's the use of having cousins and friends sitting in the Ministries? They were put into action."[57] Hellmuth appealed to his first cousin, Georg, Baron von Rheinbaben, son of his father's older sister, Klara von Gerlach, who was then a *Vortragender Rat* in the Ministry of Finance. Rheinbaben "exerted himself energetically and informed me shortly: 'Schleswig is ripe for storming!' ",[58] whereupon Hellmuth wrote to the *Regierungs-Praesident* of Schleswig-Holstein and was immediately accepted as *Referendar* in his district. Gerlach's dependence upon a family relationship arose from the fact that he lacked two of the three customary personal requisites for appointment to the administration. Altho of noble birth he was a member neither of an aristocratic student corps nor of the Reserve Officers Corps.

A fourth personal requirement reputed to be necessary for entrance into an administrative career, and perhaps the most essential, was loyalty to conservative principles and policies. This political requisite had been introduced during the reactionary regime of Robert von Puttkamer, Minister of the Interior from 1881 to 1888, when the political complexion of the bureaucracy was transformed from a moderately liberal to a conservative hue.[59] There is no indication that this requirement of loyalty to Conservative principles and interests was dropped after the dismissal of von Puttkamer in 1888. On the contrary all evidence seems to suggest that it continued to be important, if not decisive, thruout our period. One would expect a succession of more or less Conservative governments to prefer Conservative candidates. In addition, our assumption is supported by the complaints of more liberal-minded officials, even as late as 1910, about the solid phalanx of Conservatives in the administrative service.[60] It would

---

57. Gerlach (31) p. 76.
58. *Ibid.*
59. Even the moderate Conservative, Gustav Schmoller (148) "Die preussische Wahlrechtsreform von 1910 aus dem Hintergrunde des Kampfes zwischen Koenigtum und Feudalitaet," *Schmollers Jb. f. Gesetzgeb.*, 1910, p. 1267, admits regretfully, "Und in dieser Zeit liess er [Bismarck] leider den Minister des Innern, Herrn von Puttkamer, ueber die Ernennung der saemtlichen Landraete, Regierungs-Praesidenten und Ober-Praesidenten so schalten, dass das von 1810 bis 1870 ueberwiegend liberale oder politisch indifferente Beamtentum eine stark feudalreaktionaere Richtung bekam."
60. Herrfurth, von Puttkamer's successor, admitted to Miquel, "er habe die feudale Cliquenwirtschaft trotz aller Muehe nicht beseitigen koennen." About fifteen years later, in 1910, a high administrative official, presumably Clemens von

therefore seem safe to assume that Conservative convictions were still an important requisite for admission into the higher administration.

Political "reliability" undoubtedly played its part not only in the original appointment but also in the promotions in office and the ambitious young official may have often found that zeal for the Conservative party was the way to a successful career. Von Gerlach says bitterly and hence perhaps with exaggeration, "The career of a *Landrat* depended primarily upon the political representation of his Circle. If he succeeded in winning a Circle over to the Conservatives which had formerly been represented by a Centrist or a Progressist, then his ability was established. The way to the top was open to him."[61] Friedrich Wilhelm von Loebell may have been influenced by such considerations because it appears[62] that his rise to top administrative offices dates from his active participation in the Conservative party fraction and his close association with its leader, von Heydebrand.

Everything that we know of Junkers in honorary provincial offices would lead us to believe that they, too, were Conservatives. For them, of course, political convictions had no professional significance altho it might well have been one of the reasons for their selection for a provincial post. We are led finally to the conclusion that political homogeneity was an added element in the social solidarity of the Junkers and of Junker officials. If we consider the Junkers who served in the eastern provinces as members of the Provincial Executive Committee, as *Landschaft* directors, or as *Landraete* who held provincial offices as well we see that the same men were both the foremost administrators and the leading political figures of their rural areas. We have a sense of the close corporative spirit of the Junker landowners, their relatives and their satellites, which dominated the

---

Delbrueck, is reported to have told the Progressist deputy, Gothein, "Wie ist es moeglich, bei uns liberal zu regieren? Seit fuenfundzwanzig Jahren ist kein Landrat, kein Regierungsrat oder Regierungs-Praesident, kaum ein Ober-Praesident, kein Amtsvorsteher, kaum ein Gemeindevorsteher in Ostelbien bestaetigt worden, der nicht konservativ bis in die Knochen gewesen waere. Wir befinden uns in einem eisernen Netz konservativer Verwaltung und Selbstverwaltung, . . ." See *ibid.,* p. 1268; Walter Koch (89) *Volk und Staatsfuehrung vor dem Weltkrieg,* p. 24.

61. Gerlach (31) p. 91.

62. Graf Kuno Westarp (43) *Konservative Politik* . . . , v. 1, p. 369.

political and communal life of the countryside. *Regierungs-Assessoren* and *-Raete* serving in their home districts would be tied up with the local scene by their youthful association with their neighbors, some of whom might now be in provincial posts. Even a *Regierungs-Praesident* coming back from service elsewhere to his home district would feel closely related to this social and political group and would perhaps be torn between its wishes and his orders from the Ministry of the Interior. This tension was not likely to become extreme in the period from 1888 to 1914, however, because of the conservative character of the successive governments.

We should not assume, however, that all Junker officials were equally "feudal" or aggressive in their Conservative political views. Some may have been by nature more moderate, more tolerant and less partisan; others may have become so by association thru their office with the wider problems of statecraft and the broader viewpoint of the nation.[63] Gustav Schmoller recognizes the political effect of officeholding when he quotes a high Prussian official as having said to him, "We are almost all conservatives when we enter office but after two years the logic of the facts has made us liberal."[64] Again, in the field of politics, we find evidence of variations within the Junker group and again we conclude that not only individual differences but also differences of experience in the several types of offices created dissimilarities within the still homogeneous Junker group.

For some Junker officials, activity along Conservative lines was perhaps not so much a means of attaining official favor, as it may have been with many bourgeois Conservatives, but rather the occasion for their entering office at all. Junkers were for the most part conservatives by nature. Since their political philosophy was conservative in the literal sense of the word and their objective, to preserve the old, "feudal" political and social order some of the old-fashioned Junkers may have felt it their obligation to enter those offices which they could use as a bulwark against the onslaughts of the Social Democrats or the Progressists. They felt a deep sense of responsibility for keeping Prussia in the old tradition and they may

63. Rudolf von Valentini, Chief of the Civil Cabinet, appears to have become such a neutral, impersonal bureaucrat.
64. Schmoller (148) *Schmollers Jb. f. Gesetzgeb.*, 1910, p. 1269.

have looked on officeholding as a means of conserving the old political order.

Personal ambition for power and prestige, however, was sure to have been a more frequent and characteristic motive for taking up an administrative career. Economic considerations, but only a modest desire for economic security rather than the drive for economic opportunity, also played a fundamental part in prompting Junkers to become civil officials. But these primary motives for holding office were all conditioned and sanctioned by the Junker's peculiar social and cultural habits. If it was economic necessity which drove him to seek a position at all it was tradition and social custom which prompted him to go to the civil administration and the Officers Corps to find an income. The Junker's native desire to command and dominate found satisfaction in the administration of high offices or in the holding of provincial posts where he could control the local scene. The social prestige which he himself had given to the profession by generations of service in the administration now made civil offices acceptable and even attractive to him.

This aura of social imponderables together with concrete material advantages made it natural for the Junker younger son to follow the easy road of custom and enter the offices of his fathers. By so doing he perpetuated the traditional relationship between the Junkers and the administration and sustained the old sense of solidarity between the two. He preserved as best he could the old social and political influence of the Junkers on the character of the administration. He in turn was subtly but inevitably affected by his experience in office. If he were a local landowner holding provincial offices or the local *Landratsamt* his inclination to rule, to domineer and to assert himself would be accentuated by this opportunity for their free expression and his sense of feudal, corporate solidarity with his Junker neighbors and colleagues would be strengthened. If, at the other extreme, he were constantly in the central administration and were sent from east to west and if, in addition, neither he nor his father owned land it seems clear that he would be surely if slowly weaned away from his Junker attitudes toward the neutral and impersonal viewpoint of the professional bureaucrat.

The decisive factor both in the original decision to enter the administrative service and in the effect of officeholding upon the Junker appears to be the closeness of his relationship with the land.[65] The nearer he was to land-ownership the more feudal and traditional he was in his attitudes and the more easily he could afford to accept a low salary or none at all, the more he was able to hold either local posts or high offices requiring the social brilliance and the added income which flow from landed properties. If he were closely connected with a Pomeranian or Silesian knight's estate he was more certain to keep his Junker attributes and the habits of his natural social milieu, he was less apt to be conditioned by his experiences in office. His political vigor, as well, tended to be affected by his interest in the land since the main objective of the Conservative party in this period was to preserve the social and economic status of the landed proprietors. Altho the bonds between landholding and officeholding were loosening they still remained of fundamental consequence for the Junker official.

65. "Wenn nun der Bauer undenkbar ist ohne den Bauernhof, so ist es der wirkliche Junker auf die Dauer ebenfalls ohne den Besitz eines Rittergutes. Dieses macht meist die Familie eines buergerlichen Besitzers, wenn sie sich dauernd im Besitze haelt, zum Junker, aber eine adelige Familie, welche den Besitz verliert, verliert auch in ein paar Generationen die Junkerqualitaet, welche im Grunde eine feudale ist, und wird besten Falles gouvernemental-conservativ, faellt in den Beamtenadel." Rudolph Meyer (142) "Adelstand und Junkerklasse," *Neue deutsche Rundschau*, 1899, p. 1090.

IV

THE JUNKER OFFICIAL IN HIS FAMILY SETTING

THE Junkers in the reign of William II still remained faithful to the old tradition of service in the civil administration of the King of Prussia. Large numbers of them still took up civil service as a career or held honorary administrative posts in the provinces as a normal adjunct to their farming vocation. But, as we know, administrative service was only one and not even the most important occupational tradition among the Junkers. Originally they were primarily large-scale farmers associated with the local government. Then from the 17th century their sons entered the Officers Corps in large numbers until they became predominant in that body. They grew to look upon themselves as the natural military caste in Prussia and upon an army career as the preferred profession for their class. By the end of the 18th century the civil administration had taken second place alongside the Army as an accepted occupation for Junker sons. Only in the 19th century did the free professions and, to a much less extent, business begin to attract a few Junkers away from their habitual professions.

Until now we have been concerned only with those Junkers who held some office at Court, in the Prussian State administration or in provincial self-government. We have taken them out of their social surroundings and studied them as individuals and types. This concentration upon Junkers as officials, however, tends to distort the picture of the Junkers as a social group and even of the relation of the Junker official to his family and his class. In order to restore perspective we must reinsert the Junker official in his social background and look at him as only one member in his own family or clan and in the whole Junker group. Such a consideration of the Junker official in his normal place within the Junker social pattern will restore the balance in our picture of the Junkers; it will set the civil service tradition in its proper relationship to other Junker

114

traditions. Moreover, it will enrich our understanding of the Junker official himself by showing his position with relation to the other members of his family and his group and by suggesting what his social standing as an official was in his Junker group.

The best way to fill in the social background of the Junker officials serving under William II would be, of course, to trace the life history of all their relatives who were their contemporaries. This would place the official in the right perspective as only one of a number of brothers and cousins, uncles and nephews engaged in several occupations. Because of the enormity of the task it was impossible to trace the careers of all of the contemporary members of the 668 families which had men in the administration between 1888 and 1914. I have therefore selected thirteen representative families for this careful examination in the belief that these thirteen typical Junker families give an accurate picture of conditions in Junker families as a whole. These thirteen families are von Koeller, von Jagow, von Bonin, von der Groeben and Counts von der Groeben, von Saucken, von Stuelpnagel, Counts von Zedlitz-Truetzschler, Barons von Schuckmann, Barons von Seherr-Thoss, von Wolff, von Meyer-Arnswalde and von Loesch. Six of these families[1] trace their lineage back to the original migrations into the Mark and East Elbia in the 13th and 14th centuries. The von Sauckens belong to the ancient native nobility of East Prussia.[2] Four families[3] belong to that group which was early assimilated into the Junker tradition.[4] Of these, three belong to the important Silesian branch of the Junker social group.[5] The von Wolff family on the other hand comes from the Mark where it held extensive properties. After being ennobled in 1786 it apparently grew close to the Junker stock. Finally, two of the families chosen—von Loesch and von Meyer-Arnswalde—were

1. Von Koeller, von Jagow, von Bonin, von der Groeben and Counts von der Groeben, von Stuelpnagel.
2. *Jahrbuch des deutschen Adels* (15) v. 3; *Taschenbuch der Uradeligen Haeuser* (12) 1900.
3. Barons von Seherr-Thoss, Barons von Schuckmann, Counts von Zedlitz-Truetzschler, and von Wolff.
4. For a description of the three main Junker categories, see above, Chapter I, p. 40.
5. The Barons von Seherr-Thoss belong to the original Silesian aristocracy, the Counts von Zedlitz-Truetzschler come from an ancient Bohemian noble family and the Barons von Schuckmann were raised to the Imperial nobility in 1732.

not ennobled until after 1850, but their activities and attributes seem to indicate that they aligned themselves with the Junkers and hence they fall into the category of those nobles who have become like the old Junkers. The von Wolff family was the only one of the thirteen which did not possess any landed property whatsoever. It had been richly endowed with estates in the 18th century but had lost them all by 1888.

The life history of each member of these thirteen families who was alive at any time between 1888 and 1914 has been traced and analysed. This includes old people, some of whom were dead by 1889, as well as those young children who had shown an indication of their choice of a career by 1914, e.g., those who were law students or army cadets. In considering the conclusions resulting from the analysis of these thirteen families and in estimating the ratios it should be borne in mind that these families were chosen not only because they typified the Junker social group but also because they sent several of their members into the administrative service. Hence the proportion of Junker officials in these families is even larger than it would be in other families where members had served in the administration only prior to 1888 or perhaps not at all. The results are therefore weighted on the side of the administrative career.

GENERAL ANALYSIS OF THIRTEEN FAMILIES

The thirteen families had a combined total of 681 members living between 1888 and 1914. Of these 315 were women and 366 were men. Because the number of Junkers under consideration here is so small and the span of years from 1888 to 1914 is so brief individual variations and incidental factors are bound to be operative to a relatively high degree in any general deductions. I am well aware that the following broad generalizations and comparisons based on the brief case histories of these 681 Junkers cannot be conclusive because of this fact. They are nonetheless useful and important insofar as they give even a rough indication of prevailing habits and conditions among the Junkers as a whole and the figures seem large enough to preclude any basic distortion. At the least, they are interesting when considered in conjunction with the findings in other sections of this work and are therefore worthy of study and presentation here.

The 315 women have been studied only with regard to their marriage habits and the few instances of special occupations where they remained single. Of the 315 women 119 or 37.77% never married. Only sixteen of these are recorded as being occupied outside the home. Eight of these were connected with charitable foundations (e.g., *Stifte*)—five as canonesses. Four others were in the nursing profession. Two were in Evangelical cloisters and two were deaconesses in Bethanien.[6]

Of the 366 men the largest number—88 or 24.04%—made a career in the Officers Corps. Another 78 or 21.31% had served in the Officers Corps in their early years and then retired to farm their estates. Forty-seven more were in the Officer Corps in 1914 but were still so young that it was impossible to determine whether they intended to make a career in the Army or to retire later to farming. Only 57 or 15.63% became officials and pursued careers in the civil administration. Twenty-three others (6.30%) held provincial or Circle offices in conjunction with their position as local landowners. Twenty members of these Junker families were engaged only in agricultural pursuits and at no time held army or admin-

---

6. Because the number of Junker women active outside the home is so small and because their occupations shed so much light on Junker social customs it is not without value to list these sixteen women separately here:

Julie von Koeller—Diakonisse in Bethanien bei Stettin
Anna Luise von Jagow—Schwester in Augusta Hospital, Berlin
Pauline von Wolff—Stiftsdame in Stift Friedrich II in Potsdam
Anna von Wolff—Stiftsdame in Stift Geseke-Kepell, Westphalia
Charlotte von Bonin—Gemeindeschwester in Niederschoeneweide
Eleanore von Bonin—Oberin eines adeligen Fraeuleinstiftes in Schoeneberg
Margot von Bonin—Oberin einer staedtischen Krankenanstalt in Essen
Rosalie von Bonin—Stiftsdame in Geseke-Keppel in Wiesbaden
Emma von Bonin—Konventualin des Klosters Gross-Koeln am Rhein
Theodolinde von Bonin—Expekt. auf Kloster Gross-Ruhnow
Marie von Bonin—Schwester des Johanniter Ordens und Oberin des Samariterordensstiftes in Kraschnitz
Elizabeth, Countess Zedlitz-Truetzschler—Oberin und Diakonisse des Mutterhauses Bethanien in Breslau
Anna von der Groeben—Mater des Marienstifts in Koenigsberg i. Pr.
Martha von der Groeben—Ehren-Stiftsdame des Klosters Heiligengrabe in Oldenburg
Marie von Stuelpnagel—Stiftsdame von Kammin
Natalie von Stuelpnagel—im Schroederstift in Hamburg

istrative offices. As many as 73 or 19.94% followed pursuits or entered professions which lay outside the regular Junker tradition but only 24 of these engaged in definitely non-Junker occupations. To recapitulate, the 366 men fall into the following categories:

Army careers	88
Army service followed by retirement to farm estate	78
Farming only	20
In Officers Corps, still young	47
Administrative careers	57
Unusual careers	73
Others (*stud. agr., stud. jur.* and *Dr. jur.*)	3
Total	366

If we return to a consideration of the Junkers' connection with the Officers Corps as reflected in the lives of the 366 men in these thirteen families we find that as many as 270 or 73.77% had at some time or other been army officers, either in the active service or in the Reserves. The total figure of 270 comprises in addition to the 88 men who made the army their profession the 78 who left the Officers Corps for farming, the 47 young officers still in the service in 1914, those administrative officials who at one time served in the Officers Corps and those who strayed into unusual and non-Junker careers but had previously been Prussian Army officers. This figure of 270 is in striking contrast with the 80 men (21.93%)[7] who at any time held either central or provincial administrative offices. If we subtract from these 270 men the 47 who do not yet show an indication of either a permanent career or early retirement we are left with 223 officers. Of these we know that only 88 made a vocation of army service and as many as 60.54% either retired after a few years for one reason or another or else served only in the Reserves.

The proportion of Junkers who were at one time connected with the Officers Corps may at first seem amazingly high, particularly when compared with the figures for the civil administration, the other profession favored by the Junkers. But the numbers do not seem so surprising when we stop to consider some of the more

7. Fifty-seven in the Prussian State administration and 23 in offices of the provincial self-government.

obvious reasons why Junker sons entered the Officers Corps and also why such large numbers of them dropped out after a few years. The first and most evident is that all Prussian men of a certain educational standing were required to take at least one year of military training. Since they had to enter the army anyway, noblemen and especially Junkers were likely either to become Reserve Officers in due time or to prefer from the beginning to serve as active officers. Altho it cost more in time and money, service as an officer brought with it much greater satisfaction and honor. Moreover, the added number of years were of no great concern to the idle Junker son, who often had no other ambition than to continue in the Officers Corps or retire to the family estate.

A second important reason why so many Junkers entered—and left—the Officers Corps was that the time and money required to train for an officer's post were relatively small, much smaller than for a higher administrative office. In Prussia a boy could begin his military training at an early age. The cadet schools for the training of army officers were made parallel to the secondary schools, or Gymnasien, and the *Abiturienten* examination was the final step in the cadet's preliminary schooling.[8] After passing this examination a candidate was given the rank of *wirklicher Portepeefaehnrich* or ensign and assigned to a military school for six months or a year, at the end of which he took the officer's examination. Satisfactory passage of this examination automatically meant entrance into the corps of commissioned officers and appointment as a 2nd Lieutenant. Thus a boy could become a commissioned officer while he was still very young. If the average age of cadets in the *Unterprima* was seventeen years[9] then a boy could pass his *Abitur* a year later, take his officer's examination six months or a year thereafter and become a 2nd Lieutenant with a regular salary at nineteen or twenty. The very fact that an army officer began earning a salary at such an early

8. According to the royal decree of 1877. See von Scharfenort (114) *Das Koeniglich preussische Kadettenkorps, 1859-1892*, pp. 33-47. The Officer's candidate did not have to go as far as this, however. At the end of the *Obersekunda*—the third from the last year of study—he was obliged to take the *Portepeefaehnrich's* examination and if he passed he might enter the army immediately as a *Portepeefaehnrich* or ensign.

9. *Ibid.*, p. 42. The *Unterprima* was the second from the last year of study in a Cadet School, also in a Gymnasium.

age was another attractive feature about the Officers Corps and one which would tend to place it ahead of other activities in the estimation of the Junkers. Furthermore, the costs of a military education were also attractively low, much below those for other professions. It has been estimated[10] that an officer's son could be educated in a cadet school for only 6000 marks whereas parents might have to spend 25,000 to educate their son for the legal, 18,000 marks for the medical, and 15,000 marks for the theological profession.

The fact that the Officers Corps was comparatively easy and inexpensive to enter and also that it brought quick financial returns in the form of the 2nd Lieutenant's salary goes a long way toward explaining the great contrast between the numbers of Junkers in the Officers Corps and those in the civil administration. It also appears to give the most evident and satisfactory explanation of the decided difference in the length of tenure of the men in the two services.[11] Whereas the Junker who entered easily into the Officers Corps could easily afford to drop out a civil official who had spent years of his time and thousands of marks training for his profession would not lightly sacrifice them by an early retirement.

A brief service in the Officers Corps was particularly tempting to a young heir apparent who expected shortly to retire to his estate. It afforded an attractive and convenient occupation for the years before he came into his inheritance. Actually, it was not a very intelligent use of his time and would tend to have a deleterious effect upon his later farming career, the solvency of his estate and the position of the Junkers as a whole. Military training and army service were hardly the best preparation for running a large-scale and scientifically organized farm and for bringing in a profit.[12]

Another motive for serving briefly in the Officers Corps was the desire and the need to seek "connections." To be a retired or a Reserve Officer was, as I have already pointed out, an important

10. F. von Schulte (150) "Adel im deutschen Offizer- und Beamtenstand. Eine soziale Betrachtung," *Deutsche Revue*, 1896, pp. 186-87.

11. See above, Chapter II, p. 74ff.

12. Johannes Conrad (127) "Die Latifundien im preussischen Osten," *Jb. f. Nationaloek. u. Stat.*, 1888, pp. 167-68. He advocates that nobles make a serious profession of farming and devote their entire attention to that. But what Junker boy would not choose to be a dashing young Cavalry Lieutenant, or even a *Regierungs-Assessor*, rather than a dull, grubby and hard-working agricultural student?

if unofficial prerequisite for admission into the higher administrative service. We know that this motive was less common, however, from the fact that the proportion of those Junkers under consideration who served briefly as officers before making a career in the administration was relatively small. Here it applies only to those 32 out of the 57 administrative officials in our thirteen families who served as army officers.

Personal and family considerations, no matter how customary, do not by any means explain all of the early withdrawals from the Officers Corps. Many retirements were enforced, contrary to expectations, the natural and inexorable result of the pyramidal structure of the Officer Corps. For all army officers had to rise in rank after a period of years or else be retired.

There are still other and equally basic characteristics of the Officers Corps which help to explain not only the wide extent of the Junker's affiliation with it, as do the foregoing, but also his preference for an officer's career above all others when he did adopt a profession. We have found among our thirteen families, as one may recall, not only that 270 men were at one time army officers but also that 88 of these men made a career in the Officers Corps. This was our largest figure for any occupational category and exceeds by 31 the numbers of those who spent their lives in administrative careers. Our analysis of economic factors in the preceding chapter has led us to the conclusion that in the choice of an army or an administrative career, or in the preference for the one over the other, financial motives were strongly qualified by other considerations. What, in general, were those other considerations which caused the Junker to favor an army over an administrative career? The answer is, no doubt, tradition, social custom and prestige. Family tradition was important, for many a son was eager to follow in his father's footsteps. But behind that was the whole history of the Junker's development and of the unique position of the officer's caste in Prussian society. The army officer, even the ensign or 2nd Lieutenant, belonged to Prussia's first estate.[13] By the very fact of his membership in the Officers Corps he acquired social acceptance, even social brilliance.

13. Karl Demeter (59) *Das deutsche Heer und seine Offiziere*, p. 209, speaks of ". . . eine veraechtliche Devotion und Liebedienerei selbst vor dem unbesternten silbernen Achselstueck des zwanzigjaehrigen Leutnants."

For example, at any official banquet in the provinces the commanding General for the province would precede the *Ober-Praesident,* altho of equal rank, and the Captain would precede the *Regierungsrat.* The young army officer was also given no small measure of pre-eminence over his fellow men. Altho himself at the command of his superior officers the twenty-year-old 2nd Lieutenant could feel the heady rapture of power as he gave orders to the men under his command—some of them older, more mature and better educated than he. Von Schulte gives vivid expression to this social factor in the following words,

> "Especially decisive is the traditional view which is still very widespread that the Officer's estate is the first estate. When one considers that the eighteen-year-old Lieutenant is called '*Hochwohlgeboren*', can be commanded to Court balls, is socially eligible everywhere, one can understand the effect which this position has upon a young man. . . . It would be very strange if a young Lieutenant who had one-year service men under him—students, candidates for the Bar, doctors, *Referendare,* etc., all perhaps four years older than he but not yet independent,—if such a young Lieutenant did not have a very high opinion of his own position."[14]

It is equally true that the Officers Corps offered a Prussian young man his only opportunity to assume responsibility at an early age. This fact, of course, increased his eagerness to enter it.

Because such a large number of men in our thirteen families were at one time connected with the Officers Corps let us first briefly examine their backgrounds and careers. This will enable us not only to become acquainted with the lives of army officers in typical Junker families but also to make some tentative deductions regarding the habits of Junker army officers in general, in order that we may compare them with the typical administrative official. We turn first to the 88 men from the thirteen families who spent the best part of their lives in the Officers Corps and made a career of army service. Only two of these men owned land and they were two Counts von der Groeben who had inherited fideicommissa. Another had married a wife with landed property. As for the fathers of these army

14. Schulte (150) *Deutsche Revue,* 1896, p. 187. Can it be that the quality of arrogance for which the Prussian Officers Corps was so severely criticized by other European and even other German people before 1914 was due in large measure to the custom of placing power and social prestige in the hands of young men, not yet mature enough to use these forces with wisdom and a sense of responsibility?

officers, the number of those who owned estates was equalled by those who were non-propertied officers themselves or else civil officials of some sort. The ranks which these men had reached when they were retired or by 1914 are as follows:

Rank	Number
(retired or in 1914)	
General	3
Lieutenant General	5
Major General	9
Colonel	11
Lieutenant Colonel	10
Major	22
Captain (including *Rittmeister*)	25
1st Lieutenant	3
Total	88

The 50 officers with the rank of Major and below have been classified as career men for the following reasons: the Majors and Captains had either already retired without any apparent indication that it was their own choice or else they had already served in the Officers Corps for so many years that I felt convinced that they were career men; the three 1st Lieutenants were included because they had already been retired after several years (15-20) of service, and also under conditions which suggest involuntary withdrawal.[15] The proportion of men in each rank, with the exception of the three retired 1st Lieutenants, corresponds to the ratio which one would expect to find in the Officers Corps as a whole due to its pyramidal structure.

An additional 47 men from these families, were, as we have already stated, still serving in the Officers Corps in 1914 but had not yet advanced far enough either in age or in rank for us to determine whether they intended to make army service their life work or to retire to agriculture or some other occupation. Only one of these men owned real estate—a fideicommissum which he had inherited due to the early death of his father. As with the 88 career men, about half of the fathers of these young men owned landed property. In view of our findings it seems fair to assume

---

15. All 1st Lieutenants still in active service are treated below under the heading of young officers whose intentions were not yet discernible.

that those young officers who were the only or the eldest sons of men with estates would have retired from the Officers Corps after a few years of service had not the war overtaken them.

Seventy-eight officers had already retired from active service or the Reserve list in order to farm their estates or else were serving only in the Reserves in 1914 and hence spending the greater part of their time on their property. The retired men amount to 55, the Reserve officers to 21. Two are undetermined. We are particularly interested to know what ranks the 55 retired officers had reached before they left the service because this will give us some indication of the rank which the transient Junker officer tended to reach before personal and family considerations or the decision of his superior officers, or both, forced him to withdraw to his estate. We find that only 10 of the 55 had achieved the envied rank of *Major a.D.* whereas as many as 21 or 38.18% were Captains when they retired. Of these three-fourths were from the Cavalry (*Rittmeister*) and only 6 from other branches. Ten others were only 1st Lieutenants and 14, only 2nd Lieutenants. The retired Captains attract our particular attention because theirs was the rank most frequently reached before retirement, at least by our 55 retired officers with estates. Altho it is of course true that the young Junker officer was not entirely free to decide when he would retire, there are nonetheless some evident reasons not only for his being retired with this rank but for his preferring to be retired then. For instance, if a Junker planned to farm his estate he had to leave the army while still sufficiently young and adaptable to take up this new work. The rank of Major was more distinguished but it was hard to reach and in general not obtainable within the number of years which such a Junker could afford to spend in army service. Furthermore, a Major was the first to have staff work and desk work; he was moved away somewhat from the leadership of his men. But a Captain, who had direct command over a company, the largest unit where the officer had close contact with the men, worked with his men and gave them personal direction. Hence the Captaincy seems to be the rank best suited to the Junker with his special traditional habit to command and his propensities for personal authority. The rank of Captain appealed to the Junker also because the Cavalry Captain had the distinctive title of *Ritt-*

meister. This made it possible for anyone to tell just by a glance at the Cavalry Captain's calling card that he had belonged to this much more elegant and aristocratic branch of the service. In no other rank was this differentiation made and it would give a Junker great satisfaction to be able to show by the *Rittm. a. D.* after his name that he had been connected with the "right" branch of the Officers Corps.

The 21 officers who were still active in the Reserves in 1914 correspond in many ways to the Junker officials in honorary provincial offices. In general they were concerned chiefly with farming their estates and gave only incidental attention to military activities. Many of them actually held local administrative posts as well as a post in the Reserves. We do not find any Majors among these 21 men because this was a rank seldom reached by Reserve Officers. Eight were Captains, however—7 *Rittmeister* and 1 Infantryman. Another 8 were 1st Lieutenants and the additional 5 were 2nd Lieutenants. It is to be expected that in normal times these last 13 would have advanced in rank until they fell into the same pattern as their retired colleagues when they, too, retired.

When we come to consider the age at which the officers from our thirteen families first entered the Officers Corps we find that our information is not complete for all 270. However, we have the figures for a sufficient number to indicate definitely that almost without exception these Junker sons entered the active service as 2nd Lieutenants between the age of nineteen and twenty-three. This is, as we know, in striking contrast with the administrative officials who with their long academic training and apprenticeship were close to thirty before they qualified for appointment as *Regierungs-Assessoren.*[16] Those who served in the Reserves only were considerably older, i.e., twenty-eight and twenty-nine, or even thirty-one or thirty-two, before they became 2nd Lieutenants, but this is because their military training was only incidental and hence they took it up later and stretched it over a longer period. Once they began to train they had to serve one year followed by two successive periods of eight weeks each before they were eligible to become commissioned officers.

16. See above, Chapter III, p. 101 and note 43.

The lives of the 57 men, who pursued administrative careers and who have already been dealt with in a general way in the preceding study of all Junker officials, fall into those same patterns which we have discerned in the lives of the total number of officials. All but 7 held office for long terms or had only just started their careers by 1914. Of the seven who are conspicuous for their brief service two were *Landraete,* one was a courtier, three retired young to their estates—two as *Regierungs-Assessoren* and one as only a *Regierungs-Referendar*—and one unfortunate soul remained a *Regierungs-Assessor* for ten years[17] and then retired to live in Berlin. The percentage of landed proprietors is somewhat higher than for the total number of bureaucratic officials: 24 of the 57 or 40.35% (total salaried officials, 33.96%) owned estates ranging between 1250 and 15,750 acres. Twenty-two or 38.60% of the 57 men (as compared with 46.52% of the total officials) were *Landraete* and 17 of these or 77.27% (as compared with 41.76% of the total officials) owned estates. Also one courtier held landed property. Of the 34 remaining, all of whom were regular administrative officials, only six held land. Even so the percentage of landowners here is higher than for the total body of salaried officials—17.64% as against 14.58%. As to army service we can be sure that 32 (56.14% as compared with 51.49% of the total Junker officials) served in Officer Corps. Another 12 certainly never entered it and 13 are doubtful. Of the 23 men in provincial offices we shall pause only to state that all 23 owned estates—a 100% record.

Another and a large group of men from the thirteen families are particularly intriguing for us. These are the 73 who did not conform to the accepted Junker pattern and lived out their lives in exceptional ways. These men are interesting not just because they are deviations from the norm; there were always some few who failed to keep up to Junker standards. They become really important if they reveal to us, even partially, to what extent, if any, modern capitalistic and bourgeois society was threatening the solidarity of the old, exclusive, feudal Junker social group. We are eager to know if they give any evidence that the corrosives of an individualistic and equalitarian modern age were dissolving, at least around the

17. August, Baron von Schuckmann, 1895-1905.

fringes, the corporate body of the patriarchal and feudal Junker caste.

We must first write off twenty-three of these men as merely negative and without influence on the social pattern for they were without a profession and without a career. Some did serve for a brief term in the Officers Corps, others are recorded as doing nothing at all. They were apparently supported by their propertied fathers or brothers or even by their wives.[18]

Nine of the seventy-three men held public offices but these were of such a bourgeois or humble nature that they were unworthy of a Junker.[19] Another seven held judicial offices. These are interesting because the judicial service was shunned by the Junkers but the posts held—judges of local or district courts, etc.—were highly respectable. One became head of a district (*Bezirkschef*) in Southwest Africa, also a respectable office but one unusual for a Junker.

Nine entered the free professions; five became lawyers, one a doctor, one a geologist, one a mineralogy professor and one a Doctor of Philosophy.[20] Alexander von Stuelpnagel, who was a riding master, might be classed as a professional man; he was certainly a *déclassé*. Three others broke with tradition and devoted themselves to the arts; one was an author and two were painters. Only six pursued a regular business profession. Three were recorded as merchants.[21] Another, Hugo von Koeller, became the owner of the *Konstantinopler-Handelsblatt*. He later returned to Germany to be co-director of a transoceanic shipping company. His son was an official of the Hamburg-American line. The sixth businessman, Alexander von Stuelpnagel-Gruenberg, was the director of a horse-car company. Another Junker held the humble if congenial post of professional

18. The fact that one married the daughter of a *Kommerzienrat* and another married a middle-class girl from Solingen, the centre of the steel industry, gives rise to this suspicion.

19. Buergermeister; Post-Direktor; Kreis-Ausschuss-Assistent; Polizei-Inspektor; Lotterieeinnehmer; Strafanstaltsdirektor; Polizeirat; Steuerinspektor; Polizeiwachtmeister.

20. E. Sokal, in his article, "Die buergerliche Erwerbstaetigkeit des Adels in Deutschland" (152) *Die Gegenwart,* 1903, argues that so few Junkers entered the free professions because they did not foresee the need to take up some remunerative work—other than the army or administration—until a family economic crisis was upon them and then it was too late to prepare for a professional career.

21. One, Adolar von Bonin, settled in New York.

administrator of a stranger's estate (*Gutsverwalter*). Yet another is interesting because he was forced into a mésalliance and he and his children appear to have been cut off from the Junker circle — the latter entered business professions.

As many as 12 of the 366 men broke with Junker tradition by leaving Prussia and settling abroad. Six of these came to the United States.[22] Three others settled in South America, two went to South Africa and one settled in Russia.[23]

The most significant consequence of the foregoing record of unusual careers is that it shows to what a slight extent modern bourgeois and business society encroached on the Junker group. The toughness of Junker conservatism is reflected again in the hold which its traditional social patterns had on its young men. Only six of 366 representative Junker men were in business, only nine or ten entered the free professions, only three were artists and only twelve migrated permanently from the family threshold. Those seventeen who held lesser civil or judicial offices, altho outside the three great Junker professions, were not breaking with Junker traditions entirely, for even a hundred years earlier and probably before that some Junkers were, probably by the bitter choice of necessity, in humble civil offices.[24]

When we come to consider the marriage customs and trends in the thirteen families we discover some interesting and revealing tendencies. We find, first, that the women in these families, or more likely their parents, had higher and more exclusive standards than

22. The father of one, a Bonin, was killed in the Civil War.

23. There was a tradition that a man dismissed from the Officers Corps must leave the country but apparently only two, possibly three of these twelve Junkers could have moved away for this reason: Karl von der Groeben, Lt.a.D. in Patagonia, Georg von Jagow, Lt.a.D. in Africa, and perhaps Friedrich von Schuckman, heir to Auras, Ober Lt.a.D. in America.

24. Fritz Martiny (171) "Die Adelsfrage in Preussen vor 1806 als politisches und soziales Problem," *Vjschr. f. Sozial-u. Wirtschaftsgesch.*, 1938, pp. 70-71, says that in 1800 of the Kurmark nobles seventeen were surely, and an additional six were probably, in such low posts as *Postmeister, Muehlenwaagemeister, Akzise-Aufseher,* and the like. He points out the significant fact that in 1800 there were not sufficient higher administrative offices to meet the needs of the landless nobles— the opposite of the situation prevailing in 1888-1914. Martigny lists no nobles as business men for the reason that nobles were not permitted to enter business at this time but he explains that Junkers sometimes circumvented this restriction by dropping their titles.

the men. Apparently in many cases, if they could not marry one of equal social rank they preferred to remain single. Spinsterhood was inexpressably finer and more elegant than marriage with a commoner. Maiden ladies in Junker families could become canonesses in an aristocratic charitable foundation (*Stift*) or enter a cloister or flit as pale shadows around their ancestral homes waiting on their parents and brothers.[25] At any rate 119 women remained single, and in ten families more women than men did not marry. Not economic necessity, which kept some men bachelors, so much as social standards made spinsters of these women. The record also shows that more women than men married into their own Junker group. This is true in ten of the thirteen families.[26]

In all but two families—von Seherr-Thoss and von Zedlitz-Truetzschler—some daughters did marry middle-class men. The percentage for each family ranges from 3.44% to 66.66% in the von Meyer-Arnswalde family but in only six families did it go above 10% and in only one over 25%. In all, only 37 of the 315 Junker girls married into the middle class. They represent only 11.74% of the total number but as much as 18.8% of those 196 who married. It is important to take note as well of the occupations of the middle-class men who married these Junker girls. Seven were army officers and six owned estates which they farmed. Is it not probable that, in these cases at least, the Junker wife raised the bourgeois husband up to her class rather than herself sinking into the bourgeoisie? Another six husbands were medical doctors and six more were connected with the Evangelical Church—three as pastors and three as Superintendents. Three more were professors. The remainder were: an administrative official, an architect, a president of the *Seehandlung* in Berlin, a merchant, a concert singer, a mechanic, a lawyer in Brazil, an engineer in Constantinople and a Turkish Ambassador in Berlin—not a commoner but certainly no Junker!

25. See Eduard von Keyserling, *Abendliche Haeuser* (88) *passim*.
26. In the 3 remaining families the figures are as follows:

Family	No. of women	Married Junkers	Other nobles	Commoners	Single
von Saucken	21	3	2	4	12
v. d. Groeben (Uradel)	38	6	7	8	17
von Meyer-A.	3	1	0	2	0

As for the men, they married more frequently into the middle class. In eleven families more men than women, and in every family at least one man, married commoners. The percentage for each family runs much higher than for the women. Altho the total range is from 5% to 50%, in eleven families it was over 10% and in as many as five it was over 25%.[27] We do not know why so many Junkers married middle-class girls. Perhaps it was personal desire, perhaps economic necessity, perhaps it could be more easily forgiven by the Junker social moniters than a daughter's humble marriage.

To inquire further into the matter of Junker marriages we can ask whether this widespread if moderate tendency of Junkers to marry into the middle class varied in degree according to the age, prestige and rank of the noble families under consideration. Upon investigation we do find a certain similarity within and contrast between the three main Junker categories represented—old, original Junkers, families in the Junker tradition and families attached to the Junkers in the 19th century. Those four families which were assimilated into the Junker tradition maintained the most exclusive marriage standards.[28] More men and women married Junkers or remained single and fewer married into the middle class than in either of the other two categories. We are at first surprised to find that the most exclusive marriage standards were maintained not by the old, original Junkers but by those four families which had early been assimilated into the Junker tradition. We soon realize, however, that this was due not so much to their age and their Junker character as to the fact that two of them belong to the Baronage and one to the still higher rank of Counts. For if we look at the marriage statistics from the point of view of rank we find, as we would expect, that more Counts and Countesses married Junkers or other nobles and fewer

---

27. Of the total number of men in each of these five families the proportion which married commoners is as follows:

Family	Percentage
von Meyer-Arnswalde	50.00
von Loesch	41.66
von Saucken	34.37
von Bonin	30.86
von Stuelpnagel	30.43

28. Counts von Zedlitz-Truetzschler, Barons von Seherr-Thoss, Barons von Schuckmann and the von Wolffs.

married commoners than did the Barons, and again that more Barons married girls of equal rank than did the lesser nobles. It is, then, not the age or tradition but the rank which makes these Junkers of later origin appear more exclusive. As between the seven old original Junker families, of which only one family bears the title of Count, and the two recently patented families we find that marriages conform to the expected lines. The numbers of the old nobility, both men and women, who married Junkers or remained single are far above those in the two new families, whereas the proportion of marriages with the middle class is much higher with the von Loesches and the von Meyers than with either the old nobility or those longer in the Junker tradition. Some interesting exceptions to this are to be found below in the discussion of individual families.

Because of the widespread belief that the Junkers and nobles in general tended because of their exclusive standards to marry within their own families and clans I have taken particular pains to note the number of consanguineous marriages—both those between members of the same family and those between members of one family and other families with which it had conspicuously frequent marriage ties. The marriage statistics of these thirteen families show that there was little basis for this accusation of endogamy. In some families there was no evidence of frequent marriage within one or between two families and in only two families did the total number of the members who married within the same or into one other particular family exceed six. In the von Zedlitz-Truetzschler family one married another von Zedlitz and five or about 30% married into the von Rohr family. Of the Barons von Seherr-Thoss three married within the family and three married into the family of von Lieres und Wilkau, a total of 9 out of 64 members. These findings do not contradict the fact that Junkers tended to marry into neighboring families.

We are reminded here especially of a fact already mentioned and one which prevails thruout this chapter, namely, that the total numbers under consideration are too small to form the basis for any substantial generalizations. In the discussion of marriage habits or any other social custom we can only note the facts and draw rough conclusions. Comparisons between the three main Junker categories with regard to landholding and occupations are also inconclusive and show no striking variations. This would naturally be the case since both those in the Junker tradition and, more particularly, those who were ennobled in the 19th century were included in the Junker group only because their lives and customs corresponded in large measure to the pattern of the old, original Junkers. One specific analysis is interesting—that of Junkers in unusual occupations. The variations in the numbers of unusual careers appear in the following table:

Category	Family	Number of Unusual Careers	% of Total Number of Men in the Family
Old, original Junkers:	Counts Groeben	1	5.00
	von Jagow	6	15.78
	von Bonin	13	16.05
	von Koeller	6	22.22
	von Groeben (Uradel)	11	24.00
	von Stuelpnagel	11	24.00
	von Saucken	13	40.62
In Junker Tradition:	Counts Zedlitz-Truetzschler	0	0.00
	Barons von Schuckmann	1	11.11
	Barons von Seherr-Thoss	5	16.66
	von Wolff	3	23.00
Associated in 19 century:	von Meyer-Arnswalde	0	0.00
	von Loesch	3	25.00

Here again the paucity in numbers gives a biased and inconclusive picture. This is particularly true of the von Meyer-Arnswalde family which was originally chosen because three out of their four men were *Landraete* and active Conservatives. The low percentage for the Counts and Barons is more indicative since it seems to show, once again, that those of higher rank in the nobility tended to preserve more carefully the exclusive aristocratic social customs. The high figure of 40.62% for the von Saucken family is striking since it seems to show a marked degeneration of Junker standards in this ancient and distinguished East Prussian family.

Further interesting if indecisive variations between the three Junker groups and also within them will appear as we go on to examine each of the families individually. In this brief study of each family those in the class of old and original Junkers will be considered first, then those in the Junker tradition and finally the latest accretions—those absorbed in the 19th century.

VON KOELLER FAMILY

The von Koeller family belongs to the original nobility of Pomerania; it has documentary evidence to prove that Johann Collner, Knight, was a Counsellor of Bogislav IV, Duke of Pomerania in 1280.[29] In our period it had branches in Silesia as well as Pomerania. As many as six of the 27 men living between 1888 and 1914 held or had previously held central administrative offices and another two, as owners of knights' estates, served in an honorary provincial capacity, eight had left the Officers Corps for their estates and only two made a vocation of army service. Nine or 33⅓% of the men belonged to a single student corps—the Saxo-Borussen of Heidelberg. Five of these were later administrative officials, thus making 83⅓% of the von Koeller officials fraternity men.

Adolf Henrich von Koeller-Ossecken (1832-1918) lived out a typically Junker life. From the age of twenty to thirty-four[30] he was an officer in an Infantry regiment of the Prussian Army. He retired as Captain in 1866. Altho the fourth son, Adolf inherited property from his father, who was the owner of many estates. At some time he became lord of Ossecken (4070 acres), Wittenberg (2680 acres), Gross Damerkow (3092 acres) and Aalbeck (362 acres), all in Kreis Lauenburg in Pomerania. In 1883-1884 he was acting *Landrat* of Kreis Lauenburg as a Circle delegate and from 1885 to 1893 he served as permanent *Landrat* there.[31] In addition, he was a *Landschaft* Counsellor in 1883-1884 and a *Landschaft* Director in Stolp from 1885 to his death. For ten years he was a member and later the deputy chairman of the Provincial Executive

---

29. *Uradeligen Haeuser* (12) 1904, p. 449.
30. As far as I am able to determine.
31. Note that he reached the *Landratsamt* thru service in the provincial self-government rather than thru regular administrative training.

Committee. In 1914 he was chairman of the Pomeranian Provincial Diet. Adolf had married Hildegard von Waldow, of good Junker stock, and he raised a family of six daughters and two sons.

Politically more prominent if no less typical was Georg von Koeller-Kantreck (1823-1916) who for nineteen years (1879-1898) held the important office of First President in the Prussian Diet. Georg was a wealthy landowner, lord of the estate of Kantreck (15,750 acres) in Kreis Kammin, Pomerania. He was a brother of Adolf and Ernst von Koeller. There is no evidence that Georg ever belonged to the Officers Corps. He apparently trained for the civil administration and for twenty years (1848-1868) he acted as *Landrat* in his home Circle, Kammin. He later entered politics and was elected President of the House of Deputies an office which he held for nineteen successive years. He was chairman of the Pomeranian Provincial Diet for an even longer period (1877-1905). His wife was Maria von Wurmb and they had six children.

As President of the House of Deputies Georg exercised considerable political influence and attracted much public attention. In 1892 he was even offered the presidency of the Prussian ministry, before Botho zu Eulenburg, but he refused it.[32] Koeller was a true, gruff, self-assertive, independent Junker squire, "the stout archetype of all Pomeranian Junkers."[33] He did not hesitate to speak out boldly in opposition to government policies and his protests were particularly loud at the time of the disciplinary dismissal of the twenty *Landraete* after the canal affair.[34] As a Conservative and as a Junker Koeller was an important factor in Prussian politics.

Still more influential was his famous younger brother, Ernst von Koeller, at one time Prussian Minister of the Interior and the centre of an important political cabal in 1895. As the seventh son Ernst had little hope of an inheritance and so he plunged into the civil administration. By 1869 at the early age of twenty-eight he succeeded his elder brother, Georg, as *Landrat* in their home Circle of Kammin. Nineteen years later he became Police President in Frankfurt a.M. and in the following year he was appointed Under-

32. Graf Alfred von Waldersee (41) *Denkwuerdigkeiten,* v. 2, p. 236.
33. Prince Bernhard von Buelow (24) *Memoirs,* v. 2, p. 445.
34. Siegfried von Kardorff (86) *Wilhelm von Kardorff, . . . ,* p. 341.

secretary for Alsace-Lorraine. For a brief period, from 1881 to 1888, he had held a seat in the Reichstag. Ernst had served in the Officers Corps for some years and finally retired as a 1st Lieutenant. In 1869 he had married his niece, Martha von Koeller, daughter of his older brother, Hugo von Koeller-Schwenz, but they had no children.

Ernst von Koeller represents the stubborn, aggressive, socially arrogant and yet hearty official from the East Elbian squirearchy against whom the liberals railed. To Count Hutten-Czapski he appears to have "all the virtues and weaknesses of a typical Junker"[35] and Alexander von Hohenlohe, who knew him well in Alsace, describes him with the special animosity of a South German Prince:

"He had the outward appearance of a corpulent, robust Landjunker . . . and as to his education it could not have been more extensive than that of most of his fellow Junkers. As far as his political opinions were concerned, he was naturally a convinced Prussian monarchist and Conservative. In personal relations Koeller was a jovial, jolly patron and this jovialty combined with his corpulence gave him . . . a certain popularity."[36]

Because of his thorough-going Junker character and conservative convictions—and his real ability as well—von Koeller was chosen by the Kaiser for the post of Minister of the Interior in the new Hohenlohe Ministry with the intention that he should counterbalance the liberal elements in the new government and thereby placate the Conservatives and overcome their estrangement from the Government.[37] But von Koeller proved to be an unassimilable element in the new Ministry because of his bluntness and uncompromising conservatism. He soon clashed with the War Minister, Walter Bronsart von Schellendorf, and brought on a serious ministerial crisis and a trial of strength between the Ministry, which opposed him to a man, and the Kaiser. The latter insisted on keeping Koeller because " he was the very man on whose energy he was counting if it

---

35. Graf Bogdan von Hutten-Czapski (34) *Sechzig Jahre Politik und Gesellschaft*, v. 1, p. 266.

36. Alexander von Hohenlohe (32) *Aus meinem Leben*, pp. 132-34.

37. At the time of Koeller's appointment to the Ministry the Saxon ambassador to Berlin said, "Der letzterer [Koeller] ist ein sehr faehiger, streng konservativer Mann aus der Puttkamerschen Schule, von dessen Berufung S. Majestaet einen Zusammenschluss mit der konservativen Partei erhofft." See Egmont Zechlin (122) *Staatsstreichplaene* . . . , Appendix, p. 220.

should be necessary to resort to force."[38] But the Kaiser finally gave way before the threat of resignation of his whole Ministry and Koeller was dropped. In 1897 he entered public office again as the *Ober-Praesident* of Schleswig-Holstein, where he went to work with characteristic initiative and zeal to suppress the Danes. Waldersee writes in 1899, ". . . I congratulated him on his energetic campaign against the Danes and learned that he had undertaken it entirely on his own initiative."[39] In 1901 von Koeller returned to Alsace-Lorraine as Secretary of State and remained in this office until 1908.

Hugo von Koeller, eldest son of Hugo von Koeller-Schwenz, and his son, Alexander, offer an interesting and surprising contrast to the three brothers just described. From the scanty records we see that Hugo went from Prussia to Bulgaria because he married Emelie Theiser in Warna in 1882. He also acquired the title of a retired Bulgarian Cavalry Captain. It is possible that some dishonor had forced Hugo into exile. By 1904 he had moved on to Constantinople and was the owner of a newspaper there, the *Konstantinopler Handelsblatt*. He later returned to Prussia and in 1912 he was the co-director of a trans-oceanic steamship company in Berlin. Hugo's whole career is most unusual and surprising for a Junker; travel and, what is more, occupation in business enterprises were definitely outside the Junker tradition. Hugo's son, Alexander, is equally unlike the average Junker. He was born in Bulgaria, had no military record and spent his life as an official of the Hamburg-American line.

Another but quite different non-conformer is Waldemar von Koeller (1837-1889). As well as being fideicommissary of Dobberphul, Reckow and Moratz in the Koeller home Circle of Kammin, Waldemar owned three estates in Silesia. He was a Catholic, a member of the Maltese Order of Knights and Papal *Gen. Km. di Spada e Cappa*. He held no public office, not even in the Officers Corps, and appears to have devoted himself to the administration of his estates. In 1868 he married Hedwig, Countess Zieten, from an ancient and

---

38. Fuerst Chlodwig zu Hohenlohe-Schillingsfuerst (33) *Denkwuerdigkeiten der Reichskanzlerzeit*, p. 126.

39. Waldersee (41) v. 2, p. 428. Eugen von Jagemann (35) *Fuenfundsiebzig Jahre des Erlebens und Erfahrens*, p. 165, says, "Die schroffe Ausweisungspraxis des Oberpraesident von Koeller gegen die Daenen im Schleswigschen loeste manchen Streit aus."

distinguished Junker family and they had five children. It is both interesting and important to take stock of the fact that such variations and such wide deviations from the Junker tradition can occur in the heart of a single genuine Junker family.

VON JAGOW FAMILY

The von Jagow family belonged to the ancient nobility of the Mark Brandenburg and was one of the oldest and most important families of the Uckermark. It took its name from the village of Jagow near Prenzlau where it first appeared in the 13th century.[40] In 1798 the family was given the hereditary title of Master of the Hunt (*Erbjaegermeister*) in the Kurmark because of its ownership of the fideicommissum of Ruehstaedt (6000 acres).

The von Jagows had several members in public life during our period. Eight rose high in army service and another eight were in the civil administration. Of these four belonged to student corps and in all six or 15% were corps members. Seven had retired from the army to farm their estates. The most prominent of those in civil life was Gottlieb von Jagow who became Foreign Secretary in January, 1913, and directed German foreign affairs during the critical weeks preceding the outbreak of the first World War. It does not lie within the scope of this study to discuss von Jagow's capacity as Foreign Secretary or his tactics as head of the Foreign Office in 1914, but it is appropriate to give a brief glance at his background and particularly at the manner in which he made his career. Gottlieb was the third and youngest son of Karl, lord of the old family fideicommissum of Ruehstaedt. He had no land nor any expectation of a landed inheritance, altho both of his older brothers owned estates, and so he had to seek a livelihood in some form of state service. He trained for the civil administration and by 1892, at the age of twenty-nine, he was a *Regierungs-Assessor* in Potsdam. Apparently he found this work uncongenial, for in 1895 he sought to make a change and the tactics which he used to better his position are interesting and revealing. Bernhard von Buelow tells us in his memoirs[41] that while

40. *Jahrbuch des deutschen Adels* (15) v. 1.
41. Buelow (24) v. 3, pp. 32-36. Buelow's account of Jagow's procedure in seeking a better post may be accepted as reliable in the main altho Jagow is one

he was Ambassador to Italy Gottlieb's older brother, Hermann, who was "a good old comrade" in Buelow's regiment, the King's Hussars, but had retired to farm his estates, asked him as a friend to find a place for his brother in the diplomatic service. He added that Gottlieb was not only poor but sickly and would like a post in a salubrious climate. Buelow responded immediately, also perhaps because Gottlieb was a corps brother of his in the Hasso-Borussen of Bonn, and took him into the Embassy at Rome as an attaché. Von Jagow was now launched on a diplomatic career and his ambition together with Buelow's sponsorship carried him rapidly toward the top. By 1906 he was a *Vortragender Rat* in the Foreign Office and by 1908 Minister to Luxemburg. In 1910, upon the recommendation of Buelow but with the misgivings of the Kaiser, von Jagow was given the important post of Ambassador to Rome. In explanation of this appointment Buelow claims to have said that Jagow was well acquainted with Rome. "As for the rest you [Jagow] come from a very good family and so I hope you'll behave yourself accordingly."[42] In 1913 von Jagow returned from Rome to take over the Foreign Office from Kiderlen-Waechter.

Another prominent member of the family was Traugott von Jagow, the notorious Police President of Berlin who was at one time made a laughing stock by the Social Democrats. He was the second son of Julius who owned no land and had spent his life as *Landrat* of Kreis West-Priegnitz in the district of Potsdam. His mother was Thekla von Wilamowitz-Moellendorf. Traugott decided to follow his father into the administrative service and in 1896 he stepped right into his father's office as *Landrat* of Kreis West-Priegnitz upon the latter's retirement. But Traugott was energetic, ambitious and a faithful and active member of the Conservative party. After ten years as *Landrat* he was made an *Ober-Regierungsrat* in Potsdam, and, finally, the Chief of the Berlin police. During this time he rose from a Lieutenant to a Major in the Reserves of the Guard Curassiers.

---

of the many public figures whom Buelow treats with an exaggeration of malice and self-righteousness. Jagow was much more highly considered by other men in the Foreign Office. See, for example, Otto Hammann's letter to Kiderlen-Waechter in Ernst Jaeckh (82) *Kiderlen-Waechter*, . . . , v. 1, p. 251.

42. Buelow (24) v. 3, p. 34.

Traugott was now in a position of great responsibility and his most delicate and important task was to keep the large Social Democratic population of Berlin from challenging the State authority. He approached his task with true Junker directness, self-assurance and blunt imperiousness with the result that in 1910 he committed a serious blunder and weakened the authority of the Government. The Berlin Social Democrats had requested permission to hold a demonstration against the Government's electoral reform bill at Treptow Park but Jagow replied with more zeal than judgment or tact that such a demonstration was forbidden and if it should be attempted it would be prevented *by force*. He sent a large contingent of police to Treptow Park at the appointed time to break up any demonstration. Meanwhile the Social Democrats had quietly assembled in the Tiergarten in another section of Berlin and had held their demonstration according to schedule until the police discovered them there and broke up their gathering. This sly victory of the Social Democrats covered both Jagow and the Government with shame and ridicule and brought down criticism on the whole Conservative party because of Jagow's close connections with it. But von Heydebrand, who had approved Jagow's energetic action, retained his confidence in this loyal party member and continued to support and praise him in spite of further indiscretions.[43] Even after the war he often said that the office of Prussian Minister of the Interior would have been the right post for Jagow.[44] This blunt, arrogant, dogmatic, bludgeoning Police President is, then, the type of official which the Conservatives supported.[45]

An equally zealous and intransigeant, if less spectacular, Conservative official is Ernst von Jagow, one of the "Canal Insurgents." He was the fourth son of Eduard, lord of Kalbewisch and Uechtenhagen,

43. In particular, his action in the Zabern Affair. At that time (December 27, 1913) Heydebrand wrote to Westarp, ". . . er ist einer unserer besten Beamten, die wir haben und m. E. ganz berufen, noch hoehere Stellen einzunehmen." Graf Kuno Westarp (43) *Konservative Politik* . . . , v. 1, pp. 394-95.

44. *Ibid.,* p. 117. "Von Jagows entschlossenes und energisches Vorgehen fand die volle Zustimmung von Heydebrands der mir noch bis in die Nachkriegszeit hinein wiederholt von Jagow als einen Mann genannt hat, der als preussischer Minister des Innern am rechten Platze gewesen waere."

45. Traugott von Jagow was one of the leaders in the Kapp Putsch in 1920. See, *inter alia,* H. G. Daniels (57) *The Rise of the German Republic,* pp. 121, 142.

but he had no hope of an inheritance so he began at an early age to train for the civil administration. By 1880, at twenty-seven, he was a *Gerichts-Assessor* and from 1886 to 1892 he filled the *Landratsamt* in Kreis Osterburg in the Province of Saxony. He never held any army office. In 1893 Ernst was moved east to Posen and by 1895 he was *Regierungs-Praesident* of the governmental district of Posen. Von Jagow had been an active member of the Conservative faction in the Prussian House of Deputies since 1888 and when, in the summer of 1899, the question of the *Mittelland* Canal placed so many Conservative officials in a dilemma between loyalty to the government they represented and loyalty to their party von Jagow chose to stand by his party. He voted against the Government measure in the face of a threat to dismiss him for insubordination and shortly thereafter he was removed from office and placed on the semi-retired (*z.D.*) list. This was also the fate of many of his colleagues but von Jagow is remarkable because of his amazingly quick reinstatement in office. On March 30, 1901, only nineteen months after his disciplinary dismissal, Ernst was appointed *Regierungs-Praesident* in Marienwerder, West Prussia, and on October 18, 1905, he was made *Ober-Praesident* of West Prussia, an office which he still held in 1914. It is significant that he did not re-enter the Prussian Diet after 1901. A further explanation of his return to favor is his apparently close connection with von Buelow who had become Chancellor in 1900. Buelow speaks of von Jagow as "reliable" (!) and belonging to "the best class of old Prussian civil servant and that is saying a good deal."[46] Moreover, Count Westarp, the prominent Conservative party leader, complains that von Jagow deserted his party for Buelow when in 1909 he opposed a resolution of his old friend, von Oldenburg-Januschau, against Buelow's inheritance tax.[47]

There are many other less prominent but equally representative Prussian officials, army officers and landed squires in the von Jagow family. A few did not conform exactly to the Junker pattern but of these only one diverged conspicuously. This was Eugen von Jagow, fourth son of Wilhelm of Aulosen who, after a short period in the

46. Buelow (24) v. 2, p. 477.
47. Westarp (43) v. 1, p. 60.

Officers Corps, devoted himself to literary pursuits and became an author. He married a commoner, Gertrud Meyer, and died in France in 1905.

VON BONIN FAMILY

A large and thriving old Junker clan from Pomerania is the von Bonin family from Bonin near Koeslin in Further Pomerania. According to the documents it first appeared here in 1301. By 1888 it was still flourishing in many branches and had spread to Brandenburg and the Province of Saxony. Some lines were richly endowed with landed estates in the home province, others, without landed property, had moved west or to foreign countries and were drifting toward the middle class. Within the group of 156 members examined there were both many genuine old Junker types and many who had broken with tradition. Conspicuous among the latter are two merchants, one in Berlin and one in New York, and also a young man in California who was the son of the von Bonin killed in the American Civil War. Less eccentric but of unusual interest is Dr. Gisbert von Bonin, lord of Brettin (1325 acres) in the Altmark, who left a high post in the Prussian Administration—*Vortragender Rat* in the Finance Ministry —to become Director of the Ministry of State in Saxe-Coburg-Gotha and plenipotentiary representative of this State in the German Bundesrat. After three years in this post he retired from civil service entirely and was later appointed a life member of the *Herrenhaus* to represent the von Bonin family.

Another unusual figure is Joachim von Bonin, son of Lebrecht, a retired Captain without property. Joachim decided upon an administrative career and in 1888 at the age of thirty-one he was a *Regierungs-Assessor* in Schleswig-Holstein. From then on he devoted himself to the service of this new Prussian province, first as *Landrat* in Kreis Apenrade (1890-1894) and from 1895 to 1918 as *Landrat* in Kreis Stormarn. Joachim appears to have become assimilated to the life of this more bourgeois and distinctly anti-Junker, even anti-Prussian province. He married a middle-class girl from Altona, Ethel Fawcus, and as *Landrat* lived for years in Wandsbek, the chief town of Kreis Stormarn. In 1908 Joachim entered the House of Deputies as the representative for Stormarn-Wandsbek. That he was one of the few Junkers who belonged to the Free Conservative party is another evidence of his alienation from the strictest Junker standards.

The most striking Junker figure among the Bonins was Bogislav von Bonin, lord of Bahrenbusch (6512 acres) in Kreis Neustettin, Further Pomerania. He was the eldest son of Ernst, who owned several estates in the region, and of Anna, née von Holtzendorff. Bogislav trained for the civil service with the apparent intention of being a farming *Landrat* but he did not neglect army service. He took part in the campaigns of 1866 and 1870-1871 and finally retired with the habitual Junker rank of Cavalry Captain. While still a young *Referendar* Bogislav married Klara von Schlieffen-Soltikow who bore him seven daughters and a son who died at an early age.

In 1874 Bogislav became *Landrat* in his home Circle, Neustettin. He held this convenient and congenial office for twenty-five years, until 1899, and would undoubtedly have occupied it longer had he not "fallen into the Canal." Bonin had entered the Prussian Diet in 1893 as a representative for Neustettin-Belgard, that thoroughly Junker Pomeranian district, and in 1898 he was elected to the Reichstag for the same district. He was by nature independent, self-assured and stubborn. In addition he was a doctrinaire. He continued staunchly to preach and defend the old corporative ideals of the divinely ordained *Staendestaat* and of old-fashioned Prussianism. Westarp says that he was the only and last representative of the old Prussian ideas as conceived of by the von Gerlachs. He still considered the foundation of the German Empire as a great mistake.[48] Because of his intransigeant support of this position Bogislav did not hesitate to challenge the Government, in the Canal affair even in the face of the threat of dismissal. As a result he was disciplined and retired on half-pay,[49] but he continued to be elected to the House of Deputies and the Reichstag right down to the war. In both Houses he was a lone figure, almost an anachronism, because of his continued and vociferous adherence to old-fashioned, particularist Prussian Conservatism. It is characteristic of this old Junker's determination and robust self-confidence that as late as 1922 he published a pamphlet entitled *Vorwaerts zum alten Preussen.*

48. Westarp (43) v. 1, p. 362.
49. *Z. D. gestellt.*

Before leaving the von Bonins let us consider briefly the descendants of General Eduard von Bonin, the War Minister (1858-1859) of the New Era. Eduard had only one son, Arthur, who became a Major and the commander of the school for non-commissioned officers in Potsdam. He had died by 1886 but he left four sons. The two eldest, Wilhelm and Otto, do not appear to have done anything. There was no landed property in this branch of the family for them to farm. Otto may have been supported by his wife. We know that he married Adele Zander of Solingen, the great steel manufacturing city, in 1903 and she may have been an heiress. The two younger sons trained for a career and it is interesting, considering the important positions in the military profession of both father and grandfather, that they both chose the administrative service. One had become a *Regierungs-Assessor* in Muelheim a.R. by 1912, at the age of thirty-two. The other, who was serving as a Lieutenant in 1912-1914, apparently intended to become a civil official because he was also a law student. Both of these men married into the von Versen family. These few facts suggest to us the variations in energy and capacity which were bound to make their appearance even in the family of a distinguished Junker and a distinguished General.

Of all the Bonins active in our period only fourteen (17%) pursued an administrative career whereas twenty-two spent their lives as army officers and another thirteen retired from the army to their estates. As many as thirteen led lives outside the Junker tradition. Twelve or 15% of the eighty-one men were members of student corps. Of these eight later became officials.

Von der Groeben Family

When we come to consider the Groeben family[50] we find that of the Counts only two out of 40 men and women married into the middle class whereas of the plain von der Groebens 18 out of 84 or 21.43% married commoners. Because of the more extensive property-holdings of the Counts, 7 or 35% of these went from the Officers Corps to farming whereas only 6 (13%) of the plain Groebens re-

50. In this family we must carefully distinguish between the more exclusive and aristocratic branches which had been raised to the rank of Counts and those which remained plain *Uradel.*

tired to their estates. Conversely, only 4 Counts or 20% pursued a life career in the Officers Corps (2 of these had inherited fideicommissa) but 18 of the plain Groebens or 40% remained in the army. Only a very few from either side (5% of the Counts and 4.35% of the plain Groebens) were in the regular administrative service. As would be expected the Counts conformed more carefully to the aristocratic customs while the other Groebens were not so strict. Five per cent and 24% respectively led lives unusual for Junkers. Out of the 66 men in both families only two were members of student corps.

Altho both of the Groeben families originally belonged to the earliest nobility of Magdeburg they later moved to East Prussia where the Junker tradition of service was not so strong as in the Mark or Pomerania. Here some branches acquired extensive properties. Four of these large landholders set up four fideicommissa in 1711 and these properties together with the joint family foundation of 12,000 acres set up in 1772 were the basis for their elevation to the rank of Counts. The Counts von der Groeben were and are today one of the most distinguished and honoured families in East Prussia. Their less elegant cousins, the plain von der Groeben, also played their part in local and national affairs. We shall mention only Louis von der Groeben who was a vigorous leader of the Agrarian League in East Prussia. It was he who led a deputation from the East Prussian branch of the League in 1894 to petition the Kaiser to fight for "Religion, morals and order." In itself this audience with William II was not of great importance but because of the tense political situation and because of the presence of both August zu Eulenburg and his brother, Botho, at the interview von der Groeben's action took on great political significance and did much to undermine the position of Caprivi and bring about his downfall. This gave Louis von der Groeben occasion to rejoice for he was a bitter enemy of Caprivi and his commercial treaties.[51]

Von der Groeben was a landowner himself, lord of Arenstein (2720 acres) in East Prussia, and a retired Infantry Captain. He had married a middle-class girl, Bertha Linde, in 1867. Groeben carried on a campaign against his liberal and industrialist opponents from his seat in the Prussian *Herrenhaus* and in the Reichstag and

51. Zechlin (122) pp. 131-32; Otto Hammann (72) *Der neue Kurs*, p. 102.

from his post as East Prussian leader of the Agrarian League. He never held an adminstrative office.

VON SAUCKEN FAMILY

The von Saucken family is interesting to us chiefly because of the contrast between its ancient and illustrious origin and the undistinguished appearance of some of its members by the twentieth century. Modern research has produced evidence that the von Sauckens are a branch of the now extinct native East Prussian noble family of von der Wickerau. Hence they must have originally been old Pruzzen with an aristocratic lineage going back before the oldest Junker families of the Mark. In the early part of the 19th century, however, some of them belonged to the liberal group in East Prussia headed by Theodor von Schoen[52] and they acquired some liberal convictions and liberal attitudes which brought them into closer contact with the bourgeoisie than was customary for Junkers. Hence their deviation from Junker standards seems to have been due not to any lack of Junker antecedents or personal capacity but to a conscious desire to disregard the accepted social barriers between them and the middle class. The conspicuous fact about the Sauckens of the pre-war generation is that 13 or 40% of them had departed from strict Junker tradition, some of them even lowering themselves to bourgeois pursuits. One was a lottery collector (*Lotterieeinnehmer*), another a police inspector. A von Saucken became a landscape painter, three had settled in the United States and a fourth had migrated to Brazil where his daughter married a native Portuguese middle-class lawyer. Only one of the 32 men was affiliated with a student corps, the Hasso-Borussen of Bonn; he was a *Referendar a.D.*

The von Saucken marriage statistics in general indicate a similar trend away from Junker tradition. Of the 53 men and women, 15 or 28.3% married into the middle class whereas only 8 or 15% married into their own Junker class.[53] Five of the men followed army careers as compared with four who retired to their estates. Four others were in the administrative service, one as a *Landrat*. Two others held office in the provincial self-government.

---

52. See Hans Rothfels (113) *Theodor von Schoen, . . . ,* p. 5, note 4.
53. Eleven married other nobles; nineteen remained single.

Some of the von Sauckens still held fine estates in East Prussia and lived like their ancestors as distinguished country gentlemen. At least seven of the old estates still belonged to members of the family. In fact, what intrigues us most about the von Sauckens is the curious way in which some of them combined a solid Junker background with a liberal and unprejudiced attitude toward the middle class. For example, Ernst von Saucken-Tarputschen, the ancestor of some of those in our period, was a warm supporter of German Nationalism in 1848 altho he was lord of four estates in East Prussia, a retired Cavalry Captain and the husband first of Luise von Heyligenstaedt and later of Pauline von Below. On the other hand, Ernst's second son, Kurt, the only one who survived until our period, gives the appearance of being thoroughly a Junker. His reversion may be representative of a general swing away from liberalism, back toward conservatism after the economic depression of the 1870's. He undoubtedly lived from the two estates which he had inherited from his father—Tarputschen and Tataren (4020 acres) in Kreis Darkehmen. He married one of his own clan, Lina von Saucken-Julienfeld, and raised three sons and a daughter. As proof that Kurt took a considerable interest in local affairs we have the knowledge that he represented Koenigsberg in the Prussian House of Deputies and at the time of his death in 1890 he held the distinguished post of *Landesdirektor* of East Prussia.

Kurt's three sons, however, seem to have inherited some of the liberal attitudes of their grandfather. Two of them, altho they each inherited one of the two family estates, entered the judicial service and became public prosecutors. Moreover, they both married middle-class girls. The third son was the landscape painter referred to above; he remained a bachelor. Of Ernst's four other grandsons one was the above-mentioned lottery collector, two spent their lives in the army and no occupation is recorded for the fourth. Two married commoners and two married Junkers. Other branches of the family show this same mixture of Junker characteristics and bourgeois inclinations.

Von Stuelpnagel Family

The von Stuelpnagel family shows a similar if less marked departure from Junker tradition. It, too, is of distinguished heritage, dating back to the original nobility of the Uckermark in Brandenburg. By our time its greatest ties were with the army and 15 or one-third of the men examined pursued careers in the Officers Corps. Only three entered upon administrative careers whereas eight retired from the army to their estates. But again we find that a large number—11 or 24%—failed to measure up to Junker standards. One was a tax inspector, another migrated to Paraguay. The greater number of these 11 who left the Junker tradition belonged to the family of Alexander von Stuelpnagel who was the director of a horse car company. That Alexander's eldest son, Arthur, was the black sheep of the family may be gathered even from the meagre information in the pages of the dignified Gotha handbooks. Arthur's son was apparently forced to enter a business profession—he became a merchant. Arthur's brother was a riding instructor. Only three in the whole family or 6.52% belonged to a student corps but one of these, a member of the Goettingen Saxonia, was an administrative official.

FOUR FAMILIES IN THE JUNKER TRADITION

We turn now to the four families, three from Silesia and one from the Mark, which had been assimilated into the Junker group in the 18th century and hence belong in the Junker tradition. The most illustrious and politically prominent was the family of the Counts von Zedlitz-Truetzschler. The Zedlitz are an ancient aristocratic family of Silesia and Bohemia. One branch was raised to the rank of Prussian Counts in 1764 because of its wide property-holdings and the family was granted the combined name of "Grafen von Zedlitz und Truetzschler" in 1810. The family was still well endowed with property in 1888-1914. Seven of the eight men under consideration owned estates and the eighth was the son of a fideicommissary. Five of the Counts devoted themselves to the direction of their estates, four having retired from the Officers Corps. The one Count without property remained in the army until he was thirty-nine and then apparently became a rentier. Not one of the eight men was affiliated with a student corps. Two held civil offices, however, and these, father and son, possessed a modest estate. None deviated from the aristocratic tradition. Their exclusiveness is apparent also in their marriage connections—of the ten Countesses, eight married Junkers and two remained single and of the men, five married Junkers, one married a Countess who was not from a Junker family, one was a bachelor and only one married a bourgeois. The Zedlitz were closely related by marriage to the illustrious old Junker family of von Rohr in the Mark Brandenburg.

The two most prominent figures in the Zedlitz-Truetzschler family before the war and those who interest us the most are Count Robert von Zedlitz-Truetzschler, famous for his brief tenure as *Kultus-minister* in 1891-1892, and his son, Robert, a Marshal in the Kaiser's Court. The elder Count Robert was a prominent and beloved figure in Prussian politics to his death in 1914. Even those who criticised his ideas admired him for his noble idealism, his integrity, his un-selfishness and his genuine graciousness. Zedlitz had the ardent piety and the Christian Socialist ideals of an old Conservative of principle and with true Junker tenacity he stood out boldly and uncompromis-ingly for his beliefs regardless of the exigencies of the political situation.[54] Consequently he was a failure as a statesman altho he served his province of Silesia and the Prussian administration with ability and devotion for a great many years. He is also remarkable for the variety of ways in which he served; his public career was most irregular. At the age of 19 he entered the aristocratic regiment Gardes du Korps but he retired six years later to take over the administration of his father's estate, Niedergrossenbohrau (1450 acres). He later took part in the campaigns of 1866 and 1870-1871 and was finally retired as a Major. He had married Agnes von Rohr-Levetzow in 1862 and they raised a family of two sons and four daughters.

While running his father's estate Robert played an active part in the administration of his Circle and province and became chairman of the Provincial Executive Committee. Suddenly, in 1881, he was persuaded by Bismarck[55] to take the post of *Regierungs-Praesident* in Oppeln, Silesia—this without any regular training for the Prussian

54. Hans Herzfeld (76) *Johannes von Miquel* v. 2, p. 296, describes him as a man of piety and strong convictions, "durchaus konservativ und betont christlich-kirchlich . . . der menschlich zu den lautersten Persoenlichkeiten der Epoche ge-hoert."

55. According to the account of his son, Count Robert von Zedlitz-Truetzschler (46) *Twelve Years at the Imperial German Court*, pp. 1-2.

State administration. Zedlitz filled his new office with distinction and in 1886 Bismarck raised him to the position of *Ober-Praesident* of Posen and head of the newly established Colonization Commission for West Prussia and Posen. His membership in the Eastern Marches Association is another indication of his sympathy with the German colonization program in these two provinces. In 1888 Bismarck turned to Count Zedlitz again and proposed him to succeed von Puttkamer as Minister of the Interior but Frederick III and his wife opposed Zedlitz on the ground that "that would be merely a continuation of the Stoecker business, he [Zedlitz] would be just as pietistic as Puttkamer and besides he had a daughter married to a Kleist-Retzow."[56]

It is significant that Zedlitz was held in greater esteem by Frederick's son, William II, and it was at the Emperor's desire that he was appointed *Kultusminister* in 1891 with the express purpose that he draft and put thru a School Reform Bill. At the time of his appointment Zedlitz was generally recognized as a Conservative, even as a sympathizer with the Right Wing Conservatives, the *Kreuzzeitung* group, with whom he had close personal relations.[57] But this was the consequence of Zedlitz' own personal views and not of any political opportunism. Zedlitz brought all his religious and pietistic convictions to bear upon the problem of school reform and as a result he produced a bill which in its effort to give wider scope to the Evangelical Church in primary and secondary education opened the doors to extensive activity by the Roman Catholic Church as well. Altho the bill satisfied the deepest desires of the Hammerstein-Stoecker Conservatives,[58] it brought forth a storm of protest from all the liberal parties and even from the moderate Conservatives. Finally the Kaiser himself turned against the bill. Count Zedlitz, who preferred to oppose his Emperor rather than compromise his religious principles, offered his resignation scarcely a year after taking office.

56. Frhr. Robert Lucius von Ballhausen (36) *Bismarck-Erinnerungen,* p. 463. Robert's daughter, Ruth, was married to Juergen, only son of Hans von Kleist-Retzow. Wilhelm von Massow (97) *Die innere Politik unter Kaiser Wilhelm II,* p. 123, writes, "politisch wie kirchlich gehoerte er der aeussersten Rechten an; . . ."
57. Heinrich Heffter (74) *Die Kreuzzeitungspartei* . . . , p 224.
58. *Ibid.,* p. 225.

Altho in royal disfavor Zedlitz did not disappear from public life nor did the *Kreuzzeitung* Conservatives forget him. At the time of the Caprivi crisis in 1894 they proposed him to Botho zu Eulenburg as chancellor rather than suggesting Botho himself,[59] and again in 1899 Hohenlohe thought of him as a possible successor to von der Recke in the Ministry of the Interior. Actually Count Zedlitz returned to his old work in the higher administration where he spent twelve more years of loyal and distinguished service. He was made *Ober-Praesident* of Hessen-Nassau in 1898 and from 1903 to 1910 he served as *Ober-Praesident* of his home province of Silesia. In 1914 the year of his death, the Kaiser made him a life member of the *Herrenhaus*—a tardy recognition of years of noble and high-principled, if sometimes unwise, service to the Prussian State.

Count Robert's eldest son, also Robert, professed to have his father's simplicity and integrity of character and complained that he chafed under the restrictions and hollowness of aristocratic society. He says of himself that as a young man he had a strong desire to migrate to the United States and become a pioneer but with the help of his father he curbed his rebellious impulses and conformed at least outwardly to the conventions of his class.[60] He did, however, break with family and Junker tradition to the extent of marrying a middle-class girl, Olga Buergers, in 1899 when he was already thirty-six and a personal adjutant to Prince Joachim Albert. Robert had entered the exclusive 1st Foot Guards Regiment when he was twenty and in 1899, after he had become a Captain, he was assigned to attend the Prince. Four years later he was especially singled out by the Kaiser for the post of Marshal at his Court. Robert claimed that he accepted this brilliant but onerous office with some misgivings because of his distaste for court intrigue and the sycophancy of many of those in the Emperor's entourage. His autobiography is filled with criticisms of the Kaiser—his vanity, his arrogance and his incapacity—and of the servile and spineless courtiers who encouraged his egotism by their exaggerated flattery. Yet one gathers from Zedlitz' account that he himself took little initiative to offet these harmful influences. It must be said to his

59. Waldersee (41) v. 2, p. 326.
60. Zedlitz-Truetzschler (46) pp. 2-3.

credit, however, that Alexander von Hohenlohe, that severe critic of "Byzantinism" at the Prussian Court, expressly distinguished Count Robert as one of the few courtiers who could be respected.[61]

Because he found the court atmosphere so distasteful and because he became more and more "a prey to a serious conflict of feeling"[62] between his own principles and his loyalty to his Emperor, Count Robert finally begged permission to retire in 1910. He withdrew to a quiet country life on the family estate in Niedergrossenbohrau in Silesia and took over the management of the property.[63]

The other two families from Silesia who are in the Junker tradition, the Barons von Schuckmann and von Seherr-Thoss, conform so completely to the regular Junker pattern that they do not warrant any special attention. Their members neither broke away from accepted customs nor excited special interest because of prominence in public life. Of the Barons von Schuckmann three out of nine pursued an administrative career, three were in the army and two had retired from the Army to their estates. One young man, Friedrich, Baron von Schuckmann, who had inherited the old family estate of Auras, retired from the army as a Lieutenant when he was thirty-four, renounced his inheritance and moved to America. Altho he later returned to Europe he never came back to Prussia. Of the nine Barons four or 44.44% belonged to student corps; three to the Hasso-Borussen of Bonn—and these were the three administrative officials—, one to the Saxo-Borussen of Heidelberg.

The Barons von Seherr-Thoss are perhaps a degree more exclusive than the von Schuckmanns. They made almost no marriage connections with the middle class and showed a definite preference for other Junker families, particularly the von Lieres und Wilkaus. Of the 30 men studied seven followed army careers, six were in the administration and another six had left the Officers Corps for their estates. Only one member of the family, an official, belonged to a student corps. The family was closely connected with the Silesian *Landschaft* and four of its members were *Landschaft* Counsellors and Directors

---

61. Alexander von Hohenlohe (32) p. 369.
62. Zedlitz-Truetzschler (46) p. 297.
63. It was here in 1922 and 1923 that he wrote his retrospective memoirs criticizing the Kaiser and the Court.

in our period. Guenther, Baron von Seherr-Thoss rose in the administration to the office of *Regierungs-Praesident* in Liegnitz whereas
Erich was a mere Post Office Director. Eugen, who was the politician
in the family and sat in the Prussian House of Deputies, had married
Anna von Heydebrand und der Lassa, who was, however, only a
distant relative of the Conservative leader, Ernst von Heydebrand.

The von Wolff family is interesting because of its origins and
because by the time of our period it had lost all of its landed property.
The family came originally from Mecklenburg-Schwerin but by the
18th century it had settled in the Mark Brandenburg and acquired
extensive lands there. It was apparently for this reason that in 1786
Frederick William II bestowed a noble title on the two Wolff brothers
—Paul, who owned seven estates in Kreis Ober-Barnim and Adolf
who owned one estate there. By 1888 the family had lost all these
properties. Contrary to the usual course of development in noble
families it had moved from the landowning nobility into the purely
service nobility. Because there was no land each one of the men was
forced to enter upon a career. In view of the Junker official's relationship with the land it is interesting for us to see to what extent this landless family still conformed to Junker patterns. As with other families
we again find that the Officers Corps is the preferred field of service.
Of the thirteen men under consideration three were Colonels and
one a Lieutenant Colonel. Four others were serving in lower ranks
in 1914. Two pursued bureaucratic careers. Only three or 23%
entered upon unusual careers and these were very respectable. One
became President of a Senate in the Imperial German Court, another
was director of a penitentiary and a third was a professor of mineralogy. The two in the administration were father and son. Artur von
Wolff, who became head of the Central Audit Chamber, was the
son of a landless official—Ferdinand von Wolff, *Ober-Regierungsrat*
and member of a cathedral consistory. He married a girl from a noble
but not a Junker family, Elise von Wurmb. Artur's son, Horst,
followed his father and grandfather into the administration. By 1905
he was a *Landrat* in Kreis Sagan, Silesia. He still held this post in
1914 but we know that by 1920 he had become an *Ober-Regierungsrat*
in Cologne. Horst married a commoner, Margarete Lueg. Of the
thirteen men in our period three or 23% married into the middle class

while only one married a Junker. The sixteen women were much more exclusive: four married Junkers and only one married a commoner, a concert singer.

Two Newly Assimilated Families

We come now to the two families which had joined the Junker circle most recently—the von Meyers and the von Loesches. Obviously these two families have been included among the Junkers because they do conform to the Junker pattern. Hence it would be somewhat inconsistent to turn about and remark on how much they conform. Our interest here is not so much in the extent as in the manner of conformity.

Altho the von Meyer family of Arnswalde, in the Mark Brandenburg, was small in numbers and owned only the modest estate of Halpe (1280 acres) in the same Circle it is important because of its long tenure in the *Landratsamt* Arnswalde and the prominence of its members in the Conservative fraction of the Prussian House of Deputies, for the von Meyers were staunch old conservatives and took vigorous action to promote their policies. The patriarch of the family was Leuthold Meyer. Son of a physician in Berlin, he decided to enter the administrative service. By 1848, at the age of thirty-two, he had become *Landrat* of Kreis Arnswalde in a conservative and backward rural area of the Mark. Here he either acquired or inherited the estate of Halpe. In 1865, while still *Landrat* as well as a landowner and a retired Cavalry officer, Leuthold Meyer was elevated to the Prussian nobility. He continued to be *Landrat* of Arnswalde for another 19 years, until 1884. In 1875 he had already become *Landesdirektor* for the Neumark and General Director of the Neumark fire society. Leuthold also entered the field of politics and from 1871 to 1892 he sat in the Prussian House of Deputies. He joined the Conservative fraction and sat on its extreme Right. He became famous for his proverbial native wit and also for his stiff-necked adherence to his political convictions, even in the face of party discipline. He stood "rugged and independent in opposition to the Government and his own fraction. . . . Even in important questions he was stubborn enough to go his own way and not that of the Conservative Party. . . ."[64] In 1886

64. Heffter (74) p. 10.

he came out in support of the Poles against the colonization law because he considered that it attacked the Conservative principle of the inviolability of property rights. He withdrew at that time from the Conservatives and became a "Wilder." As late as 1891, the year before his death, Leuthold rose in the House of Deputies to attack the Government's bill for the reform of the local communes (*Landgemeindeordnung*) because it reduced the authority of the local owners of knights' estates. Leuthold combined reactionary convictions with a high degree of that stubbornness and individual self-assurance so characteristic of the Junkers.

Meyer had married Masie Treumann in 1846 and she bore him two sons. Nineteen years later he married Anna Barth of Arnswalde who was the mother of another son and a daughter. Meyer's eldest son, Richard, entered the Officers Corps and became a 1st Lieutenant in the Field Artillery but he retired at the age of thirty-six and lived in Berlin. Michael, the second son, followed his father into the administration and in 1885 he succeeded Leuthold as *Landrat* in Kreis Arnswalde. He also succeeded him as General Director of the Neumark fire society. On Leuthold's death in 1892 he inherited the family estate of Halpe.

Michael died in 1895, at the early age of forty-four, leaving a wife, Martha Booth, and two daughters, one of whom inherited the estate. The *Landratsamt* of Arnswalde now passed out of the family for a few years but Heinrich von Meyer-Arnswalde, son of Leuthold and his second wife and eighteen years younger than Michael, took up the family tradition in the administration. By 1901 he was a *Regierungs-Assessor* in Muenster, Westphalia, and by 1906 he had been appointed to the family office of *Landrat* in Kreis Arnswalde. Twelve years later, in 1918, he was still in office there but by 1921 he had been retired, probably as a consequence of the Revolution. Thus the family von Meyer-Arnswalde has the remarkable record of holding the office of *Landrat* in Kreis Arnswalde for seventy years with only a short break of ten years from 1896 to 1906 when there was no one in the family qualified to fill the post.

Unlike his step-brother Michael, Heinrich served as an army officer as well, first as a Reserve Officer in the Light Infantry and then in the militia. He resembled both his father and brother in his conservative convictions. Rudolf von Valentini writes of him, "Landrat von Meyer in Arnswalde . . . was a queer duck who administered his office entirely in the conservative and agrarian traditions of his father and his grandfather who had filled the post before him."[65] As is often the case with new adherents these 19th century Junkers seem more thoroughly Junker-like than some members of the genuine old Junker families.

The von Loesches present a somewhat different picture. The family was considerably larger, owned much more property and had a greater variety of interests. It originated in Silesia and had gradually acquired estates there. It was this fact, apparently, that prompted William I to elevate five heads of families to the nobility—one in 1863 and four in 1872—for each of these men owned one or more estates and each had no official title except a modest rank in the Officers Corps. Of the twelve men in our period two were *Landraete* and one an apprentice in the forestry service (*Forstreferendar*). Five others had left the army for agriculture and two of these were *Landschaft* Counsellors. Another had trained to be a *Referendar* only to retire to his property. Only one of them was associated with a student corps, the Saxo-Borussia in Heidelberg. One von Loesch married an English girl and moved to England, a second became a painter and lived in Dresden and a third became a geologist. Thus only 25% of the men failed to conform to the usual Junker patterns. Oddly enough none made a career of the army profession. As for marriage connections, 5 or 41.66% of the men married middle-class girls but the women were more exclusive and only one of them married a bourgeois—a merchant. Two married Junkers.

The preceding study has been very useful in clarifying our perspective of the Junker official and in widening and enriching our knowledge of the Junkers as a sociological group. Our interest has been quickened by an acquaintance with a great variety of personalities and we are particularly impressed with the wide range of individual variations within this group of 681 Junkers. It brings a realization that the Junker was not stereotyped but had his own individuality which might differ considerably from that of other Junkers and still

---

65. Rudolf von Valentini (40) *Kaiser und Kabinettschef*, p. 90.

be consistent with the general Junker pattern. For example, altho we know that the farming of a knight's estate or an army career were both preferred by the average Junker to an administrative career and that, in general, family councils considered the administrative service as a third choice when deciding the future of a young member of the clan, nonetheless we find that some Junkers and even some families reached more important positions and acquired a greater reputation in the administration than in the army. Again, we know that some members of staunch old Junker families joined obscure student corps, married into the middle class and served in ordinary posts in the army or administration whereas men from more recent and less distinguished Junker families sometimes joined the most "feudal" corps and regiments, married into famous old Junker families and farmed the estates in Pomerania or the Mark which had first been acquired by their fathers. In fact, there seems to be a general tendency for the Junkers in the category of those recently absorbed into the Junker group to be the most careful about conforming to strict Junker standards. In general, altho there is a certain consistency in the way in which members of each of the three categories of Junkers conform to the Junker standard, each category does it in a somewhat different way and, as we have seen, there are also individual variations within the general pattern of each category.

Some men from both the old, original Junker families and from those later absorbed into the Junker tradition conformed thoroughly to the strict Junker pattern and by so doing they sustained and strengthened the central Junker stock. Others, but only a very few, wandered far from Junker traditions and seemed to lose all sense of loyalty to Junker standards. One gathers the impression, however, altho it is impossible to establish it on the basis of the material here at hand, that these deviations from the Junker norm, these aberrations in the conduct of an individual Junker or of a single branch in a Junker family are in the majority of cases only temporary and that altho the original wanderer might remain alienated his sons and grandsons tended to return to the fold, by marrying back into Junker families, by joining the right student corps and regiments and in other ways.

We are attracted here not only by the indication that deviations from the norm were not necessarily permanent but by the fact, which is of primary importance, that they were actually very small to begin with. As we know, only 6 of the 366 men entered business, only 9 entered the free professions and in all only 31 or 8.47% led lives which were definitely beyond the Junker pale.[66] This indicates a remarkable conformity to accepted Junker traditions—traditions which did, however, leave room for considerable individual variation. But it should not be lightly taken as proof that the Junkers were little affected by bourgeois influences. For against the small number of men who actually entered bourgeois professions must be set the larger but indeterminate number of Junker officials treated in Chapter II who had apparently become assimilated to the bourgeois way of life because of generations of bureaucratic service together with separation from the land. In fact, one cannot escape the impression that service by landless Junkers in the regular administration, especially if extended over two or three generations, did more to mould the Junkers into the bourgeois pattern than any other factor and that the greatest encroachment of bourgeois customs on the central Junker stock was thru this channel.

66. Six were in regular business; 9, in the free professions; 3 were artists; one, a riding master; 12 had left Prussia and settled abroad.

V

THE ROLE OF THE JUNKER OFFICIAL IN THE PRUSSIAN ADMINISTRATION

IN THE preceding chapter the attempt was made to restore the balance in the Junker social pattern by reinserting the Junker official into his general family background. Here another attempt will be made to give balance and perspective by placing him in his proper position in the Prussian administration as a whole. We already know that approximately 1500 Junkers served in an official capacity, either in the higher administration of the Prussian State government or in the provincial self-governing bodies, at some time between 1888 and 1914. But the number of Junker officials takes on far greater meaning when we know what proportion they represent of the total number of Prussian higher officials. We are not greatly concerned with total figures of both Junkers and officials, however. Since these lump *Ober-Praesidenten* with surveyors and Ministerial Directors with Provincial Supreme Court judges they are not very revealing either as to Junker habits and preferences or as to the political significance of the offices Junkers held. But an analysis of the administration office by office and of the numbers of Junkers in each gives, I feel, a real insight into the sociological and political position of the Junker official. By this method we gain a clear and rather striking picture of the Junker's preference for certain types of offices and one which tends to corroborate the conclusions drawn in the preceding pages regarding his characteristics and his habits when choosing a profession.

We also want to know not only how many Junkers were *Landraete* or *Ober-Praesidenten* between 1888 and 1914 but—what is even more important both sociologically and politically—how many *Landraete* and *Ober-Praesidenten* were Junkers. Here we go on to a thorough analysis of the Junker official as a political phenomenon.

For we are interested in him not merely as a member of Prussian society but even more so as a factor in the political supremacy of the Conservatives in Prussia before the last war. The objective is to determine insofar as possible the potentialities for political influence in the hands of the Junker officials. Our first and most obvious concern is to establish the proportion of Junker officials in each department of the government, for if the percentage is large it would tend to indicate that Junker social and political views would be dominant in that department. This general conclusion must be modified, however, by the expectation, and in some cases the knowledge, that Junker officials vary among themselves in the degree of force and aggressiveness with which they promote their Junker views.

It is not only the proportion of Junker officials in a branch of the administration but the nature and political significance of the office itself which determine the potential political influence of its Junker incumbent. There are wide variations in the political importance of the Prussian administrative offices and these are due in large measure to the particular historical growth of each type of office. Hence, a brief historical review of each type of office will give us a better understanding of the political weight of the office itself by the end of the 19th century and in addition a further explanation of the Junker's traditional social preference for certain offices.

Beyond our interest in the political potentialities of the Junker official under William II is our concern to know if his opportunity to influence the government was increasing or diminishing during the twenty-six years of the Kaiser's reign before the war. The best and most concrete way of discovering changes and trends in influence is to trace the fluctuation up and down of the numbers of Junkers in each department and to note any consistent movement in either direction. In this operation it is necessary to take into account the relative political importance of the office and also the changes in the absolute number of Junkers as opposed to the proportion of Junkers in the total number of offices. Other, more intangible factors affected the Junker official's relative position between 1888 and 1914. Altho often indefinite and impossible to compute they, too, have an important bearing on changes in the Junker's capacity for influence and an attempt will be made to estimate their effect as well.

In this study of the Junker official's relative position office by office—this analysis of the historic importance of each office and the numbers, changing or constant, of Junkers in each—let us consider first the offices in the Prussian State administration from *Ober-Praesident* right down to *Regierungs-Assessor*. These form the main framework of the whole Prussian administrative system and it is here that we find the real Prussian bureaucrat and the passive power of the permanent official. Yet we shall find that even here in the central bureaucracy there are many variations due not merely to the hierarchy of ranks, but also to the different character of the several offices.

PROVINCE

The office of *Ober-Praesident* had a distinctive character. Its importance and prestige were the result of its peculiar historical evolution. The *Ober-Praesident* was the single political and administrative head of an entire province. He had a staff of assistants in the *Ober-Praesidium* to help him but the whole responsibility for the political direction and a part of the regular administration of the province rested in his hands. He held office directly under the Minister of the Interior. His office was created in 1808 by Freiherr vom Stein who wished to combine modern administrative centralization with a measure of communal self-government and a respect for historical particularism. Stein divided Prussia into provinces along historical lines and set the *Ober-Praesidenten* over them as political heads. In this way he retained something of the legacy of the old "provincial" ministers of the General Supreme Finance, War, and Domains Directory. At first the office was linked with such distinguished personalities as Theodor von Schoen, Sack, etc. Hence from the beginning the *Ober-Praesident* enjoyed a high degree of authority, independence and prestige and he was thought of somewhat as a patriarch.[1] As the political representative of the central government in the province he had to see to it that all official bodies in his province, whether a part of the Prussian State administration or an organ of the provincial self-government, kept in line with the general interests of the State.

1. Franz Schnabel (117) *Deutsche Geschichte* . . . , v. 2, p. 279.

He also performed certain administrative functions for the central government. He had general oversight over the *Regierungs-Praesidenten* in his province and served as a link between them and the Minister of the Interior. He carried out special orders from the Minister of the Interior and acted as head of all general administrations in his province, such as the Medical Advisory Committee, the School Board, etc., except for such bodies as were under the several *Regierungs-Praesidenten* or a special administration.

Each province was a self-governing unit as well as a division of the State government and the *Ober-Praesident,* as head of the province, also supervised the provincial self-government for the Prussian State. He had oversight over all the self-governing affairs and public institutions of his province. He was a member ex officio of the Provincial Diet, the Provincial Executive Committee and the Provincial *Landschaft.* He also had authority over the provincial budget. Thus he functioned in a dual capacity, both as the director of his province for the Prussian State government and as supervisor of the provincial self-governing organs. The central government and the local government were united in the person of the *Ober-Praesident.*

It is clear that the *Ober-Praesident* enjoyed considerable political authority and prestige.[2] Indeed, his office was more political than any other except that of Prussian Minister and it required him to give political leadership and direction. The lines of this political direction, however, were determined in large part from above, for the *Ober-Praesident* took his general instructions from the Minister of the Interior and, beyond him, from the Prussian Ministry. By our period the *Ober-Praesident* generally enjoyed more prestige and authority than independence. He possessed honour, position and political importance but not the political discretion of a Minister. Hence his office was frequently used as a convenient post to which to relegate

2. Graf Bogdan von Hutten-Czapski (34) *Sechzig Jahre Politik und Gesellschaft,* v. 1, p. 127, describes the office as follows: "Die Stellung der preussischen Ober-Praesidenten war eigenartig: Sie war formell nur eine Durchgangsinstanz zwischen den Regierungs-Praesidenten und den Ministern. Ein tuechtiger Ober-Praesident war aber ein maechtiger Beherrscher seiner Provinz; juristische und verwaltungstechnische Kenntnisse waren fuer ihn weniger erforderlich als Menschenkenntniss, klares Uebersehen der jeweiligen Lage, und vor allem Takt und noch einmal Takt."

Ministers or other high officials whom the Minister President or the Kaiser wished to remove from key political positions.[3] Of the 19 Junker *Ober-Praesidenten* in our period four had previously been Prussian Ministers and two others were *Ober-Praesidenten* both before and after serving as Ministers.

The *Ober-Praesident's* close connection with the provincial self-government contributed greatly to his ability to dominate the political affairs of his province. It gave him continual personal contact with the people and with their problems. Hence he had an opportunity to exert an immediate pressure and, conversely, he could be reached and influenced by prominent landowners and political leaders who lived in his province. Two references to the actual work of the *Ober-Praesidenten* will serve as the best illustration of the nature of their political influence. In 1882-1888 the *Ober-Praesident* of East Prussia was Dr. Albrecht von Schlieckmann, a man but recently assimilated into the Junker group. Rudolf von Valentini, who as a brand new *Regierungs-Assessor* was assigned to von Schlieckmann, praises him in his memoirs and says that he was able thru his great political skill to transform the strongly "progressive-liberal" sentiment in East Prussia into a conservative one so that the Reichstag elections of 1887 took a course which was very favorable to Schlieckmann's efforts.[4] Again, Adolf Ernst von Ernsthausen, who was no Junker but who served as *Ober-Praesident* of West Prussia from 1879 to 1888, writes in his memoirs that he must be careful to be discreet when describing his work there. "Not all [proceedings] are now suitable for publication, especially not those, for example, with regard to Reichstag and Diet elections, the relationship of the State administration to the press and the expulsion of Poles of Russian citizenship."[5] Of course, not all *Ober-Praesidenten* exercised their political

---

3. Fuerst Chlodwig zu Hohenlohe-Schillingsfuerst writes in his memoirs (33) *Denkwuerdigkeiten der Reichskanzlerzeit*, p. 269, ". . . da jetzt Gelegenheit waere, Wedell als Ober-Praesident in Schleswig unterzubringen." Von Wedell-Piesdorf was Head of the Royal Household in 1896 when this was written and as things turned out he remained in that office and was not made an *Ober-Praesident*.

4. Rudolf von Valentini (40) *Kaiser und Kabinettschef*, p. 31.

5. A. Ernst von Ernsthausen (28) *Erinnerungen eines preussischen Beamten*, p. 399. Altho Ernsthausen was not a Junker his remarks give illuminating evidence of the political activities of *Ober-Praesidenten* at the end of the century.

powers with equal effectiveness. If bureaucratic and unimaginative an *Ober-Praesident* might act merely as the passive political agent of the government, or submit to the pressure of provincial leaders. If aggressive, commanding and of strong convictions he might be a powerful political factor in his province. Since the real Junker was by nature self-assertive he was likely to have a positive influence. Men such as Robert, Count Zedlitz-Truetzschler, who was a leader in the Prussianizing of the eastern marches,[6] or Ernst von Koeller who as *Ober-Praesident* in Schleswig-Holstein began a campaign against the Danes on his own initiative,[7] or Ernst von Jagow who was dismissed from office because of his opposition in the Canal affair but who was later made *Ober-Praesident* of West Prussia[8]—such men made the fullest use of the *Ober-Praesident's* office to promote their own views or the views of their province even in opposition to the central government.

How many Junkers held this high and important office in our period? In 1888 six of the twelve *Ober-Praesidenten* or 50% were Junkers but in 1914 their number had fallen to three or 25%. This remarkable decline was not constant, however, as the following table shows:

Year	Total no. of offices	Junkers	Other nobles	Commoners	Percentage of Junkers
1888	12	6	4	2	50.00
1890	12	5	6	1	41.66
1895	12	4	5	3	33.33
1900	12	5	6	1	41.66
1905	12	4	5	3	33.33
1910	12	5	6	1	41.66
1914	12	3	7	2	25.00

At the first we are struck with the contradiction between the small and declining number of Junkers in this high post and the general conception of Junker domination in the higher administration. The Junker's potential political strength here falls below our expectations. But we must remember that because of the small total an average even of one-third gave an extensive opportunity for political

6. See Chapter IV, p. 149.
7. See Chapter IV, p. 136.
8. See Chapter IV, p. 140.

influence. The numbers of Junker *Ober-Praesidenten* were higher in the east but the figures also show that their influence spread into the western part of Prussia as well:

	Seven eastern provinces			Five western provinces		
Year	Junkers	Other nobles	Commoners	Junkers	Other nobles	Commoners
1888	4	2	1	2	2	1
1890	4	3	0	1	3	1
1895	4	3	0	0	2	3
1900	3	4	0	2	2	1
1905	3	3	1	1	2	2
1910	5	2	0	0	4	1
1914	2	4	1	1	3	1

Moreover, there were among the nineteen Junkers who at any time held the office such striking personalities as Robert V. von Puttkamer, Count Botho zu Eulenburg, Friedrich Wilhelm von Loebell, Wilhelm von Waldow, as well as Count Zedlitz-Truetzschler, Ernst von Koeller and Ernst von Jagow. What is more, four of the nineteen Junker *Ober-Praesidenten* later became Ministers; this shows again the special importance of the office of *Ober-Praesident* as a potential source of Junker influence.

The *Ober-Praesident* had a staff of bureaucratic officials who assisted him in the conduct of the affairs of the Prussian State administration but who had no connection with the provincial self-government. The foremost of these and the first assistant to the *Ober-Praesident* was the *Ober-Praesidialrat,* a high bureaucratic official, somewhat above the rank of an *Ober-Regierungsrat* and chosen generally from among these or the *Landraete.* The *Ober-Praesidialrat* acted as deputy for the *Ober-Praesident* in many capacities, such as chairman of the Provincial Council. Altho his office was in the regular administration and concerned with more or less routine duties, and hence less attractive to the Junker, the *Ober-Praesidialrat* might thru the importance of his post as deputy and his constant association with the *Ober-Praesident* exert influence on the latter and on the general political atmosphere in the province. He also had direct contact with political leaders in the Provincial Council. The proportion of Junkers serving as *Ober-Praesidialraete* was, as to be expected, smaller than the number of *Ober-Praesidenten:*

Year	Total no. of offices	No. of Junkers	Percentage of Junkers
1888	12	2	16.66
1890	12	2	16.66
1895	12	3	25.00
1900	12	3 (1 in west)*	25.00
1905	12	3	25.00
1910	12	4 (2 in west)*	33.33
1914	12	3 (1 in west)*	25.00

* Only in these four instances did Junker *Ober-Praesidialraete* hold office in one of the five western provinces.

The most striking fact here is the rise in the number of Junker *Ober-Praesidialraete* from 1888 to 1914. This is the only instance of an increase in the proportion of Junkers in any department of the Prussian State administration but due to the nature of the office it is not of great political importance. On the other hand, it is significant that on an average 45%[9] of the Junker *Ober-Praesidialraete* were assigned to *Ober-Praesidenten* who were not Junkers themselves. So far as the Junker influence is concerned the appointment of a Junker *Ober-Praesidialrat* in such cases would tend to compensate for the fact that the *Ober-Praesident* himself was not a Junker.

In addition to the *Ober-Praesidialraete* the *Ober-Praesident* was aided by from one to nine *Regierungsraete* and *Regierungs-Assessoren* who had been assigned to him. These officials from the regular bureaucracy were apparently sent about with little regard for their origin and the numbers of Junkers serving in the twelve *Ober-Praesidia* during this period do not fall into any consistent pattern. The total

9. Year	Number of Junker *Ober-Praesidialraete*	Number with *Ober-Praesidenten* who were not Junkers
1888	2	1
1890	2	1
1895	3	0
1900	2	1
1905	3	2
1910	4	2
1914	3	1

number of Junkers is as follows:

Year	Total no. of offices	No. of Junkers	Percentage of Junkers
1888	18	10	55.55
1890	21	5	23.80
1895	30	5	16.66
1900	36	7	19.44
1905	54	9	16.66
1910	63	9	14.28
1914	68	10	14.70

The rise from five in 1895 to ten in 1914 merely corresponds to the general increase in the total numbers in this office. For the striking drop from ten in 1888 to five in 1890, I can offer no explanation. At no time were there more than two Junker *Regierungsraete* or *Assessoren* in a single *Ober-Praesidium*.

The *Ober-Praesident* was also assisted in the administration of the affairs of the central government by the Provincial Council composed largely of local residents. There were six members and six deputy members of the Provincial Council, of whom five and five respectively were elected by the Provincial Executive Committee whereas one member and one deputy were appointed by the Minister of the Interior. The *Ober-Praesident* acted as chairman and the *Ober-Praesidialrat* as deputy chairman. This Council, which was a residue of Stein's *staendisch* ideas, functioned only in the realm of State affairs and here only in an advisory capacity. It had no jurisdiction whatsoever in the provincial self-government.[10] Elected members held honorary offices and served without pay. Because five-sixths of the members were local men elected by a provincial body it was natural that a large proportion of the members in the eastern provinces should have been Junkers and that no Junkers should serve in the west. Indeed, we find that at no time was a Junker an elected member of the Provincial Council in any one of the five western provinces. In Saxony there was but one Junker member—Ludolf von Bismarck-Briest—from 1888 to 1914. Conversely, in the East Elbian provinces the proportion of Junkers is high, according to expectation, reaching 60% or 70% in the Provincial Council of Brandenburg or Pomerania. The political importance or influence of a local member of the Provincial Council would depend largely on his individual personality and interests. If

10. Conrad Bornhak (52) *Preussisches Staatsrecht*, v. 2, pp. 356-60.

he were active in politics, the representative of his district in the House of Deputies and a member of the provincial *Landschaft* and Agricultural Chamber as well[11] he might have a considerable voice in the Provincial Council and in discussions with the *Ober-Praesident.* If he were concerned entirely with farming his estate and did not rise above the local horizon his attitudes might not be influential.

GOVERNMENTAL DISTRICT

The next area of government below the Province in the Prussian administration was the *Regierungs-Bezirk* or governmental district. With the exception of Schleswig-Holstein each province was subdivided into two or more governmental districts. The total number in Prussia was 34 until 1906 when the governmental district of Allenstein was added in East Prussia and raised the number to 35. At the head of each governmental district was a *Regierungs-Praesident.* From the beginning this official was primarily an administrative agent of the central government. At no time did he have any connection with communal affairs or the institutions of self-government. His function was to direct all the administrative affairs of the central government within his governmental district and since the governmental district was the vital administrative centre of the whole Prussian government he held a key position administratively and hence, by indirection, politically as well. But the *Regierungs-Praesident* was only *primus inter pares,* for the governmental district had a semi-collegial organization, that is, questions of a general nature were handled by the *Regierungs-Praesident* with his *Ober-Regierungsraete* and *Regierungsraete* acting together in committee. The *Regierungs-Praesident* was not a single independent, responsible official like the *Ober-Praesident.*

The collegial organization of the governmental district, its strictly administrative character and its key position all stem directly from its origin in the Chambers for War and Domains set up by Frederick William I during his administrative reforms in 1723. These Chambers for War and Domains were created to be simply the administrative organs of the central authority. They took their orders from the King and the General Supreme Finance, War, and Domains Directory and

---

11. For illustrations see Chapter II.

were allowed little or no initiative. Originally they were essentially financial bodies but they rapidly acquired many—and always more—administrative functions as an outgrowth of their financial duties. Their organization was strictly collegial and the *Kammerpraesident* was only chief of the *collegium* altho he had to act as spokesman for the committee and bear the brunt of the responsibility. He was assisted in the work of the Chamber by one or two colleagues and a staff of ten or a dozen Counsellors (later known as *Regierungsraete*) and fifteen to twenty *Assessoren* and *Auscultatoren* (apprentices in the administration, later known as *Regierungs-Referendare*). The Chamber for War and Domains had jurisdiction over all administrative subdivisions within its confines, that is, over all Circles, royal domains, and cities. Hence it had oversight over both the *Landraete* in the rural districts and the *Steuerraete* in the cities. It also had a certain judicial authority but here it came into conflict with the old mediaeval, feudal *Regierungen* which then functioned as local courts.[12]

Under Frederick II the *Kammerpraesident* grew in importance as an administrative agent, for the King maintained direct relations with him over the head of the General Supreme Finance, War, and Domains Directory and ran Prussia thru him and and his *collegium*. An indication that the *Kammerpraesidenten* had some personal discretion even in the 18th century is the fact that Frederick II selected them almost exclusively from among the ranks of the *Landraete* because these latter would have had experience in individual responsibility and quick, independent decisions.[13] Moreover, *Landraete* were generally nobles and landowners who had had some practical farming experience and hence were better suited to be *Kammerpraesidenten* in the eyes of Frederick II, altho he did not hesitate to appoint a bourgeois if he had conspicuous capabilities.

During the great reform era of Stein and Hardenberg the Chambers for War and Domains were remodelled and given essentially the form which they have had ever since. Their judicial functions were taken from them and they became strictly administrative organs.

12. Otto Hintze (78) *Behoerdenorganisation,* pp. 218-33.
13. Martin Hass (166) "Friedrich der Grosse und seine Kammerpraesidenten," *Festschrift zu Schmollers siebzigsten Geburtstag,* pp. 205-06.

Their name was changed to *Regierungen*[14] and their heads became *Regierungs-Praesidenten*. Originally the *Regierung* was given the entire internal administration of the district and it handled all the practical affairs of government within its borders. In time new administrative organs for special fields were set up within the governmental district, each with a prescribed competence, until by our period one must say that the jurisdiction of the *Regierung* extended to all affairs of internal administration not explicitly given to another authority.[15] The *Regierung* was under the *Ober-Praesident* and, beyond him, the Ministry of the Interior. For the most part the *Regierung* took its instructions from the Minister of the Interior but it might also receive orders directly from other Ministries with regard to special functions, e.g., from the *Kultusministerium* concerning the regulation of the division for Church and Schools.

Since the reforms of 1807-1815 the *Regierung* has enjoyed much wider discretion in running its affairs. Altho still the agency of the central government for the district administration it has been allowed to govern fairly independently and direction by the higher authorities has been greatly reduced. The *Regierungs-Praesident* also came thru the reorganization with an increase in individual authority. Altho the organization of the governmental district remained partly collegial, the *collegium* or committee composed of the *Regierungs-Praesident*, the *Ober-Regierungsraete* and the *Regierungsraete* still meeting to discuss general *Regierung* affairs and to make collective decisions for the district as a whole, the *Regierungs-Praesident* now had individual authority over his own subdivision of the *Regierung*, i.e., over the division for the general conduct of the regular administration of the governmental district and over its corps of officials. Thus the *Regierungs-Praesident* personally had direct supervision over the *Landraete*. This subdivision of the *Regierung* was clearly the most important of the three.[16] Of the other two one was for church and schools and

14. The old *Regierungen* had now become the Provincial Supreme Courts.

15. Bornhak (52) v. 2, p. 322. For example, the administration of indirect taxes which had once been partly in the hands of the *Regierungen* was transferred to the Provincial Tax Direction; the division of common land in the villages was given to the general commissions; institutions of higher education were placed under the Provincial School Boards. See Graf Hue de Grais (81) *Handbuch der Verfassung und Verwaltung*, pp. 69-70, note 3.

16. Valentini (40) p. 89.

the other for direct taxes, domains and forests. Both were under the personal jurisdiction of individual *Ober-Regierungsraete*. The *Regierungs-Praesident* had added authority as the formal chairman of the *Regierung* and as the official link between the Minister of the Interior or the *Ober-Praesident* and the governmental district. He was required to give semi-annual reports on public opinion in his governmental district. He might exercise some personal initiative in vetoing acts of the *Regierung* or a subdivision and in urgent matters he might act alone for the *Regierung*. The extent to which he kept his eye on the affairs in the other two divisions and controlled the officials directly under him depended in large measure on the character of the *Regierungs-Praesident*.[17] Considering the great importance and authority of the post it is surprising that it was held by relatively few Junkers during the period from 1888 to 1914. The following table shows that the proportion of Junkers in the office of *Regierungs-Praesident* never reached 42% and also that in spite of some fluctuations there was a tendency for it to decline.

Year	Total no. of offices	Junkers	Other Nobles	Commoners	Percentage of Junkers
1888	34	13	15	6	38.20
1890	34	14	13	7	41.17
1895	34	12	15	7	35.29
1900	34	9	14	11	26.47
1905	34	12	11	11	35.29
1910	35	12	9	14	34.28
1914	35	11	7	17	30.57

On an average $34\frac{1}{2}\%$ of the *Regierungs-Praesidenten* from 1888 to 1914 were Junkers. This is slightly lower than the average of 38% for *Ober-Praesidenten*. It is significant that during the same period the number of bourgeois *Regierungs-Praesidenten* rose steadily

---

17. *Loc. cit.* Valentini, who is a rather perfunctory Junker official, describes his contact with the other divisions as follows: "Die Steuerabteilung ueberliess ich ganz der Leitung ihres tuechtigen Dirigenten . . . und auch die Herren von der Domaenen- und Forstverwaltung stoerte ich moeglichst wenig in der sorgfaeltig gehueteten Selbstaendigkeit ihres fiskalischen Ressorts. Die bis ins Detail gehende Zentralisierung dieser Verwaltung in der Hand des Landwirtschaftsministers liess fuer ein Eingreifen des Praesidenten auch nur geringen Spielraum." Graf Kuno Westarp (43) *Konservative Politik* . . . , v. 1, p. 4, writes, "Energische Regierungs-Praesidenten, die auch dem Landrat gegenueber genau wussten, was sie wollten, habe ich mehr geschaetzt als solche, unter denen der Referent herrschte."

from seven to seventeen, thus surpassing by 1914 the top figure of fourteen for Junker *Regierungs-Praesidenten*. As for the geographical distribution of Junker *Regierungs-Praesidenten,* the figures are as follows:

Year	No. of Junkers in 17 Govt. districts of 7 eastern provinces	No. of Junkers in 17 Govt. districts of 5 western provinces
1888	9	4
1890	8	6
1895	7	5
1900	6	3
1905	9	3
1910	9	3
1914	10	1

Here where the number of governmental districts is the same for the five western provinces as for the seven eastern provinces we can clearly see that, in this instance, at least, there is a definite tendency to keep Junkers in the east. It is also noteworthy that the decline in the number of Junker *Regierungs-Praesidenten* came in the west.

Altho the numbers of Junker *Regierungs-Praesidenten* seem small, we must take into account the fact not only that the position was one of great importance and authority and offered considerable opportunity for political pressure but also that the total number of such offices was small and hence ten or twelve Junker *Regierungs-Praesidenten* could exert influence over a wide area. Moreover, considering the nature of the office, it seems significant that so many Junker candidates were available at all. For it involved more bureaucratic routine than the office either of *Ober-Praesident* or *Landrat* and it had retained a certain bourgeois tradition since the days of Frederick William I. It is also notable that so many Junkers were qualified for the post since it required a first rate administrator and one who had been well trained in the ranks. Considering these facts it seems safe to submit that the government preferred Junkers so far as they were available and qualified and that Junker *Landraete* and *Regierungsraete* had a good chance of reaching this important office if they showed ability and the right political attitude.

The *Ober-Regierungsraete* who were the associates of the *Regierungs-Praesident* in the direction of collegial affairs and who headed the two remaining subdivisions of the central government in the district were also men of influence and authority—and also essentially bureaucrats concerned primarily with directing the general administrative affairs of their departments. Each *Regierungs-Praesident* had at least three *Ober-Regierungsraete* to work with him, one who acted as his deputy and assisted him in the conduct of the first or general administrative division, a second who headed the division for church and school affairs and a third at the head of the division for direct taxes, domains and forests. These latter had the same directoral power over their departments as the *Regierungs-Praesident* had over the whole *Regierung*.[18] The years from 1888 to 1914 show no indication that Junkers were preferred for one department of the *Regierung* administration rather than another. Altho the *Regierungs-Praesident's* deputy possessed more prestige and a larger salary there was no preponderance of Junkers in that post. Nor did the Junkers maintain a superiority among the *Ober-Regierungsraete* in general. Moreover, their relative position was adversely affected by the marked tendency to increase the number of *Ober-Regierungsraete* serving in a single governmental district. Some of those added were specialized technical advisers, others were unspecialized administrative aides. Since the former were never Junkers and among the latter there were no more Junkers than heretofore, the percentage of Junker *Ober-Regierungsraete* dropped off markedly altho the actual numbers remained fairly constant, as one can see from the following table:

Year	Total no. of offices	No. of Junkers	Percentage of Junkers
1888	113	15	13.27
1890	116	16	13.80
1895	122	22	18.03
1900	133	21	15.78
1905	149	21	14.09
1910	158	19	12.02
1914	176	17	9.65

This table, together with the corresponding one for the *Regierungs-Praesidenten*, gives a clear indication, however, that the small and constant number of Junker *Ober-Regierungsraete* had a relatively much better chance of advancement than the large and increasing number of bourgeois *Ober-Regierungsraete*. For the ratio of pro-

18. Bornhak (52) v. 2, pp. 313-14.

motions to the total number of Junker *Ober-Regierungsraete* is far above the ratio for middle-class *Ober-Regierungsraete*. Even as *Ober-Regierungsrat* the Junker could exert a political influence if he had the force and will because the office was endowed with considerable authority and discretion and placed him in close touch with important affairs and people.

Below the *Ober-Regierungsraete* were the *Regierungsraete* and *Assessoren* who handled the regular administrative business of the governmental district under the direction of the *Regierungs-Praesident* and the *Ober-Regierungsraete*. Their work was often humdrum and many of them belonged to that great body of generally anonymous officials who carried on the day to day affairs of the Prussian State government. On the other hand it was possible for a simple *Regierungsrat* who worked on the drafting of laws to have a considerable influence on the course of legislation. Moreover, it was from among the *Regierungsraete* as well as the *Landraete* that appointments were made to higher posts. Hence the office might be only one step in a good career and the *Regierungsrat*, if aggressive and ambitious for a promotion, might take considerable initiative in public affairs and exert some political influence. If interested only in his papers and documents his influence might be negligible. The proportion of Junkers serving as *Regierungsraete* or *Assessoren* was not large, never as high as 20%. Since these are regular bureaucratic officials there is, as one would expect, little variation in their numbers from east to west.

The significant feature with regard to the *Regierungsraete* and *Assessoren*, as with the *Ober-Regierungsraete*, is the tremendous increase in their numbers in every governmental district. This is particularly true of the strictly technical *Raete* such as surveyors or mining officials, due to the rapid increase in technical installations in the districts. Thus we find that the members, excluding the *Regierungs-Praesidenten*, of the seventeen governmental districts in Prussia's seven eastern provinces were only 327 in 1835 but 673 in 1901, an increase of over 100%. The increase in technical *Raete* is even more striking—from 106 in 1835 to 280 in 1901.[19] Since

19. Albert Lotz (139) "Ueber die Notwendigkeit der Reform der Verwaltungs-organisation in Preussen," *Schmollers Jb. f. Gesetzgeb.*, 1902, p. 238.

the added *Raete* were seldom Junkers this development had the effect of reducing the percentage of Junker *Regierungsraete*.

The rapid growth in the size of the *Regierung* staffs which certainly had a tendency to make them top-heavy and unwieldly brought criticism and reform proposals from several sources by the turn of the century. We find men of such widely different outlook as Octavio von Zedlitz-Neukirch, a Junker leader of the Free Conservatives, and Hugo Preuss, a liberal politician and journalist, demanding the abolition of the governmental district.[20] Both complained that the *Regierungen* had become congested and clumsy in administration and that they suffered from an excess of bureaucratic red tape and departmentalism. Because they were wholly concerned with the regular administration they lacked the vitality and sense of reality which came from direct contact with the people. Both men recommended decentralization, greater self-government and local control and the apportioning of the *Regierung's* activities to the *Ober-Praesident* and to the *Landrat*. Von Zedlitz-Neukirch's insistence on greater local independence and on increased jurisdiction and authority for the *Landrat* makes one suspicious that he was trying to strengthen the hold of the Junker landlord-*Landrat* in East Elbia.

The *Regierung* officials did have one tenuous connection with the local residents of their district thru the District Committee. This committee was composed of the *Regierungs-Praesident* as Chairman and six members with six deputies. Two members and two deputies were appointed by the King for life. The remaining four members and deputies were elected by the Provincial Executive Committee which in turn had been elected by the Provincial Diet. The function of the District Committee was to act as an administrative court to handle administrative conflicts and disciplinary questions.[21] Hence it was concerned entirely with the Prussian State administration and had no connection with local affairs. As with the Provincial Council[22] its elected members were generally local landowners and pillars of society. They held honorary posts and served without pay. Again,

20. Frhr. Octavio von Zedlitz und Neukirch (158) "Neueinrichtung der preussischen Verwaltung," *Preuss. Jb.*, 1902, pp. 24-43; Hugo Preuss (146) "Verwaltungsreform und Politik," *Z. f. Polit.*, 1907, pp. 95-126.
21. Bornhak (52) v. 2, pp. 319-22.
22. See above, p. 166f.

like the members of the Provincial Council their political influence depended on their political interests and activities in general and their connections with other branches of government. As is to be expected the number of Junkers was high in East Elbia and non-existent west of the province of Saxony.

CIRCLE

The next administrative area below the governmental district was the Circle. The governmental district was divided into a number of Circles and each of these, with the exception of the urban Circles, was under the administrative direction of a *Landrat* who was immediately subordinate to the *Regierungs-Praesident*. As we already know, the *Landrat* served both as the agent of the Prussian State administration and as the director of local self-government for the Circle. Because of the uniqueness of its dual nature and all the consequences that flow therefrom and because of the peculiarly satisfactory and congenial environment which it offered the Junker official, the *Landratsamt* is the most remarkable and significant office under our consideration both for the administration as a whole and for the Junker official. It functioned as the nerve centre of the Prussian government.

Both the uniqueness of the office and its great political importance have their roots in the early history of Prussia, for they grow out of the period of the *Staendestaat*. The Circle, or area under the *Landrat's* jurisdiction, was originally a communal association of knights and its geographical frontiers were determined more by history than by administrative planning. During the Thirty Years' War, when the rudimentary central government failed to function, the Circle assumed its administrative activities and became the general administrative district for the the rural areas. The Circle Assembly was composed only of owners of knights' estates, i.e., of nobles.[23] In some places but not in all the Circle Assembly was headed by a Circle Director, a prominent local knight who conducted the public affairs of the Circle for the Assembly.

The heavy costs of the Thirty Years' War brought about the introduction in Brandenburg of a new State land tax called the *Con-*

23. Hintze (78) *Behoerdenorganisation*, p. 259.

tribution. This tax had to be collected in the rural districts and troops had to be quartered there, so the Elector found it necessary to designate officials, known as *Kriegs-* or *Marschkommissare,* to perform these new duties for the State. In some Circles where a local Circle Director already existed the Elector made him the *Kriegskommissarius* as well and thus himself fused the two functions of local *staendisch* director and princely official.[24] In other districts, such as Priegnitz or the Mittelmark where the local assembly of knights had not set up a Circle Director or *Landeshauptmann,* the Elector appointed his own princely *Kriegskommissarius* and this official, altho originally a servant of the prince, soon took on the functions of director of the self-governing affairs of the Circle as well and began to lean more toward knightly than toward princely interests. This was due in large part to the fact that the Elector's appointees were local knights, *Raete vom Hause,* and naturally their interest centered in the affairs of their own class and territory. It was in this way that the functions of a State administrative officer and a local feudal executive were fused in the person of a single official—indeed, of one knight. Everywhere the *Kriegskommissarius* was the motivating factor in this development and yet paradoxically enough until the 18th century the character of this dual functionary was predominantly *staendisch.*[25]

In Pomerania and Magdeburg the *staendisch* Circle Directors, known as *Landraete,* and the princely *Marsch-* or *Kriegskommissare* existed side by side and were not combined until 1713 when Frederick William I forced the *Landraete* to surrender much of their local authority and take on the functions of the royal officials. It was because the *Landraete* or communal officials of Pomerania and Magdeburg had retained their purely feudal and local authority thruout the 17th century that the officials with dual capacities in the Mark petitioned in 1701 that they, too, be permitted to use the title of *Landrat.* They felt that altho it would not make them more feudal in authority this name would underscore their *staendisch* character.

During the 18th century, as might be expected, the royal functions

24. This whole description of the origin of the *Landratsamt* is based on the material and theory presented by Otto Hintze in his article, "Der Ursprung des preussischen Landratsamts in der Mark Brandenburg" (168) *Forsch. z. brandenburg. u. preuss. Gesch.,* 1915, pp. 357-422, especially pp. 366-380.
25. *Ibid.,* pp. 383-85.

of the *Landrat* were expanded and strengthened and he was integrated much more closely into the central administrative system. In addition to the apportionment and collection of the *Contribution,* the regulation of the marching and quartering of troops in the Circle and the settlement of lesser judicial questions he was given jurisdiction over police affairs by the central government and became the royal police officer for the Circle. True, he did not enjoy such wide police and judicial powers as the *Steuerrat* in the city, because he had to share these powers with the local noble landlords, but since he was himself one of these noble landlords and as such not only exercised but prized his rights as a landed proprietor he would not object to the limitation of his powers as a *Landrat* by his rights as a *Gutsherr.*

After 1723 the *Landrat* became the executive organ of the Chamber for War and Domains in the Circle and as such he was the administrative agent of the central government and the servant of the King in the rural areas. He took his orders from the Chamber for War and Domains and had to fulfill them, being allowed only to request a change, giving his grounds. In spite of the fact that he was growing more and more to be a functionary—and a key functionary—of the central administration the *Landrat* retained in full his old characteristics as director for his peers of the local self-government. He stood as a bond between the local self-government and the bureaucracy of the absolute state. In stressing this distinctive feature of the *Landrat,* Hintze says, "The *Landrat* does not have the purely bureaucratic character of the *Steuerrat.* He is not primarily an official but a nobleman and a landowner."[26] The custom that a *Landrat* be a nobleman was made law in 1769 when Frederick II decreed that commoners were excluded from the office. This continued until the reform era of 1807-1815.

26. Hintze (78) *Behoerdenorganisation,* p. 267. In the same work (p. 260) Hintze summarizes the dual character of the *Landrat* as follows: "Der Landrat ist fuer das platte Land was der Steuerrat fuer die Staedte ist: ein einzelner localer Bezirksbeamter mit finanziellen und polizeilichen Functionen, der Repraesentant der koeniglichen Gewalt im Kreise. Aber das Landratsamt hat doch einen wesentlichen anderen Charakter als das Amt des Steuerrats. Der Steuerrat ist ein rein koeniglicher Beamter von bureaukratischem Typus; der Landrat hat einen halb staendischen Charakter, der zwar in der Zeit Friedrich Wilhelms I teilweise unterdrueckt erscheint, nachher aber wieder deutlich hervortritt. Er ist zugleich ein Organ der koeniglichen Verwaltung und ein Vertrauensmann der Kreistaende. Das ist das Ergebniss der Bildungsgeschichte dieses Amtes."

In these reforms Stein wished to break down the rigidly centralized bureaucratic government of Prussia and promote decentralization and self-government in the provinces and Circles. The Junkers, however, were able to keep this local self-government on a feudal and reactionary basis and thus maintain their control over it. It was not until the liberalizing reforms of 1848, 1872 and 1891 that their feudal grip on the Circle and village was relaxed.

In 1888, as we know, the *Landrat* still stood with one foot in the local Circle government and one in the central administration. In accordance with the Circle constitution of 1872 he conducted the communal administration of the Circle in conjunction with the Circle Executive Committee. This local executive committee was elected by the Circle Assembly and chaired by the *Landrat*. The *Landrat* and the Circle Executive Committee together carried out the statutes passed by the Circle Assembly, the local legislative body. The Circle had power to conduct local affairs and levy taxes to meet its own expenses. Thus in communal affairs the *Landrat* worked very closely with the local inhabitants and their leaders and took many of his instructions from them. Of course, he was often one of them. When carrying out his duties as the agent of the central government in the Circle the *Landrat* was, functionally at least, an outsider sent in by the Minister of the Interior to supervise the self-government of the Circle—thus, curiously, supervising himself—and to conduct police and military affairs and the collection of the State's direct taxes for the government. As an organ of the central government he was simply a bureaucratic official filling his niche in the administrative hierarchy. Obviously it was quite impossible for one and the same individual to keep these two occupations separate and in fact one of the virtues of the *Landrat's* peculiar combination of duties was that he formed a point of contact between a mechanical and often ingrown bureaucracy and the daily life of the people. But it was equally impossible for the *Landrat* to maintain a nice balance between his responsibilities and interests as servant of the central government and as director of the local affairs of his Circle. In the beginning, that is, in the 17th century, the scales were heavily weighted on the side of local interests, but the tendency was constantly toward developing the royal and bureaucratic side of the office, until by our period the *Landratsamt* was frequently considered merely as one step in a civil service career. This held true particularly of those *Landraete* without property who were ambitious to rise to the top and who were sent off to administer distant Circles. Junkers disliked and resisted this tendency to bureaucratize and impersonalize the *Landratsamt*, for they felt that the *Landrat's* interest and attention should be centered on the Circle which he administered and not on Berlin and some higher rank in the service. Bismarck had strong views on this subject and expressed the sentiments of the Junker class when he wrote as follows:

"The governed *contribuens plebs* no longer has that guarantee against clumsy interference which used to be inherent in the *Landrat's* activities when residents of the Circle were selected as *Landraete* and these generally intended to remain in the Circle their whole life long and shared the joys and sorrows of the Circle. Today the post of *Landrat* is the lowest step in a career in the higher administration and sought after by young *Assessoren* who have the justifiable ambition to make a career for themselves; for this they need the favor of their minister more than the goodwill of the inhabitants of the Circle. . . ."[27]

Bismarck refers, however, only to a growing tendency and it would be wrong to assume that the *Landrat* who devoted his life to his Circle, such as von Rauchhaupt or von Bonin-Bahrenbusch, had already disappeared. In fact we know that of the 328 Junker *Landraete* of our period only 20% held the office for a short time and then went on to higher posts.[28]

It now becomes very apparent why the *Landratsamt*, altho low in the administrative hierarchy, was of paramount importance for the Prussian government and the favorite office of Junker officials. The *Landrat* was a single official invested by the central government with the entire administration of a Circle. As such he filled a position of real authority. He was in constant contact with the *Regierungs-Praesident* and might exert an influence on him and thru him on

27. Otto von Bismarck (22) *Gedanken und Erinnerungen*, v. 1, p. 30. See also Zedlitz-Neukirch (158) *Preuss. Jb.,* 1902, p. 34; Georg Gothein (70) *Agrarpolitisches Handbuch*, p. 451.
28. One of the *Landraete* dismissed in 1899 writes as follows, *Deutsches Wochenblatt,* Aug. 26, 1899, p. 1443, "Und es gibt doch auch Landraete genug, die keine Carriere machen und machen wollen. Unter den jetzt Beseitigten befinden sich solche, die laengst Grossvaeter, langjaehrige Abgeordnete und . . . noch immer Landraete sind, oder, richtig gesagt, bis vor wenigen Tagen waren."

the Ministry. In addition he was in charge of all the communal affairs of his Circle and here again he had wide powers of discretion and authority. Gothein reaches the conclusion that "in the last analysis Prussia is ruled by the *Landrat*"[29] and von Kleist-Retzow gives the following striking description of the *Landrat's* position in 1845:

"Independent toward the district government above as well as toward the inhabitants of the Circle below, it [the office] brings me in every way into vital association with the latter and gives me entire responsibility. I can and must work in it more thru my own personality than thru the administration of the laws. Of course there are many petty details which I have to regulate and smooth out and it is hardly likely that a *Landrat* as such would find a place in one of your brother's [Leopold von Ranke's] history books. But he has all the more opportunity for fidelity in little things and all the more chance of being remembered for generations. . . . The *Landrat* still has an authority which often frightens me. When people tell their children that the Pope is not allowed to marry then they ask if the *Landrat* has forbidden it."[30]

A position of such administrative importance and command was sure to be attractive to Junkers. Moreover, as we already know,[31] they enjoyed holding office in their own neighborhood. They fostered the old feudal tradition of selecting *Raete vom Hause*, i.e., of the appointment of a local noble landlord, and they were glad of the opportunity to combine their administrative duties with the farming of their estates.[32] The aura of feudal tradition enhanced the authority of the local Junker *Landrat* over the peasants and farmers of the Circle. We may, therefore, conclude that the administrative character of the office and its traditional prestige, quite apart from its strictly political importance, gave it a particular appeal for the Junker.

Furthermore, *Landraete* were especially preferred for promotion to higher offices. Altho, as we have noted, the tendency to look

29. Gothein (70) p. 453.

30. From a letter by von Kleist-Retzow in Hermann von Petersdorff (106) *Hans von Kleist-Retzow*, p. 84.

31. See above, Chapter II, p. 59ff.

32. See the description of a *Landrat* farmer which Otto Kuesel-Koenigsberg gives in "Rudolf von Brandt, Landeshauptmann der Provinz Ostpreussen" (136) *Altpreussische Monatsschrift*, 1908, pp. 139-40.

on the *Landratsamt* merely as a stage in an administrative career was frowned upon by many Junkers and altho the proportion of Junker *Landraete* in our period who were promoted was as small as 20%, it is nonetheless a definite fact that the *Landratsamt* gave more opportunity and promise of promotion to higher posts than any other office of a similar rank. We know this to be true from a survey of the careers of the Junker *Regierungs-* and *Ober-Praesidenten* in our period. Of the 42 Junker *Regierungs-Praesidenten* as many as 35 or 83.33%[33] had at one time been *Landraete* whereas only 5 had previously been *Regierungsraete.*[34] Among the 19 Junker *Ober-Praesidenten* there were 14 (73½%) who had once served as *Landraete.* This decided preference of the government for *Landraete* when selecting officials for higher offices meant that ambitious Junker—and middle-class—*Regierungs-Assessoren* were eager to be appointed to a *Landratsamt.* The remarkable fact for us is that so many of the Junkers succeeded in becoming *Landraete,* as we shall see,[35] and, what is even more important, that the proportion of the Junker *Regierungs-Praesidenten* is even higher than the proportion of Junkers among the *Landraete.*

In addition to these personal considerations there is the fact that the *Landratsamt* because of its peculiar characteristics offered the greatest opportunities for direct political influence of any administrative office. Because of its key position as a point of contact between the government and the people the office was manifestly the cornerstone of political influence in Prussia. The importance of this aspect of the *Landrat's* activities cannot be exaggerated. It was he who saw to it that the will of the government was carried out in the Circle and with his police power and his close relations with the people he was able to make sure that failure to comply would bring disagreeable consequences for the individual offender. Because of his constant association with the local inhabitants he was also able to keep his *Regierungs-Praesident* and the government informed of public opinion in the Circle. He was the one sure channel of communication

---

33. Of these thirty-five, four were raised directly from the *Landratsamt* to the office of *Regierungs-Praesident* and 31 passed thru intermediate stages.

34. The two remaining *Regierungs-Praesidenten* were brought in from outside the administration.

35. See below, p. 188.

between the government and the people—yet much more than a mere channel, rather a person of responsibility and authority who, because of the strategic importance of his post was able to exert great influence both on the government above him and on the local population under him. This even extends to legislation, for the Ministry frequently consulted the *Landrat* regarding local conditions and public opinion when legislation was being drafted.

As a political official the *Landrat* served as the means for the exercise of political influence by the government on the Circles. In particular the royal edict of 1882 and the proclamation of the Prussian Ministry of 1899 regarding the official responsibilities of government officers in political questions required that they represent and promote the policies of the government in the Circles. Since the Prussian Ministries from 1888 until the war were largely Conservative the promotion of government policies by these *Landraete* was carried on enthusiastically—with a few conspicuous exceptions. In general there was considerable complaint by liberals and Social Democrats about the government "mobilization" of the *Landraete* in support of its program. For example, in its issue of October 26, 1911 the *Frankfuerter Zeitung* complained that an official notice had been sent out to all *Landraete* in which they were ordered to report on attacks against the government in the press or in handbills within their Circle which might influence the Reichstag elections. They were also asked to suggest ways in which to refute these attacks.[36]

It was at election time that the *Landrat's* political influence in favor of the government's interest—and his own—was greatest and most effective, for the *Landrat* had certain official duties concerning the organization of elections which gave him an opportunity to influence them. Moreover, his police powers gave him frequent opportunities to favor the organs of one political party and to discriminate against others. The selection of the supervisors (*Vertrauensmaenner*) in every village was in the hands of the *Landrat*.[37] He was also in a position

36. Walter Koch (89) *Volk und Staatsfuehrung vor dem Weltkriege*, pp. 98-99.
37. Westarp (43) v. 1, p. 21, writes as follows, "Auf die Beteiligung an der Wahlagitation habe ich trotzdem, um den Kreis Bomst fuer das Deutschtum zu behaupten, nicht verzichtet. Diese und die Beschaffung der Mittel dafuer lag im Bomster Kreis im wesenlichen in meiner Hand. Ein deutscher Wahlverein unter-

to dominate the precinct and communal managers (*Amts- und Gemeindevorsteher*).³⁸ Thru his police powers "King *Landrat*" had wide opportunities to aid Conservative voters and their party organs and to injure economically those in his Circle who opposed the government. He might refuse to grant anti-government organizations permission to meet or to use a certain hall. Thus it might be possible for the Conservatives to assemble and agitate freely, whereas all other parties were kept from meeting at all. A conscientious Conservative *Landrat* would keep a sharp watch over the political views and activities of all of the inhabitants of his Circle.³⁹

Specific charges of undue and illegal influence by *Landraete* at election time were made again and again during our period. A reading of the Diet debates alone would bring to light frequent references to these cases. Altho this study is concerned with the potential rather than with the actual political influence of Junker *Landraete* one or two examples of such influence might well be quoted here as illustrations of the kind of thing any *Landrat* might do. Count Westarp relates in his memoirs⁴⁰ that in 1894 while *Landrat* in Kreis Bomst he and the *Landrat* from the neighboring Kreis Meseritz signed under their official title an electoral manifesto for the Free Conservative Reichstag candidate, Stephan von Dziembowski—also a Junker by nature. Because of this action by Westarp and his colleague the election of Dziembowski was declared illegal and a new election was held, but Westarp continued in office. In this case apparently the support of a candidate by the *Landrat* had been so flagrant as to lead to State action.

Shortly before the war the Junker *Landrat* of Kreis Grimmen in Pomerania, Axel, Baron von Maltzahn-Gueltz, was party to the trial of a Progressist landlord in his Circle and a subject of debate in the Diet because of his alleged political activities as *Landrat*. The Progressist landlord, Becker-Bartmannshagen, had been charged

---

stuetzte sie und gab die Firma her. Die Auswahl der deutschen Vertrauensmaenner in jedem Dorf und der persoenliche Verkehr mit ihnen erfolgten durch mich. Im Jahre 1895 mussten wir uns also noch einmal bemuehen mit dem Erfolge der Wiederwahl von Dziembowskis."

38. Koch (89) p. 11.
39. Gothein (70) p. 452.
40. Westarp (43) v. 1, p. 20.

with insulting von Maltzahn and was eventually imprisoned for one year in spite of the fact that during the trial among other things the following facts were established: that Maltzahn had attempted to injure Becker economically by trying to persuade a member of the Circle Executive Committee to stop buying horses from Becker; that the *Landrat* had refused permission to the Ulanen band to play in a certain beer hall because the Progressists had held a meeting there; that another beer hall had been punished by the withdrawal of the Kaiser's birthday festival from its rooms because allegedly a reconciliation meeting of Progressists and Social Democrats had taken place in it; that the *Landrat* had made the paper of the Agrarian League[41] the official Grimmen organ for the publication of notices of meetings, etc.[42]

One can easily see that the *Landrat* had a multitude of opportunities for petty but effective political influence and that in particular he was in a position to "mobilize" the Circle at election time in support of the government's, and in most cases of his own, Conservative candidate. It was upon the *Landraete* above all that the Conservative party and the government depended for the large Conservative fraction in the Prussian Diet and the Reichstag. It is for this reason that Wilhelm von Kardorff laments the dismissal of so many Conservative *Landraete* in the Canal affair, saying, ". . . since the Conservative elections depend in a great many Circles upon the influence of the *Landraete* a majority friendly to the government will be threatened in future elections."[43] It is for the same reason that the Centre party and the National Liberals were continually agitating for a better representation in the *Landratsaemter*,[44] for apparently the best assurance of an electoral victory in a district was to have one of your own men *Landrat* there.

In view of the above it is not at all surprising that so many *Landraete* were also members of the House of Deputies. The *Landrat* could use the whole administrative machinery of the Circle to win his election. In arch Conservative areas such as Further Pomerania

---

41. See below, p. 227ff.
42. Koch (89) p. 76.
43. Siegfried von Kardorff (86) *Wilhelm von Kardorff*, . . . , p. 338.
44. Hans von Dallwitz (25) "Aus dem Nachlass des . . . Ministers des Innern von Dallwitz," ed. von Mutius, *Preuss. Jb.*, 1928, pp. 147-48.

he could use it brazenly, in other districts he needed to be more discreet, but everywhere he enjoyed a distinct advantage over his opponents. This characteristic of the *Landratsamt* is an important—but not the only—explanation of the fact that of the 328 Junker *Landraete* in our period 41 or 12.80% were in the House of Deputies at the same time that they were *Landraete,* whereas of the 489 other salaried officials only 11 or 2.24% were deputies. This relatively high percentage of *Landraete* is due as well to the dynamic and many-sided character of the *Landratsamt* which naturally drew its incumbent into the political as well as all other aspects of life in his Circle and which conversely made the office unusually attractive for aspiring and aggressive politicians. There is a powerful fundamental affinity between the *Landratsamt* and politics.

The *Landrat* who was also a deputy of the Prussian Diet had a dual and even a triple allegiance—to his superiors in the administration, to the self-governing bodies of the Circle and to his political party or his own personal political convictions. For the most part during our period the *Landrat*-Diet deputy from East Elbia was not troubled by conflicts of loyalty because the Prussian Minister of the Interior, the Government and the Conservative Junker *Landrat* all worked harmoniously along general conservative lines. In case of a divergence of views between the Government and the Conservative party apparently the *Landrat* frequently obeyed his party and stood by his political convictions rather than submit to the orders of his administrative chief.[45] This was certainly the case in the famous Canal Affair. Here the Conservative party and the Conservative *Landraete* who were deputies stubbornly refused to support the Government canal bill because of their opinion that the construction of a canal from west to east in Germany would be injurious to the agrarian interests east of the Elbe, i.e., to their own interests. The Kaiser supported the Government's bill and warned the *Landraete* who were deputies that if they persisted in their opposition they would be placed on the retired list.[46] These deputies refused to be

---

45. W.(?) writes in Gothein (70) p. 454, "Die konservativen Parteien im Abgeordnetenhaus, Herrenhaus und Reichstag schuetzen auch die gegen ihre vorgesetzten Behoerden frondierenden konservativen Landraete. Diese fuerchten das Missfallen ihrer Minister weit weniger als das der Agrarkonservativen."

46. *Z. D. gestellt.*

intimidated by the Kaiser's threat. A score or more voted against the bill and it was defeated. The Kaiser then carried out his threat and ordered the dismissal of approximately twenty *Landraete* and two *Regierungs-Praesidenten*[47] on the charge of insubordination as royal officials. Here the two allegiances of the *Landrat*-Diet deputy were brought into sharp conflict and when it came to a showdown he placed his party, his political convictions and his independence as a legislator above his allegiance to his Kaiser and his administrative superiors.

The Canal Crisis was as brief as it was severe, and tolerable relations between the Government and the Conservatives were quickly restored. What is more, some of the disciplined Conservative officials were reinstated and even promoted to higher offices.[48] Of the seven Junker officials whom we know to have been victims of the Canal Affair[49] we find that Hans von Dallwitz, Ernst von Jagow and Kurd, Count von Berg-Schoenfeld went on to higher posts[50] and that Fritz von Bockelberg-Vollard was reappointed *Landrat* in Kreis Ost-Sternberg. It is a significant indication of the particular political

47. Kardorff (86) p. 341; Westarp (43) v. 1, p. 4.

48. Wilhelm von Massow (97) *Die deutsche innere Politik unter Kaiser Wilhelm II*, p. 166, gives the explanation that the government later recognized the unfairness of its treatment of the deputies who were *Landraete* and tried to make amends by reappointing and advancing them. Hutten-Czapski (34) v. 1, p. 365, implies that their dismissal was never intended to be more than temporary when he writes, "Gleichzeitig wurde eine Anzahl von ihnen in den einstweiligen Ruhestand versetzt." The Opposition said of those promoted, "dass sie die Treppe hinaufgefallen seien."

49. We can be certain that the following Junker officials were dismissed because of the Affair: Hans von Dallwitz, Ernst von Jagow, Bogislav von Bonin, Eugen von Brockhausen, Fritz von Bockelberg-Vollard, Octavio von Zedlitz-Neukirch and Kurd, Count Berg-Schoenfeld. It is possible that Viktor von Wrochem, Ludolf von Kotze and Dr. Erich von Fluegge were dismissed for the same reason. Thus we know that 31.81% and we suspect that as many as 45.45% of these rebellious officials were Junkers.

50. Hans von Dallwitz became a *Regierungsrat* in 1900 and a *Vortragender Rat* in the Ministry of the Interior in 1901. In 1909 he was appointed to the high post of *Ober-Praesident* in Silesia. Ernst von Jagow, who had been *Regierungs-Praesident* in Posen in 1899, was made *Regierungs-Praesident* of Marienwerder in 1901 and *Ober-Praesident* of West Prussia in 1905. In the clash between the Conservatives and the government in 1909 over a Finance Bill he took an opposite stand and supported the government. Kurd, Count Berg, returned to active service as a *Regierungsrat* in 1902 and by 1909 he had become *Regierungs-Praesident* in Stade in Hannover. Hutten-Czapski writes (34) v. 2, p. 14, that Count Berg "hatte sich ganz entschieden und teilweise parteipolitisch einseitig konservativ betaetigt."

activity and importance of the *Landraete* that of the twenty-two or more officials dismissed at least twenty held that office. This should not surprise us, however, since we already know that the proportion of politicians was much higher among *Landraete* than in any other lesser office in the service.

The government's disciplinary action in the summer of 1899 did have a decisive effect upon the numbers of Junker *Landraete* sitting in the House of Deputies, as we can readily see by looking at the figures for our period.

Diet of	*Total Junkers in House of Deputies*	*Also Landraete*	*Percentage*
1884	66	20	30.30
1889	71	16	22.53
1894	79	14	17.72
1900	67	1	1.49
1904	67	2	3.00
1909	67	6	9.00
1914	59	6	10.17

The number falls off sharply in 1900; but it is important that in the following years it climbs up steadily from this low point. This seems to indicate that the government had interrupted but not destroyed the Junker—and the Conservative—custom of sending *Landraete* to the House of Deputies and we may surmise that the number of Junker *Landraete*-Diet deputies would have continued to rise had it not been for the war and the revolution.

In 1909 when Chancellor von Buelow was promoting his Finance Bill another acute crisis arose between the Conservative party and the government. The comment of Count Kuno Westarp, the prominent Conservative leader, indicates that this time, when the government made an explicit attempt to mobilize the *Landraete,* the Conservative *Landraete* and even a former Canal Rebel were more docile and compliant to government direction, even at the expense of the party.

"At the beginning of April, 1909, the Prussian Ministry of the Interior appears to have been entreated to instruct the *Landraete* in strictest secrecy to arrange for the reprinting in the Circle papers of articles and reports from the *Neue Correspondenz* on the subject of the inheritance tax. An incident in Danzig[51] shows that even thoroughly Conservative political

51. He refers to Ernst von Jagow. See above, Chapter IV, p. 140.

officials did not evade this request to step in and support a government
policy which was directed against the Party."[52]

Since the *Landratsamt* is of such exceptional administrative and
political importance the proportion of Junkers who held this office
and any variations in that proportion are of particular significance.
The figures for the years 1888 to 1914 are as follows:

Year	Total no. of offices	Junkers	Other nobles	Commoners	Percentage of Junkers
1888	490	143	143	204	29.19
1890	490	142	134	215	28.97
1895	491	140	119	232	28.51
1900	491	138	130	222	28.10
1905	491	127	156	207	25.86
1910	491	121	160	210	24.64
1914	489	117	158	214	23.92

We are struck first with two important facts: the low percentage
and its steady decline—a decline which is absolute since the total
number of offices remained constant. Here, again, apparently, is
material proof that the Junker's potential domination of the Prussian
administration was not so extensive as generally believed. And indeed the numbers of Junkers have in every instance fallen below
the figures which I had been led to expect from a reading of general
discussions of the Junker's hold on the administration. More important for the Junker's political and administrative position is the
steady and relentless decline in their numbers in the *Landratsamt*,
for this indicates a decided weakening of their ability to maintain
even their potential influence on this strategic office. Even if there
had been no war or revolution the Junker *Landraete* seemed bound
to decline.

The percentage of Junker *Landraete* is, however, of larger importance than the bare figures imply. As we know, the *Landrat* was
traditionally a resident of the Circle where he served. Altho this
Indigenatsrecht[53] was observed less and less due to the above mentioned tendency to bureaucratize the *Landratsamt*, the weight of
tradition was still very great. Hence there were as many as 230
Landratsaemter in the five western provinces of Prussia where the

52. Westarp (43) v. 1, p. 60.
53. The rights of natives.

appointment of a Junker *Landrat* was the exception. That they were appointed at all here has a particular significance because Junkers in the west were often an indication of a quite opposite tendency from administrative bureaucratization. They were sometimes sent here for the express purpose of "feudalizing" the inhabitants of the more liberal western Circles. It is well to note from the following table that both as few and as many as 4 to 6% of the western *Landraete* were Junkers.

Year	Total no. of offices	Junkers	Other nobles	Commoners	Percentage of Junkers
1888	231	15	100	116	6.55
1890	231	15	91	125	6.55
1895	232	11	83	138	4.78
1900	232	13	91	128	5.65
1905	232	11	97	123	4.78
1910	232	9	99	124	3.91
1914	230	10	94	126	4.38

We should not overlook the fact, however, that from 1905 to 1914[54] as many as 12-13% of the *Landraete* in the seven eastern provinces were nobles from western Germany. Their presence in the east does not have the same political and sociological significance, however, since the nobles from the west were much less aggressive and dynamic than the Junkers.

The figures for the Junker *Landraete* in the eastern provinces show us how much greater their proportion was here than for Prussia as a whole and remind us again how truly the east was the stronghold of the Junkers.

Year	Total no. of offices	Junkers	Other nobles	Commoners	Percentage of Junkers
1888	259	128	42	89	49.42
1890	259	127	42	90	49.10
1895	259	129	36	94	49.90
1900	259	125	40	94	48.26
1905	259	116	59	84	44.79
1910	259	112	62	85	43.24
1914	259	107	64	88	41.31

Here the numbers of Junker *Landraete* even overshadowed the middle-class *Landraete* whereas in the west these outnumbered not only the Junkers but also the other noble *Landraete*.

54. The only years examined in this regard.

There were also variations within the area of the seven eastern provinces as, for example, between the arch Junker governmental district of Koeslin in Pomerania, the more cosmopolitan governmental district of Potsdam and the newer and somewhat less Junker district of Liegnitz in Silesia.

Percentage of Junker Landraete

Year	in Koeslin	in Potsdam	in Liegnitz
1888	83.33	57.14	42.10
1890	75.00	64.28	42.10
1895	91.66	64.28	68.42
1900	83.33	71.43	63.15
1905	85.00	64.28	57.89
1910	58.33	64.28	57.89
1914	58.33	57.14	47.36

There is evidence here of an interesting tendency for the proportion of Junker *Landraete* in these three different governmntal districts to become equalized by 1914.

When we recall that the *Landratsamt* was the most vital political centre in the whole Prussian administration we are impressed, altho not surprised, by the fact that so many Junkers held the office during our period. When we know that in 1895, 64.28% of the *Landraete* in the governmental district Potsdam, 68.42% in Liegnitz and 91.66% in Koeslin were Junkers we can well imagine what the political atmosphere was in those districts. Moreover, the proportion of Junker *Landraete* in the seven eastern provinces as a whole is so high as to make us believe that they were numerous enough to have a decisive political influence there. Even the general percentage, altho it drops to 23.92 in 1914, is still substantially above the percentage of *Regierungsraete* who were Junkers and this leads us to the conclusion that the government preferred to put Junkers into the highly important political post of *Landrat* rather than the more bureaucratic office of *Regierungsrat*. It also suggests that the government wished to be sure of having a good supply of Junker officials on hand to draw on for higher offices, since we know that the *Landraete* were almost always preferred for such promotions. Assuredly the Junker, whether patriarch or "climber," would rather hold the *Landratsamt* than any other office of equal, and many even of higher, rank both because it was more congenial and because it offered more promise of a career.

CONCLUSIONS ON PRUSSIAN STATE ADMINISTRATION

It is important to note as we look back over the whole structure of the Prussian State administration that the highest proportion of Junkers was in those offices which possessed the greatest political influence and authority, namely, the *Landratsamt,* the office of *Regierungs-Praesident* and that of *Ober-Praesident.*[55] It is even more significant that the proportion of Junkers increases with each step up in office. For *Landraete* the average percentage of Junkers over the 26 years was 27%, for *Regierungs-Praesidenten* it jumps to 34% and for *Ober-Praesidenten* it was 38%. This sharp rise in percentages is a striking indication that the government preferred to have the Junker officials in the most important political offices and also that it preferred to have them as *Regierungs-Praesidenten* and particularly as *Ober-Praesidenten.* What is more, it could have them. Altho the proportion of Junkers among the *Landraete* and the *Regierungsraete* was not large the numbers of Junkers in these offices were more than enough to assure the government of a sufficient supply of Junkers for the much less numerous posts of *Regierungs-Praesident* and *Ober-Praesident.* Conversely, only a few Junkers could move up.

It is, of course, also striking that the government appointed a large and an increasing number of commoners to these three important political· offices. Among the *Landraete* as a whole the number of commoners was well ahead of the number of Junkers and among the *Regierungs-Praesidenten* it surpassed the number of Junkers by 1910. Only in the office of *Ober-Praesident* did the number of Junkers keep ahead of the middle-class appointees; and this was the most important and distinguished of the three offices. The first impression which these figures give should be modified, however, by some other considerations. We find, for instance, that the proportion of Junkers among the *Landraete* or *Regierungs-Praesidenten* or *Ober-Praesidenten* in the seven eastern provinces was almost always high enough to be decisive and control of the eastern provinces would give the Junkers a very strong position in Prussia as a whole. Perhaps this is one explana-

55. Hutten-Czapski (34) v. 1, p. 366, writes, "Die Ober- und Regierungs-Praesidien so wie die Landratsaemter waren ausschliesslich im Besitz gewisser Staende und Kreise. Ich konnte nicht leugnen, dass dadurch rein administrativ im grossen und ganzen Nachteile nicht entstanden und diese Beamten ihre Pflicht erfuellten."

tion of the indication that the government did not try, at least not very consistently or successfully, to distribute the Junker officials more equally over the whole country.

Furthermore, we find that, altho the midde-class *Landraete* were more numerous than either the Junkers or the other noble *Landraete,* they never exceeded the number of these two combind nor were they ever more numerous than Junker and other noble *Regierungs-Praesidenten* combined altho they came close to it in 1914.

The most important fact to bear in mind in this regard is that the middle-class officials were not the opposite of the Junkers or even antagonistic toward them. On the contrary, many of them, altho still commoners, were undoubtedly as conservative and as "feudal" in their outlook as the Junkers and turned to the latter as their models. Those bourgeois officials who had been "feudalized" would not offset but would, rather, reenforce the influence of the Junker officials.

In general, there can be no doubt that the moral domination of the Junkers over the "feudalized" bourgeoisie both in and out of office greatly extended and multiplied the Junker's opportunities for political influence. The Junkers had been increasingly active during the 19th century in attaching to their social group as a kernel larger and larger numbers of the bourgeoisie who, either thru snobbishness and social ambition or fear of the Social Democrats, adopted the social and political attitudes of the Junkers.[56] The Puttkamer Regime (1881-1888) did much to subjugate bourgeois officials to the Junker's "feudalizing" influence. For Puttkamer would admit to office only reliable Conservatives and the middle class consented to this condition in order to get into office.[57] Once they had submitted they were under the direction of their Junker preceptors. It is unfortunately difficult if not impossible to measure exactly the numbers of bourgeois officials who had adopted the Junkers' "feudal" views. This is true largely because the great masses of the middle

56. See, *inter alia,* Eckart Kehr (170) "Zur Genesis des Kgl. preussischen Reserveoffiziers," *Die Gesellschaft,* 1928; (169) "Das soziale System der Reaktion in Preussen unter dem Ministerium Puttkamer," *Die Gesellschaft,* 1929; Max Weber (156) "Parlament und Regierung im neugeordneten Deutschland," *Gesammelte politische Schriften,* pp. 126-260; Hugo Preuss (109) *Die Junkerfrage,* p. 7; Alexander von Hohenlohe (32) *Aus meinem Leben,* pp. 327-39.

57. Kehr (170) *Die Gesellschaft,* 1928, p. 494.

class remain anonymous whereas nobles have their lives recorded merely because they are nobles.[58] But often in eastern Prussia the ennobled and the un-ennobled were equally Junker in their attitudes.

Altho it is not possible to tell exactly how the numbers of bourgeois officials who had become "feudalized" compare with the numbers of Junker officials there are some indirect and incomplete answers to our question which are important insofar as they give any indication of the extent of this process. I have selected the office of *Regierungs-Praesident* as a test case because the numbers are relatively small and easy to handle and the position is important both administratively and politically. There were thirty-nine commoners who held the office of *Regierungs-Praesident* between 1888 and 1914, but due to the serious dearth of biographical material on middle-class men I have been able to find information indicating Junker or non-Junker characteristics for only eighteen of these men. Of the eighteen only six show any definite signs of having been "feudalized."[59] The careers of another five give some definite sign[60] that they were not "feudalized." The careers of the remaining seven give no positive indication one way or the other. Clearly the results of the examination are meagre. It is probable that the seven who cannot be assigned to one group or the other belonged to that large body of officials who were non-partisan or, at the most, *gouvernemental*[61] in their outlook and who felt no particular allegiance either to the middle class or to the nobility but rather an esprit de corps and a loyalty to the government *qua* government. The six middle-class *Regierungs-Praesidenten* who give evidence of not being "feudalized," all of whom served in the west, may also belong to this group or they may have had a definitely

58. It is possible to look up the background and career of any German noble in the Gotha Handbooks but almost impossible to find information about bourgeois officials unless they became sufficiently prominent to appear in *Wer Ist's*, the *Politischer Almanach* of Mueller-Jabusch, etc.

59. Each had one or more of the following characteristics: service in East Elbia, membership in the Conservative party, affiliation with aristocratic regiments, rapid careers. One worked up thru offices in the Evangelical Church. None of the eighteen middle-class *Regierungs-Praesidenten* about whom we have information married Junkers.

60. Such as Catholic faith, service in western Prussia only, industrial connections, posts in one of the bourgeois Ministries such as the *Handels-Ministerium*.

61. The German word *gouvernemental* contains the sense of loyalty to and faithful representation of the political policies of the Prussian Ministry.

bourgeois and perhaps even a liberal viewpoint. If it is safe to make any assumptions on the basis of this scanty information one must conclude that of the eighteen middle-class *Regierungs-Praesidenten* on whom we have information as many as but no more than one-third were "feudalized."

Another interesting test is to examine the numbers of Junkers and commoners in the provincial administrative bodies in certain provinces in a single year. Let us look at the figures for the year 1900:

Province	Provincial Executive Committee				Landschaft			
	Total	J.	Noble	M.Class	Total	J.	Noble	M.Class
Brandenburg	21	9	2	10	24	15	7	2
Pomerania	23	15	1	7	16	13	2	1
Posen	24	5	9	10	14	2	7	5
Silesia	29	9	8	12	134	67	36	31

It is very unlikely that a commoner would be elected to either the Provincial Executive Committee or the *Landschaft* of Brandenburg, Pomerania or Silesia unless he had become one with the Junkers. In Posen it may have been more likely. Therefore these figures give us a further indication of the extent to which the Junkers were meeting the problem of the bourgeois large landholders by drawing them into their own circle and assimilating them.

Another situation which suggests this process of assimilation is the presence in the Conservative fraction of the Prussian Diet of a number of commoners about equal to the number of Junkers. Moreover, the former was increasing as the latter declined:

Election year	Junkers	Commoners
1903	61	55
1908	60	63
1913	54	63

Altho probably not all of these commoners had become "feudalized" surely some of them, particularly those elected east of the Elbe, were assimilated to the Junkers.

We recognize the type of the "feudalized" bourgeois in such prominent Conservative leaders as Stoecker, Roesicke, Hahn and Wolfgang Kapp. The last named, who is notorious for his leadership of a reactionary *Putsch* in 1920, is a splendid example of the "feudalized" bourgeois. He acquired property in East Prussia, identified himself thoroughly with the Junkers and Conservatives there and was elected General *Landschaft* Director of the East Prussian *Landschaft*. Thru this position he became a leader in politics and the guiding spirit in the colonization reforms. He had a pronounced Conservative influence on the province.

Even on the basis of these few analyses and examples it seems safe to submit that the Junker process of "feudalizing" the bourgeoisie, in particular the middle-class official, had a certain measure of success, both quantitative and qualitative, but that it also had certain definite limitations. Its effectiveness was probably restricted geographically to East Elbia. Here the interplay of cause and effect undoubtedly enhanced the Junker character of the administration but in the west the "feudalizing" environment was lacking. Middle-class men who held office in the provincial self-government or who served for years as *Landraete* in eastern Prussia were almost certain to be "feudalized." On the other hand, we cannot assume that *Regierungsraete, Ober-Regierungsraete*, etc., in the *Regierungen* even of East Elbia were necessarily "feudalized." They might well belong to the large and substantial group of neutral officials who were first and foremost government agents. Even *Regierungs-Praesidenten,* so far as we know from the above analysis, could be *gouvernemental*. Indeed, with them it was even more likely because of their longer service and acquaintanceship with administrative affairs. In fact, that same experience of officeholding which, when combined with other factors, made some Junkers bureaucratic and bourgeois would assuredly also shape many bourgeois officials into the governmental mould. But one must remember that the governmental mould thruout our period was predominantly conservative so that for the most part it harmonized with the Junker viewpoint.

On the whole one must conclude that the "feudalized" bourgeois made a real contribution to the political power and influence of the Junkers, who were their models and their leaders, but that the extent of this contribution is very difficult to measure. The important qualifications here suggested definitely preclude any assumption that all or even most of the bourgeois officials were "feudalized," even under the Puttkamer regime in 1881-1888. Probably the greater part of these officials were neither liberal nor "feudalized" but simply *gouvernemental*.

PROVINCIAL SELF-GOVERNMENT

Now that we have examined the position of the Junker in the territorial subdivisions of the Prussian State administration let us look briefly at the structure and personnel of the local self-governing bodies. As we know, the Prussian system of government provided for extensive self-government in purely local affairs within the village, Circle, and province but we shall confine our examination to the organs of provincial self-government, in particular to the Provincial Diet, the Provincial Executive Committee, the office of *Landeshauptmann* or *-Direktor* and the *Landschaften*.

These bodies have a long history, for they go back to the early days of the *Staendestaat* when the local assemblies of knights handled the most important questions of government, both local and territorial. In those days the Junkers assumed that they as local owners of knights' estates should comprise the entire membership of these bodies in their own provinces. They were able to hold a strong position in the personnel of these provincial organs from feudal times right down to the present day altho in the 19th century they were forced to give place increasingly to bourgeois owners of knights' estates—who, however, might in no way have affected the social and political orientation of these bodies. But if the personnel and outlook remained approximately the same the powers and functions of the provincial bodies were entirely changed. Altho the feudal institutions remained, the marrow had been drawn from them by the absolute monarchy and its bureaucracy. Gradually, under the Great Elector, Frederick William I and Frederick the Great the old provincial institutions lost their wider political and administrative importance and were confined more and more to local communal affairs. Important matters were transferred to the new central bureaucracy. Of course, as we already know, Junkers were able to make an important place for themselves in the new Prussian State administration but they were never able to achieve the strong position which they enjoyed in the old *staendisch* organizations in their own provinces. And here they now enjoyed the position without the power.

It is true that the reforms of the 19th century which reversed the trend toward bureaucratic centralization and provided for considerable self-government in local areas did widen the powers and activities of the old *staendisch* bodies.[62] But their jurisdiction was definitely limited to purely local affairs. They had no voice in State affairs, for the King was anxious to prevent any return to the old feudal dualism of prince and nobles. Even the reorganized Provincial Diets had no power over State tax appropriations or legislation. They could merely advise. Therefore, even if we do find that the Junker was as previously in a position to control the still existing but reoriented provincial bodies in his own provinces his position was only a historical residue. Altho prestige remained he had been shorn of any real power and we are reminded of the words of the Great Elector, "I let the wind of the Diet blow."[63]

The Provincial Diets in 1888 were composed of deputies from the rural and urban Circles who were elected by these districts. Representation was based on economic groups; owners of knights' estates, whether nobles or bourgeois, elected a certain number of deputies. This meant that in the eastern provinces a large proportion of Junkers was assured. The Provincial Diet was called at least every two years by the King and the *Ober-Praesident* was present as a royal commissioner.[64] It had the power to make laws and ordinances for the province, to be confirmed by the King, put into effect by the Provincial Executive Committee and administered by the *Landeshauptmann*.[65]

A casual survey of the membership of the Provincial Diets within the seven eastern provinces in our period shows that the number of Junkers ranged between 10% and 15% in peripheral provinces like Posen and Saxony and 40% in Pomerania.

In the Provincial Executive Committee in each of the seven eastern

---

62. Bornhak (52) v. 2, p. 328, says, "Aus dem Zusammenwirken der allgemeinen Landesverwaltung der Provinzen mit den ursprunglich gar nicht fuer kommunale Zwecke gebildeten Provinzialstaenden entwickelt sich erst allmaehlich die kommunale Bedeutung der Provinzen."
63. Bernhard Erdmannsdoerffer (62) *Deutsche Geschichte* . . . , v. 2, p. 498.
64. Bornhak (52) v. 2, pp. 338-44.
65. *Ibid.,* p. 348.

provinces the proportion of Junkers was somewhat higher, running from 12-28% in Posen and Saxony to 65% in Pomerania. These figures become more significant when we consider that the members of the Provincial Executive Committee were few in number—only seven to thirteen—and more narrowly chosen, being elected by the Provincial Diet for six years.[66] Also they enjoyed considerable executive powers within the limits of purely provincial affairs. It was their duty and privilege to prepare and execute acts of the Provincial Diet, to administer provincial property and to appoint provincial officials where not appointed by the Provincial Diet, e.g., the members of the Provincial Council and the District Committee, and to oversee their administration.[67] The Provincial Executive Committee assembled about every three months for two or three days and its meetings, like those of the Provincial Diet, served also as agreeable social gatherings where provincial leaders had a fine opportunity to get acquainted and talk politics. These meetings might, then, have some general political significance, not because of their official business but because of the informal discussions over the dinner table among outstanding political figures of the province.

It is immediately apparent that a member of the Provincial Diet or Executive Committee had *as such* no wide political influence. If he did have a voice in the wider affairs of politics it would be because of his personal interests and character and not because of his office. Indeed, it might easily be that he held his provincial office as a result of his general political activities and influence rather than the contrary. The political influence of Junker provincial officials would depend, then, upon their own character and not on the office they held.

It is well to be reminded here that both of the provincial offices just described and likewise the offices in the provincial *Landschaften* are honorary offices and have no salaries attached. It should also be clearly stated altho implicit in all that has been said about provincial institutions, that at no time did a Junker hold a provincial office in any one of the five western provinces.

The most interesting and important official in the whole provincial

66. *Op. cit.*, pp. 344-49.
67. *Ibid.*, pp. 350-54.

administration is the *Landeshauptmann* or *Landesdirektor*, as he was sometimes called. He alone among the higher officials received a salary—and a good one. He alone enjoyed individual authority and responsibility, all the others being members of collegial bodies. He acted as the continuing head of the whole provincial self-government and directed all its affairs with the aid of a corps of subordinate officials. The *Landeshauptmann* was elected by the Provincial Diet for six to twelve years and was inducted into office by the *Ober-Praesident*. His election had to be confirmed by the King.[68] Within the limits of provincial self-government the *Landeshauptmann* enjoyed considerable independence and authority. These attributes of the office with the added factors of a good salary and the tradition of Junker rule in the eastern provinces made the post especially attractive for Junkers and we find that it was often held by them. The figures for the seven eastern provinces are as follows:

Year	Total no. of offices	No. of Junkers
1888	7	4
1890	7	4
1895	7	2
1900	7	5
1905	7	5
1910	7	6
1914	7	7

The office of *Landeshauptmann* differs from other provincial posts as well in that the office itself gave an opportunity for political influence. The extent to which it was used depends on the character of the *Landeshauptmann*, but the office did put him in a favorable position for such influence.

A provincial organization peculiar to eastern Prussia was the *Landschaft* or co-operative land credit institution. Since the *Landschaften* were self-governing corporations of noble origin and closely related to the Junkers as owners of knights' estates even in our period it is well to consider their nature and personnel. These bodies originated after the Seven Years' War when Frederick II wished to create a land credit organization for the aid of propertied nobles. The first *Landschaft* was founded in 1770 in Silesia and was a purely

68. *Ibid.*, pp. 344-48.

staendisch affair, excluding all but noble landowners. The Pomeranian *Landschaft,* established in 1781, was also strictly confined to nobles but the *Kur- und Neumaerkische ritterschaftliche Kredit-Institute,* established in 1781, included non-noble owners of knights' estates. The East and West Prussian *Landschaften,* founded by Frederick William II, also included bourgeois property owners. The functions of the *Landschaften* were purely financial. They made loans on the lands of certain members with the property of all members as security. They set up their own organization and ran their own affairs. The provincial organization consisted usually of a general provincial board of directors with regional directors and *Landschaft* Counsellors under them. In Brandenburg the *Landschaft* was known as as a *Ritterschaft.* In Silesia the General *Landschaft* Directors had under them an extensive organization of *Fuerstenthums-Landschaften* where the Counsellors had the name, peculiar to Silesia, of *Landes-Aelteste.* In 1873 a Central *Landschaft* was set up in Berlin to give stability and flexibility to the provincial *Landschaften.* It, too, was self-governing and representative and consisted of delegates sent by all the member *Landschaften* with the Chief *Ritterschaft* Director of Brandenburg acting as executive.[69]

The *Landschaft* Director or Counsellor held an honorary post, without remuneration except for expenses.[70] He was elected to office at the general assembly of all those landowners who were members of the *Landschaft.* Because of the large number of Junker landlords as well as the *staendisch* traditions of the *Landschaften* the Junkers had a good representation among the Directors and Counsellors, running from 10% in Saxony to 45-50% in Silesia and 85-90% in Pomerania. Altho in no way a political body the *Landschaft* could exercise considerable political influence thru its financial services. And it also provided a convenient meeting place for local landowners. Therefore a *Landschaft* dominated by Junkers such as that in Brandenburg or Pomerania was in a position to exert political pressure in the interests of its Junker members.

69. Wilhelm von Bruenneck (54) *Die Pfandbriefsysteme der preussischen Landschaften;* Walter von Altrock (48) *Der landwirtschaftliche Kredit in Preussen.*
70. See above, Chapter III, p. 91, note 24.

CHURCH. PROVINCIAL AND ADMINISTRATIVE SUPREME COURTS

In each province there was also a royal consistory of the Evangelical State Church. Altho not self-governing but under the direction of the Evangelical Supreme Church Council in Berlin and altho composed mostly of clergymen, these provincial consistories are important to us because of the Junkers among their secular members. As we know, the Junkers were devout Protestants and for the most part zealous members of the State Church. It is therefore according to expectation to find several Junkers serving as lay members in the consistories of the eastern provinces. Frequently in our period the chairman of the Provincial Synodal Committee and two or three, sometimes as many as five or the six lay members were Junkers. The general average was about 40%. Though these men held positions of dignity and respect they drew no political power from their office, for the lay members of the consistories were under the influence of the Churchmen who in turn were servants of the King—their *summus episcopus.*

Junkers also had a goodly representation among the lay members of the General Synodal Executive Committee (*General-Synodal-Vorstand*) in the Evangelical Supreme Church Council in Berlin. Of the twelve extraordinary (lay) members and alternates of this Committee four were consistently Junkers. Thus one-third of the seats in the General Synodal Executive Committee and one-sixth of the seats in the whole Supreme Church Council thruout all of our period were held by Junkers. Frequently one of the four Junkers acted as chairman for the extraordinary members.

There is one other provincial body which should be given brief consideration—the Provincial Supreme Court. These courts were courts of 3rd instance and there was no appeal beyond them, except in a few restricted matters to the *Kammergericht*[71] in Berlin or to the Reich Supreme Court. Therefore they were highly important judicial bodies and their Presidents, Senators and Judges were men carefully selected and trained in jurisprudence. It is this latter fact together with social custom which made them unpopular with the Junkers in spite of the prestige and salaries which they offered. We are, therefore, not surprised to find that there were never more than one or two

71. See p. 72, note 71.

and more frequently no Junkers among the twelve to thirty-five members of the Provincial Supreme Court in each of the seven eastern provinces. In the west there were never Junkers in these courts. At no time were there more than six Junkers serving in all of the seven eastern provincial courts combined—including the Berlin *Kammergericht* with its 88 members. Among this handful of Junkers there were three who at one time held the high position of President: Otto von Kunowski in Silesia from 1888 to 1900, Carl von Plehwe in East Prussia from 1900 to 1910[72] and Dr. Theodor von der Trenck in East Prussia in 1914. This seems to be an indication that of the few Junkers who did enter the judicial service a goodly number were able to reach top positions.

Even in the Supreme Administrative Court for appeals in the adjudication of administrative disputes and the protection of citizens from administrative injustice the number of Junkers was extremely low, never as high as 10%. This is somewhat surprising since this administrative court functioned in the field of the Prussian State administration in which the Junker had a particular interest. It may be due to the judicial nature of the work and also to the fact that it was a career *cul de sac,* since there was no chance of further promotion from this office. The most prominent Junker who served in this court was Graf Kuno Westarp, leader of the Conservative fraction in the Reichstag.

STAATSMINISTERIUM AND MINISTRIES

We come now by way of the Supreme Administrative Court to a consideration of the governmental organs at the capital, that is, the various Ministries and above all the Prussian *Staatsministerium.* In spite of frequent outcries against an "arch-Prussian institution"[73] and the "victorious East Elbian Junkers"[74] the *Staatsministerium* was not predominantly Junker. On the contrary, the percentage of Junkers was remarkably low. Of the ten to twelve Prussian Ministers[75] never

72. See above, Chapter II, p. 72f.
73. Chlodwig von Hohenlohe (33) p. 290.
74. Quoted by Graf Alfred von Waldersee (41) *Denkwuerdigkeiten,* v. 2, p. 400.
75. The heads of the nine Ministries plus the Secretary of State for the Interior, the Secretary of State for Foreign Affairs and the Secretary of State for the Reich Navy Office.

more than four were Junkers—but never less than one. The figures
for the whole period are as follows:

Year	Total no. of officials	Junkers	Other nobles	Commoners
1888	9	3	3	3
1890	10	1	8	1
1895	11	2	6	3
1900	12	3	4	5
1905	11	3	5	3
1910	11	2	6	3
1914	11	3	4	4

In all, eighteen Junkers served as Prussian Ministers at some time
between 1888 and 1914. Of these five were War Ministers, four,
Ministers of the Interior and one, Secretary of State for the Interior.
Three were Ministers of Agriculture; two were *Kultusminister* and
two were Ministers for Foreign Affairs; one, Georg, Baron von
Rheinbaben, was Finance Minister. The five War Ministers were all
army officers and four of them came directly from a command;
Heinrich von Gossler served briefly as Director of a department in
the War Ministry before becoming its head. The two Ministers for
Foreign Affairs had worked up in the diplomatic service and in the
Foreign Office, and Georg von Rheinbaben, the Finance Minister, was
trained in his own Ministry as *Regierungsrat* and *Vortragender Rat*.
The four Ministers of the Interior had all come up thru the ranks
in the Prussian State administration and one of the *Kultusminister,*
Gustav von Gossler, had worked up from *Landrat* and Judge
in the Supreme Administrative Court to become Undersecretary of
State in the *Kultusministerium* in 1880. The following year he was
made Minister. Wilhelm von Heyden-Cadow, who became Minister
of Agriculture, also trained in the Prussian State administration. He
was serving as *Regierungs-Praesident* in Frankfurt a.O. when he was
appointed Minister of Agriculture. Two other Ministers, Robert,
Count Zedlitz-Truetzschler and Arthur, Count Posadowsky-Wehner,
had had most of their experience in the provincial self-government,
but they had also served for a time in the Prussian State administration. Only two Ministers of Agriculture—General Viktor von Pod-
bielski and Bernd von Arnim-Criewen—were entirely outside the
administrative field. They had had only a practical farming experience.

Thus we find that twelve of the eighteen Junkers became Ministers in the departments of government in which they had trained. Two were trained by the Prussian State administration for Ministries other than the Ministry of the Interior; two had experience both in the Prussian State administration and in the provincial self-government and only two Ministers came to their posts from outside. The fact that six of these Ministers—or seven if we include Georg, Baron von Rheinbaben, in the Finance Ministry—came up thru the ranks of the administration is important, because it gives definite proof that a Junker bureaucrat had a real chance of being appointed to a top political office.

In general the Prussian Ministry had no unity or solidarity and therefore the influence of a single Minister on the King or upon the general direction of State affairs was a matter of individual personality and opinion. Even Junker Ministers varied as to the degree of vitality and conservative conviction which they brought to bear on the Ministry. For instance, Botho zu Eulenburg or Robert, Count Zedlitz-Truetzschler, had a much more reactionary influence on State policies than did the War Minister, Walter Bronsart von Schellendorf or Arthur, Count Posadowsky-Wehner, Secretary of State for the Interior. There is no need to speak of the political influence inherent in the office of a Prussian Minister of State because it is obviously so great. No one except the Minister President or the King himself officially commanded greater political power in Prussia than a Minister of State.

There were regularly four administrative officials in the *Staatsministerium* to assist the Minister President in his duties as chief of the Ministers, namely, an Undersecretary of State and three *Vortragende Raete*. Only once in our period, in 1914, was the Undersecretary a Junker—Johann von Eisenhart-Rothe. Of the three *Vortragende Raete* two were Junkers until 1900 and thereafter only one was a Junker.

We come now to a survey of the nine Ministries administering the several departments of the Prussian State. In reckoning the proportion of Junker officials each Ministry has been studied up to its *Ressorts* or subsidiary departments and all higher officials such as Directors,

Vortragende Raete, and all assistants with the rank of *Regierungs-Assessor* and above have been counted.

Our first Ministry is the Office of Foreign Affairs and it falls into two sections: Ministry officials in Berlin and Envoys, together with all the civilians on their staffs. The proportion of Junkers among the Ministry officials is low, only once exceeding 10%, but it tends to show a slight increase by 1914. This is the more remarkable because the total number of officials increased rapidly between 1888 and 1914.

The number of Junkers among the envoys is slightly higher and averages about 17% but here there is a definite decline in the proportion of Junkers over the twenty-six years, altho the actual numbers of Junkers remain about the same as we see by the following table.

Year	Total no. of offices	No. of nobles (including Junkers)	No. of Junkers	Percentage of Junkers
1888	88	67	18	21.95
1890	80	70	11	13.75
1895	85	73	16	18.82
1900	93	84	17	18.28
1905	110	99	20	18.18
1910	116	101	18	15.51
1914	120	106	18	15.00

The striking fact here is that such a high proportion of the envoys are nobles altho few are Junkers. This seems to substantiate the general assumption that nobles were preferred for the diplomatic service because of their aristocratic background and position but that Junkers, because they were often blunt and even rustic, were not as well suited for diplomatic missions as nobles from South or West Germany. It may also be explained in part by the fact that the Prussian Foreign Office served for the whole Reich as well and therefore diplomatic appointments had to be spread over all of the German States. The influence of a Junker diplomatic envoy on the course of German foreign relations might be very great, as in the case of Hans Lother von Schweinitz, the Ambassador to Russia in 1890, but his effect on internal politics would probably be slight unless he had contact with internal affairs thru other channels. Clearly the Junkers were never in a position of sufficient strength in the diplomatic service to influence the government thru that particular department.

What was the situation in the Ministry of the Interior which

stood at the head of the whole system of the Prussian State administration and hence offered congenial work to Junkers and directed the
considerable group of them who served in the civil service? We
should expect to find a good number of Junkers here. The all-im-
portant office of Minister of the Interior was held by a Junker for
eleven out of the twenty-six years during our period or 42% of the
time. Three of the Ministers, R. V. von Puttkamer, Botho zu Eulenburg and Ernst von Koeller, were stanuch and forceful Conservatives;
the other two, Georg, Baron von Rheinbaben and Hans von Dallwitz,
were perhaps hardly less so. We know from the career of R. V. von
Puttkamer and from the attacks made on other Ministers of the
Interior that this office was of tremendous political importance, for
the Minister had control over all administrative appointments and
could require Conservative "reliability." He could also mobilize the
whole system of officials in support of government candidates at
election time. A Junker Minister such as R. V. von Puttkamer could
in a few years' time develop an iron-clad system of Conservative
officials which it would take years to remove. And yet the contrast
between the large number of Junker Ministers and the small proportion of Junker officials in the Ministry itself is striking and
significant:

Year	Total no. of offices	No. of Junkers	Percentage of Junkers
1888	17	3	17.60
1890	17	2	11.70
1895	17	3	17.60
1900	20	3	15.00
1905	21	4	19.04
1910	24	2	8.33
1914	38	6	15.79

There seems to be no notable tendency for the percentage either to
increase or decline here, which shows that in this instance the Junkers
were able to keep pace with the general increase in the number of
officials.

Why should the numbers of Junkers be so small in this key
Ministry? The answer may be in part that a Junker Minister could
control and dominate his assistants and needed few Junkers under
him. Also, he would need some technical assistants who were highly

trained and less apt to be Junkers. It is also very important to note that altho the proportion of Junkers here is low—only 15% on an average—it is nonetheless higher than in any other Ministry. Thus the Ministry of the Interior does stand forth, as we would expect, as the most "Junkerized" Ministry in Berlin.

The Ministry of Agriculture was also a department of the government which could make good use of Junkers and, indeed, we find that among the higher officials serving here on an average 10% were Junkers. Altho a small percentage it nonetheless places the Department of Agriculture in a high position with relation to the remaining Ministries. Moreover, here even more than in the Ministry of the Interior the need for trained technicians was large. In the *Kultusministerium* or Ministry for Religious, Educational and Medical Affairs, where one might expect to find Junkers because of their interest in the church, the proportion is only 3½%. Here again the number of Junkers is kept down by the specialized training required in many instances. There is a real tendency for the proportion of Junkers to increase in this department in spite of the growth in the total number of officials. But since their numbers at best were so negligible this is of no importance.

In the Ministry of Justice the proportion of Junkers practically reaches the vanishing point.

Year	*Total no. of offices*	*No. of Junkers*	*Percentage of Junkers*
1888	32	1	3.12
1890	29	1	3.44
1895	28	0	0.00
1900	29	0	0.00
1905	38	0	0.00
1910	50	0	0.00
1914	68	1	1.47

Even our previous knowledge of the Junker's distaste for the legal profession does not prepare us for these extremely low figures. The antipathy between Junkers and judicial leaders was apparently mutual.

In the ministries of Finance, Trade and Commerce, and Public Works we would naturally expect to find a very small number of Junkers because of the highly technical and specialized business in these departments and also because of the bourgeois character of their work. Actually we find the proportion of Junkers rather higher than we had anticipated, considering the general low level. In the Department of Trade and Commerce the average was 6% but the trend was downward, due to the fact that the total number of offices quadrupled and that the number of Junkers was and remained only one or two. The Finance Ministry shows a comparatively substantial number of Junkers, that is from three to seven out of 90 to 150 officials. The general average was 5%. Here again the Junkers were unable to keep up with the increase in the total number of officials. In the Ministry of Public Works the average is only 1½% and there was generally one and never more than two or three Junkers out of a group of 65 to 145 officials in this department. The figures are too small to make any trends either apparent or important.

The War Ministry presents some interesting figures and problems. First, we must bear in mind that many of the men serving in the War Ministry were regular army officers detailed to desk work in the Ministry for a short period. Therefore, they were not regular officials. Many of the Junkers in this department were therefore actually army officers. This many account in part for the somewhat higher proportion of Junkers. The number ranged around 10% and remained fairly constant in spite of the increase in the whole Ministry from 70 to 109 officials. Of course, the Junker's great interest in the army might also account for the larger numbers. But against this we must weigh the fact that the War Ministry was concerned rather with the civil aspects of army administration and that the General Staff tried to keep it within these bounds.[76]

In all of the Ministries the regular work of the officials, other than the Minister and one or two Directors, was routine. Frequently, in some departments more than others, it was also highly specialized and technical. Such work would not have a great appeal for the ambitious and politically aggressive Junker. This goes far toward explaining why Junkers preferred the *Landratsamt* or even an appointment as *Regierungsrat* in a province or governmental district to a desk job in Berlin. Furthermore, the real Junker preferred provincial and

76. Waldersee (41) v. 2, pp. 18-21.

rural life to year-round residence at the capital. It is, of course, true that a Ministerial Director or even a *Vortragender Rat* would have considerable authority and influence. He had the familiarity with the office and command of materials which is the great latent power of permanent officials. But, unless he were in the Ministry of the Interior, it is unlikely that his opportunities for general political influence would be great.

COURT

A great contrast both in numbers and potential political influence can be seen between the Junkers serving in the Ministries in Berlin and those holding high offices at the Royal and Imperial Court. The figures, at least, give some justification for the continual complaints of liberals about the pernicious influence of Junker Court Marshals and adjutants who surrounded the Kaiser. These figures are the more surprising since the Court was Imperial as well as Prussian and hence there was need for a certain distribution of Court offices among the nobility of other parts of Germany. There is also the hindering fact that most Junkers were not wealthy and could hardly afford to maintain the costly standards of a Court office.

The greatest proportion of Junkers was in the Royal Household (*Hofstaat*) where the average was about 49%.

Year	Total no. of offices	No. of Junkers	Percentage of Junkers
1888	53	24	45.28
1890	52	24	46.15
1895	51	24	47.06
1900	51	29	56.86
1905	50	27	54.00
1910	45	22	48.88
1914	46	20	43.47

It is apparent that there was no marked change in the number of Junkers here between 1888 and 1914.

In the Military Retinue the average number of Junkers was approximately the same, being 48%, but, as the following table shows, there was a definite falling off in their numbers from a high point in 1888 to a low point in 1905 from which no complete recovery had been made by 1914.

Year	Total no. of offices	No. of Junkers	Percentage of Junkers
1888	37	22	59.45
1890	51	30	58.82
1895	44	22	50.00
1900	46	18	39.13
1905	42	16	38.09
1910	43	20	46.51
1914	44	20	45.45

In the Ministry of the Royal House the proportion of Junkers was somewhat smaller, due probably to the technical character of some of the offices and the presence there of several commoners as well as non-Junker nobles. The figures for this department of the Court are as follows:

Year	Total no. of offices	No. of Junkers	Percentage of Junkers
1888	23	11	47.82
1890	24	13	54.16
1895	26	11	42.30
1900	26	9	34.61
1905	26	6	23.07
1910	25	8	32.00
1914	26	10	38.46

Again we note a marked decline in the number of Junkers which reaches its lowest point in 1905, the same year in which the number of Junkers in the Military Retinue was the smallest. Here, too, there was a definite but in no way a complete recovery by 1914.

The slump in the number of Junkers in both the Military Retinue and the Ministry of the Royal House has a particular significance because appointments to these positions were made by the King and Emperor himself. Hence any decline would seem to indicate a certain cooling of the old cordial relations between the Junkers and the Crown. The Junkers had been the preferred class from which the King of Prussia had selected his courtiers and advisors for centuries and the former considered themselves predestined by birth and custom for these royal posts. Even under William I, as we can see from our figures, the tradition was very strong. But William I was at heart an old Prussian soldier and patriarch. For him as for the Junkers Prussia was the real Fatherland. The new Kaiser, William II, was quite a different person.[77] He was too modern, too broad in his

77. See, *inter alia*, Elard von Oldenburg-Januschau (37) *Erinnerungen*, pp. 58-59.

interests, too versatile, too unstable—even too German[78] for the Junkers. His personality was foreign to theirs and they never felt truly at ease with him nor he with them. Altho the Junkers continued loyal to the Crown and the old partnership was perpetuated by the weight of hallowed tradition the uncongenial, volatile personality of William II often troubled and irked the conservative and tradition-bound Junkers. They found it hard to know on what basis their relations with the Kaiser really were. For example, von Rauchhaupt, an old *Landrat* and Conservative leader who had often opposed the King's ministers, was suddenly honoured by the bestowal of a decoration in 1891. Yet at the same time that William II presented him with the medal he said to Rauchhaupt, "voluntas regis, suprema lex" and then turned to a noble standing near him and said, "I gave the old greybeard a good scolding."[79]

This incident illustrates another royal trait of character which was offensive to the Junkers—an inclination to rule absolutely and by Divine Right without regard for the special position and privileges of the landed nobility. This trait comes out clearly in William's treatment of the Civil and Military Cabinets (*Geheime Kabinette*). He preferred to rule thru these Cabinets, which were composed of his own secretaries, rather than thru the Ministers who had far greater public responsibility and authority. Hence he was accused of establishing a "personal rule" and of attempting to restore the old Cabinet government of Frederick II. In 1897, when William II bestowed the Black Eagle decoration on Lucanus, Chief of the Civil Cabinet, von Kardorff expressed the general public reaction in these words, "This action has the distinct meaning of putting the supremacy of the Cabinet over the *Staatsministerium* in the right light and it is understood by clear-thinking politicians as an anti-constitutional demonstration."[80]

Altho an office in a Cabinet did not carry any intrinsic importance the opportunities for influence were always great and much greater under William II than under his grandfather. The number of offices in either of the Cabinets was small, only three in.the Civil and eight in the Military Cabinet, and hence the proportion of Junkers fluctuates

78. See, *inter alia,* Hutten-Czapski (34) v. 2, p. 131.
79. As described by Waldersee (41) v. 2, p. 220.
80. Kardorff (86) p. 313. See also Hutten-Czapski (34) v. 1, p. 311.

wildly between 0 and 100%. It is therefore difficult to arrive at any definite conclusions as to the extent or consistency of Junker influence thru these offices during our period. I have found no evidence that they exerted a decisive influence.

William II's penchant for absolute rule included a tendency to interfere in and take over the running of various departments of the State, particularly the army.[81] William II was without doubt a brilliant and gifted man, but by 1888 to run the Prussian state single-handed would have been an impossible task even for a ruler more conscientious and constant in his purpose than William II. Because of his desire to rule himself the Kaiser preferred to be surrounded not with strong and capable administrators but with men who by flattery and servility encouraged him in his vanity and conceit. As a result the climate at Court was fetid with adulation and sycophancy. This excess of flattery was given the name of "Byzantinism" and it was against this that men like von Reventlow and Alexander von Hohenlohe complained. Reventlow objected to the "attitude of subservience" at Court and the tendency to praise the Kaiser for all that he did no matter what or how well. Such indiscriminate flattery encouraged the Kaiser in his vanity, love of display and feeling of Divine Right and smothered any attempts at honesty and frankness.[82] Hohenlohe describes the crush of men around the King, each elbowing his way in a rude and vulgar fashion in order to reach the front row and attract the royal attention.[83] The ladies at Court showed more courage and frankness, says Zedlitz, due he thinks to naivete and "a certain fanatical devotion to the truth created by their strong religious leanings."[84]

Servility and obsequiousness were certainly foreign, even obnoxious to the deepest instincts of the true Junker. His relations with the

---

81. War Minister Bronsart von Schellendorf complained about "die fast taeglichen Eingriffe des Kaisers in die Dienstgeschaefte, insbesonders hinsichtlich der Bewaffnung, wodurch grosse Summen ganz zwecklos verausgabt wuerden." Hutten-Czapski (34) v. 1, p. 285.

82. Graf E. von Reventlow (111) *Kaiser Wilhelm II und die Byzantiner.*

83. Alexander von Hohenlohe (32) p. 371. Others who criticized the servility among the courtiers were Count Robert von Zedlitz-Truetzschler, General von Waldersee and von Buelow altho they themselves were not above the use of "Byzantinism" at times.

84. Count Robert von Zedlitz-Truetzschler (46) *Twelve Years at the Imperial German Court*, p. 37.

Crown had been simple, direct and based on mutual respect.[85] Such an atmosphere of adulation together with the antipathy between the personality of the Emperor and those of the Junkers would tend to drive the latter away from the Court and may explain in large measure the decline in their numbers among Court officials.

What of the considerable number of Junkers who did serve at Court in spite of these obstacles? From the information available it seems that some retained their Junker independence and bluntness while others tended to succumb to the servile Court atmosphere and join the chorus of flatterers. Such apparently was Georg von Huelsen, General Director of the Royal Theater at Wiesbaden and later at Berlin. He was often with the Emperor and generally accompanied him on his North Cape cruises where he made himself pleasing and entertaining. But Zedlitz-Truetzschler complains that he won William II's favor by exploiting his weakness for external show; that his policy was, "How can I flatter the taste of my All Highest Master?"[86] Buelow also writes that it was said of Huelsen in jest that he was "much too complacent to the Kaiser's taste toward mediocre music à la Meyerbeer."[87]

Georg von Huelsen's older brother, Dietrich, Graf Huelsen-Haeseler, was evidently quite a different type of person. He had started out as an army officer, had later been appointed Adjutant in the Military Retinue and finally became a General and Chief of the Military Cabinet. Dietrich was staunchly loyal to the Kaiser. But along with a strong sense of duty he apparently had the courage to be frank with the Kaiser and speak openly to him about his mistakes.[88] It was perhaps his hearty wit and his shrewd remarks which made his criticisms acceptable to William II. At any rate the Kaiser liked him for all his independence; he frequently took him on his cruises and was genuinely grieved by his sudden death in 1908.

Heinrich, Count Lehndorff, a stout old Junker who had been an

85. Prince Bernhard von Buelow (24) *Memoirs,* v. 1, p. 87, writes, "I have often had occasion to notice that liberally inclined chamberlains, adjutants and Court Marshals are more complacent and actually more servile to the 'greatest' than stout conservatives and true Junkers."
86. Zedlitz-Truetzschler (46) p. 208.
87. Buelow (24) v. 1, p. 203.
88. *Ibid.;* Zedlitz-Truetzschler (46) pp. 203-04; Hutten-Czapski (34) v. 1, p. 410.

Adjutant-General under William I and continued to serve for many years under his grandson, was another unbending spirit. Altho loyal and devoted to the dynasty he kept his own opinions and his wisdom and shrewd judgment had a beneficial influence at Court.[89] On the other hand, Wilhelm von Hahnke who became Chief of the Military Cabinet in August, 1888, was one who had a tendency to be complaisant. Waldersee complains that he didn't know how to take a stand and point out the mistakes the Kaiser was making in the military command.[90] Philipp zu Eulenburg accuses him of being one of those responsible for deceiving the Kaiser at the army manoeuvres which he directed in order to make it appear that the Kaiser's commands had been carried out without a hitch.[91] The Kaiser himself commends him because he was entirely of the same opinion as his master and remained attached to him in exemplary loyalty until his death.[92]

Whether the influence of a Junker at the Court fostered the Junker spirit there or not depended on whether he had retained his independence and frankness or become complaisant. But there can be no doubt that a Junker Adjutant or Court Marshal had an opportunity to exercise great influence over the Kaiser. He was often in attendance and able to converse freely with him. It was possible for two or more Adjutants to work in co-operation to promote a certain view or policy and they often brought down on themselves the complaint of "Adjutant politics."[93] It is clear that the influence exerted would generally be of a political nature and, considering the paramount constitutional importance of the Crown, that it would be of very great significance.

The ordinarily great potential political importance of the Junker Court officials was made greater during the reign of William II by the fact that relations between the Kaiser and the Conservative Party, in

89. Baron Hugo von Reischach (38) *Under Three Emperors*, p. 66; Buelow (24) v. 1, pp. 85-86; Hutten-Czapski (34) v. 1, p. 42.

90. Waldersee (41) v. 2, p. 180.

91. Prinz Philipp zu Eulenburg (29) *Aus 50 Jahren*, p. 285.

92. Kaiser Wilhelm II (45) *Ereignisse und Gestalten* . . . , p. 20.

93. One will recall the reference of Zechlin (122) *Staatsstreichplaene* . . . , p. 133, to the host of aides-de-camp and other Court people hostile to Caprivi who had free access to William II at a hunting party in the critical days of the Chancellor crisis in October, 1894.

whose ranks most Junkers stood,[94] were frequently strained. Junker and other Conservative Court officers were at times the only means of direct contact between the leading political party and the Crown. It is true, however, that they were not used as they might have been, because the Prussian Conservative leader, von Heydebrand, did not value them very highly.[95]

The connection between the Conservatives and the Crown had always been close because the Conservatives' first principle was loyalty and devotion to the monarchy and the Hohenzollern dynasty. Under William II this principle of fidelity to the King still bound the Conservative to the Crown but the relationship was complicated by the modern and impulsive character of the Kaiser—and also by the self-centred, materialistic ambitions of the agrarian wing of the party. Altho an absolutist, William II was no Conservative,[96] and when he tried to introduce modern innovations such as a navy, a canal system or an extension of the franchise in Prussia, he ran into opposition from the old Conservatives and the agrarians. Relations became so bad that regular direct contacts between the Kaiser and the official leaders of Prussia's most monarchial party were often tenuous, even non-existent.

In spite of the fact that the official relations between the Conservative Party and the Kaiser were so unsatisfactory it is nonetheless very probable that this party had closer connections with the monarch than any other political party under William II. The reason for this is that so many Junkers and other Conservative nobles had contacts with the Kaiser at Court. William II gives explicit recognition to this advantage of the Conservative when he writes in his memoirs, "The Conservative party possessed many members who had direct connections with the Court and also with me personally. Hence it was easier for this party than for any other to learn about my plans in the

94. See below, p. 218
95. Westarp (43) v. 1, p. 350.
96. William II writes in his memoirs (45) p. 94, "Vielleicht liegt das [strained relations] daran, dass ich zwar meiner Tradition nach den Konservativen nahe stand aber nicht parteipolitisch konservativ war." But he expected the Conservative party to give him unfailing support and in his Koenigsberg speech of September 6, 1894, he said, "Eine Opposition des preussischen Adels gegen den Koenig ist ein Unding. Die hat nur dann Berechtigung, wenn sie den Koenig an ihrer Spitze weiss." Quoted by Massow (97) p. 147.

political and other fields."[97] Junkers and in particular Junker Court officials were, therefore, in an admirable position to talk with the Kaiser and influence him in favor of their interests.

As an example we may consider Wilhelm von Wedel-Piesdorf, Minister of the Royal Household from 1890 to 1907 and a prominent Conservative. Wedel seems to have succumbed to the Court atmosphere somewhat and to have become rather over-eager to carry out the royal will and also to advance the fortunes at Court of his son-in-law, von Bismarck-Bohlen.[98] Yet he retained sufficient independence and Conservative partisanship to be a strong member of the party, so much so that William II refused to consider him as Chancellor in 1900.[99] After he had resigned as Minister of the Royal Household, Wedel represented the Conservative fraction in the *Herrenhaus*, of which he later became President. Wedel's particular value to the party was his good and close relationship with the Court and the Kaiser. He undoubtedly tried hard to improve relations between the Party and the Crown but he could not accomplish a great deal because von Heydebrand did not put much stock in this means of advancing the party.

PRUSSIAN DIET

Reference has been made both here and elsewhere to the predominantly Conservative complexion of the Junker officials and of the Junker group in general. Therefore, altho Junker deputies in the Prussian Diet were not, strictly speaking, officials, it would seem necessary and proper to examine insofar as we are able the proportion of Junkers in both Houses of the Diet and in the Conservative Party.[100]

In the *Herrenhaus*, the more august but less dynamic upper house

---

97. Kaiser Wilhelm II (45) p. 93. Earlier in the same work (p. 25) William II writes, "Mit der konservativen Partei bestanden naturgemaess zahlreiche Beziehungen und Beruehrungspunkte, da die Herren vom Landadel auf Hof und Jagden viel mit mir zusammentrafen oder zu Hofe kamen, auch in Hofstellungen Dienst taten." See also Massow (97) p. 86.

98. Zedlitz-Truetzschler (46) pp. 192-95.

99. Buelow (24) v. 1, p. 434.

100. Since there are no records of the party affiliations of the regular voter there is, of course, no absolute means of establishing the politics of our 1500 Junker officials or of Junkers in general but there are some oblique indications of the relationship between Junkers and the Conservative party which point us toward certain conclusions.

in the Prussian Diet, the Junker representation remained around eighty members or 30% of the whole body. That the proportion was as high as this is due to the fact that in 1850-1853 when the composition of the upper house was being determined the Junkers were able to prevail upon the King to increase their representation by adding a large number of life members to be elected for presentation mostly by groups of old and established landholders (*Verbaende des alten und befestigten Grundbesitzes*). This provision not only ensured the Junkers a subtantial representation in the *Herrenhaus* but also related membership to landholding, at least for this large group and two or three smaller ones, and the *Herrenhaus* turned out to be a body representative rather of large landholders than of the Crown.[101]

We know from the history of our period that the *Herrenhaus* was a predominantly conservative body and had a conservative influence on Prussian politics and the considerable representation of Junkers assuredly contributed to its conservative character. In fact, there is reason to believe that the Junkers formed the most reactionary and fanatically conservative group in the *Herrenhaus*. But their extreme influence was moderated by the more objective, more broadminded, wealthier and more secure *grands seigneurs* and mediatized princes. For the *Herrenhaus* was more conciliatory toward the government and more impartial in its views than was the Conservative fraction which dominated the House of Deputies.

The Junkers enjoyed certain constitutional advantages in the composition of the House of Deputies as well and here they were of greater significance because of the larger importance of the lower house. Both the three-class electoral law and the old unreformed division of electoral districts which favored the rural areas ensured that Junker landlords would be elected in many parts of the eastern provinces. A look at the election statistics of the years 1903, 1908 and 1913 confirms this fact and shows as well the party affiliations of these Junkers.[102]

101. Sigmund Neumann (104) *Die Stufen des preussischen Konservatismus,* p. 120.

102. Figures taken from Georg Evert (129 & 130) "Die preussischen Landtagswahlen des Jahres 1903 (1908) und fruehere Jahre", *Z. d. Kgl. preuss. Stat. Landesamtes,* 1905 & 1909, *Ergaenzungshefte* 23 & 30; H. Hoepker (134) "Die preussischen Landtagswahlen des Jahres 1913", *Z. d. Kgl. preuss, Stat. Landesamtes,* 1916, *Ergaenzungsheft* 43.

Year	Total no. of deputies	No. of deputies in 7 east. prov.	No. of Junkers in 7 east. prov.	Percentage of deputies in 7 east. prov. that were J.
1903	433	248	65	26½
1908	443	251	64	25½
1913	443	251	58	22½

Only one Junker, Joachim von Bonin, *Landrat* in Kreis Stormarn, Schleswig-Holstein, was elected outside the seven eastern provinces.

When we consider party affiliations we find that practically 100% of the Junker deputies belonged to the Conservative Party:

Year	Total No. of Junker Deputies	Conservative	Free Cons.	Nat. Lib.
1903	65	61	3	1
1908	65	60	4	1
1913	59	54	4	1

These figures lead us to believe that the Junkers were Conservatives almost without exception.[103] Altho we are dealing here only with Junker deputies it seems reasonable to conclude that approximately the same proportion of Junker voters—and hence of Junker officials—were Conservatives. The few Junker deputies who were not Conservatives probably represent the maximum of political dissension in the whole Junker group.

Our election statistics also give us information on the equally important question of the proportion of the Conservatives who were Junkers.

Year	Total no. of Cons.	Percentage of Cons. in House of Deputies	No. of J. Cons.	Percentage of Cons.	Other Nobles	Commoners
1903	143	33.0	61	42.60	28	55
1908	152	34.3	60	39.47	29	63
1913	148	33.4	54	36.50	31	63

Some figures quoted by Count Westarp, altho he refers to the Reichstag fraction of the Conservative Party, give some further indication

103. The election statistics also give us some interesting figures on the distribution of all of the Conservative deputies throughout Prussia:

Year	Total No. Cons. Deputies	No. Cons. in 7 east. prov.	Percentage of total No. of Cons.	Percentage of Cons. Deputies in 7 east. prov. that were J.
1903	143	125	87.	50.
1908	152	129	84.90	52.
1913	148	124	83.70	50.

This gives striking evidence of the way in which the Conservative party strength was concentrated in eastern Prussia, the home of the Junker.

of the position of the Junkers and landlords in general in this party. Westarp gives the following figures on the Conservative Reichstag fraction in 1908:[104]

     29 noble large landowners
     19 bourgeois landowners and peasants
      2 big industrialists
      9 officials and professional men
      3 representatives of the middle class

He also gives the composition of the Conservative Party Committee of Eleven as follows:[105]

     *Baron von Manteuffel-Krossen, Chairman
     *von Buch-Carmzow
     Dr. Baron von Erffa
     *Dr. von Heydebrand
     Dr. Klasing
     *von Kroecher
     Dr. Mehnert
     *Count von Mirbach-Sorquitten
     *von Normann
     von Pappenheim
     Stackmann

Of these eleven, six or 54½% were Junkers. It is important to note that the proportion of Junkers in this steering committee is somewhat larger than for the Diet fraction, for this seems to indicate that the smaller and more influential the group the larger was the proportion and influence of the Junkers. In other words, both the ratio and the influence of the Junkers appear to have been greater in the smaller and more important Conservative organs than in the larger and less important ones. Because of tradition and background as well as political ambitions and machinations it was to be expected that the Junkers' actual strength in the Conservative party would be much greater than that indicated by their numerical position.

104. Westarp (43) v. 1, p. 36. Of the Free Conservative Reichstag fraction von Kardorff says, (86) p. 282, that in 1893 it consisted entirely of agrarians except for four mining people and one jurist.
105. Westarp (43) v. 1, p. 41, *indicates a Junker.

VI

CONCLUSION

A S WE conclude our study of the Junker official we realize that by a steady accumulation of findings and observations we have acquired certain definite new impressions and facts regarding his character and his opportunity for political influence. We recognize, first of all, that altho we have been dealing with "the" Junker official actually there is no definite single mould for the Junker administrator. We know now that it would even be impossible to draft a theoretically typical Junker. Our 1500 Junker officials represent a wide range of individual variations; and yet we have not been wrong in referring to the Junker official as a distinctive species because all of these men correspond in some ways or in others to the character of the central Junker stock. Moreover, altho Junker officials do not conform to a stereotyped pattern on the whole they are easily recognized as different from other officials.

Individual differences in background, career and temperament have their bearing upon the qualitative potentialities for political influence of Junker officials. If all were not equally "feudal" and aggressive in their conduct of their office then the significance of the numbers of Junkers serving in the various departments of the government must be qualified in this respect. Junker *Landraete* were generally dynamic political factors but even they varied in the degree of their political activity. In general there appear to have been three different kinds of *Landraete*—and probably of Junker officials in general. There was the old-fashioned *Landrat* who was independent, patriarchal, motivated largely by principles and interested above all in the welfare of his Circle. The old-fashioned Prussian particularist, Bogislav von Bonin-Bahrenbusch, belonged to this type. Then there was the "climber" or ambitious official[1] such as Hans von Dallwitz or Friedrich

1. Rudolf von Valentini (40) *Kaiser und Kabinettschef*, p. 90.

220

Wilhelm von Loebell, who sought by a zealous promotion of government policies and party interests to earn an advancement in the ranks and who was not interested primarily in the local district. Such a *Landrat* might have very great political influence but not as great independence of views. Lastly, there was the neutral bureaucrat such as Rudolf von Valentini, become somewhat bourgeois perhaps thru years of service, whose political influence would depend largely on the direction and encouragement which he received from the *Regierungs-Praesident* and from Berlin. But no matter how much of a routine bureaucrat a Junker official might become and no matter how little personal initiative he assumed in political affairs he would still be a factor of conservative influence because he took his orders from a series of conservative governments and because the basic conservative convictions of the Junker stock with which he was identified would prevent him from ever becoming a liberal.

Paradoxically enough the group of Junker officials and the families from which they came also possessed a high degree of social solidarity. As we know from our introductory survey they were bound together by certain historic traditions and fundamental traits which all of them possessed to some degree. In particular, they were united by a common desire to possess and exercise authority. Hence they preferred administrative to judicial offices and a *Landratsamt* to a post as *Regierungsrat*. Their ability to command and dispose, developed by the experience of centuries, also tended to make them preferred material for those offices which required the exercise of personal discretion and authority.

The social solidarity of the Junkers and their peculiar characteristics were preserved and perpetuated by their still highly exclusive marriage customs and their consistency in the choice of a career. It is remarkable that about half of the Junker officials studied here married within their own Junker group and that less than a quarter married commoners and made a break with aristocratic custom. Of the men in the thirteen typical Junker families, which include some failures and unusual characters, the number who married middle-class girls was less than 30%. Furthermore, one middle-class marriage did not necessarily mean a permanent deviation from the central Junker stock. The spouse might adopt the Junker code and viewpoint and the children frequently went back into the Junker fold when it came their turn to marry.

The first essential for the stability and preservation of the Junker social group—the maintenance of the birthrate—was provided for by the Junker custom of raising large families. Even in the face of economic reverses the Junkers continued not merely to perpetuate but actually to increase their numbers absolutely if not relatively by a birthrate which at its lowest was at least 2.85 per marriage. This fact has its political as well as its sociological significance, for it meant that the government still had at its disposal a reservoir, albeit a gradually shrinking one, of material for officials who would be politically reliable. Conversely, it made it possible for the Junker to maintain at least his absolute position in the administration and to keep the opportunities for political influence which this gave him.

Our findings on the habits of the Junker lead us to the further conclusion that he was even more exclusive and faithful to social custom in his choice of a profession than in his choice of a wife. One will recall that the great majority of the men from the thirteen typical families pursued the three traditional careers of farmer, army officer and administrative official. Only a very small proportion entered business or the free professions and the proportion of all those who entered upon definitely non-Junker pursuits was less than 10%. This fact together with our knowledge of the modest economic opportunities offered by the civil administration, the Officers Corps or the farming of a small estate, particularly after the agricultural depression, leads us to the conclusion that Junkers as a whole were more interested in the preservation of their traditions and in social respectability and security than they were in economic gain.

But they were determined that the economic position which they did possess, in particular their ownership of landed property, should not slip away from them. In their struggles to keep their estates going, which became more intense as agricultural prices dropped, they were fighting not only for their own economic survival but also, either consciously or unconsciously, for the preservation of their whole Junker group. For it was land-ownership above all which nourished the Junker spirit and was the essential factor in creating and preserving the solidarity of the Junkers as a social group. The ownership and cultivation of a knight's estate in East Elbia was the surest way of making a Junker out of a bourgeois and, conversely, continued separation from the land would inevitably starve and weaken a Junker's characteristic traits. The fact that the Junkers' estates, even in our period, lay almost without exception in East Elbia contributed to the solidarity of the group by giving it geographical unity and compactness.

In former times land-ownership fostered the independent and self-reliant spirit of the Junker. As long as grain prices were high he and his sons were not entirely dependent on the government for salaries or for legislation and they could afford to withdraw at will "behind the cannons of Schoenhausen." After the agricultural depression had set in the situation became quite different. Now the ownership of land produced insecurity and fear of bankruptcy and Junkers sought administrative offices not only to augment their slender incomes but also to use the political influence inherent in these offices to bolster up their position as landholders. The struggle of the Junker for his agrarian interests modified his character somewhat by drawing out certain qualities and suppressing others but it strengthened the sense of unity in the Junker group and reenforced the connection between the Junker character and landholding. It is undoubtedly true that the degree of political vigour and aggressiveness of the Junker official was determined in large part by the closeness of his connections with the land. If the Junker official owned a knight's estate he was probably resolved to exploit his office to promote agrarian interests no matter whether such action was in support of or in opposition to the government. Hence it sometimes happened as in the Canal Affair that the Junker's very insecurity made him more intransigeant in his opposition where his own interests were involved.

In this regard it is significant to recall that those offices in the Prussian State administration which showed the highest proportion of Junker landowners were the very offices which offered the greatest opportunities to exercise political influence and authority. About 37% of the Junker *Regierungs-* and *Ober-Praesidenten* and about 42% of the *Landraete* owned land. Thus, in general, the Junkers who wanted the most from their offices and who had, at least, the greatest need to exercise political vigour and audacity were in the posts which gave them the greatest opportunity.

In the regular administration, below the rank of *Regierungs-*

Praesident, only 10% of the Junkers owned land and among all the salaried Junker officials two-thirds were without landed property and over one-fourth were at least two generations removed from the land. This separation from the land, particularly in conjunction with administrative service, surely had a tendency to starve the Junker's peculiar characteristics until they withered away.

But loss of contact with the land was only one, if perhaps the most important, of many factors which tended to efface the essential Junker character of the Junker official. There were several aspects of the Junker's service in the Prussian State administration which united to make the Junker if not a bourgeois at least a bureaucrat with a point of view that was more *gouvernemental* than Junker. As we have noted, two or three generations of service in the administration, particularly when a family had lost its contact with the land, weakened the Junker character and tended to imbue the Junker official with a bureaucratic viewpoint. The transfer of Junker officials from their natural environment in the east to the more bourgeois and liberal west of Prussia had a similar effect which, again, was intensified by the officials' loss of contact with the land. The sense of economic security which came with an administrative office because of the policy of fixity of tenure and the pension system would also tend to transfer the Junker official's loyalty and allegiance from his own social group to the government, again especially if his connections with his group had been weakened by his loss of landed property. Long tenure itself and years of experience in office, if not a *Landratsamt* or provincial office, would also have a tendency to transform the Junker official into a bureaucrat and a government agent. Thus, altho the government might require certain qualifications for appointment to administrative office such as conservative principles and the "feudal" viewpoint of certain aristocratic students corps and regiments—qualifications which the Junkers were particularly well prepared to meet—nonetheless the Junker who entered office as a Junker and a conservative might be converted by long years of service to a more liberal point of view.[2]

2. One will recall the statement of a high government official, "Wir kommen fast alle konservativ ins Amt und nach zwei Jahren hat uns die Logik der Tatsachen liberal gemacht." Gustav Schmoller (148) "Die preussische Wahlrechtsreform von 1910 auf dem Hintergrunde des Kampfes zwischen Koenigtum und Feudalitaet", *Schmollers Jb. f. Gesetzgeb.,* 1910, p. 1269.

Obviously not all offices had an equally bureaucratizing influence on the Junker officials. Indeed, one could expect that years of service in a *Landratsamt* in East Elbia might have the opposite effect. For the *Landratsamt* was the one office in the Prussian State administration which was especially suited to the Junker character and which therefore tended to preserve and foster it. Because of its peculiar characteristics the *Landratsamt* was the dynamic centre of Junker influence in the administration as well as the nerve centre of the Prussian administration itself. Its semi-communal, even semi-feudal character, its frequent association with local and provincial self-governing offices and in particular its close contact with landholding, for about 42% of the Junker *Landraete* in our period were landholders, made it in East Elbia a natural and congenial post for the Junker. The fact that it could be entered directly from communal offices and that it was generally considered as an end in itself[3] emphasized its "feudal" as against its bureaucratic character. Because of the opportunity which it offered for political activity, the *Landratsamt* was the office in the Prussian State administration which was most frequently combined with a seat in the Prussian Diet. This was an added attraction for the Junker, particularly the Junker landholder who was agitating for agrarian legislation, because it gave him added opportunity to promote his Junker interests.

Paradoxically enough the *Landratsamt* was attractive not only to the thoroughgoing Junker as an end in itself but also to the ambitious bureaucrat as a step to higher offices. For we know from our analyses that the *Landrat* had a better chance than any other official of the same rank of being promoted to higher offices. It has become very evident in the course of this study that the *Landratsamt* was the one office in the Prussian State administration which offered the greatest opportunities to the Junker, the career official and the politician.

After reviewing the several ways in which administrative offices, with the exception of the *Landratsamt,* might bureaucratize the Junker official we are forced to the conclusion that where several of these influences came to bear upon the same individual he was likely to lose much of his Junker character. Indeed, one may go so far as to say that the transformation of the Junker character by administrative

3. Only 20% of the Junker *Landraete* examined here went on to higher offices.

service was the greatest single force undermining the solidarity of
the Junker group and drawing Junkers away from their own genuine
central stock. But if officeholding made Junker officials less thoroughly
Junker it did not necessarily make them bourgeois. Undoubtedly it
drew them in the direction of the middle class and some of them
may actually have become thoroughly bourgeois. What is more likely
is that they became simply service nobility and *gouvernemental* and
were identified with that large group of civil officials with its own
esprit de corps which has been called the "aristocracy of office."

It is obvious that the process of bureaucratizing the Junkers had
its effect upon the capacity for political influence of the already small
numbers of Junkers holding office between 1888 and 1914. We find
we cannot assume that all the Junkers serving in the administration
were equally strong in their Junker attitudes and would exert an
equally Junker influence thru their offices. The degree of Junker
influence as first suggested by the figures alone is diminished by this
process. But it is counteracted to some extent by the corresponding
Junker process of "feudalizing" the bourgeois officials. We assume
from the accounts of their contemporaries and from our own rough
analyses[4] that the Junkers did "feudalize" a large but indefinite
number of bourgeois officials and that this development would increase both the numbers of officials with Junker attitudes and the
potentials, if not of the pure Junker influence, at least of that peculiar
"feudal" and agrarian Conservatism which was an outgrowth of the
Junker traditions in eastern Prussia. We are much more certain of
the fact that Junker officials were bureaucratized and drawn away
from the Junker circle by the tradition and experience of officeholding.
It is impossible in either case to make specific deductions or additions
to the given figures because of the intangible and imponderable nature
of these influences.

The party affiliations of the Junker official and his standing in
his party are other intangible factors which modify the meaning of
the plain figures when one is considering the capacity for political
influence of the Junker official. We have every reason to believe both
that the vast majority of Junker officials and of Junkers in general

4. See above, Chapter V, p. 193f.

were associated with the Conservative party and also that it was the Conservative party which controlled the political situation in Prussia.[5] This substantially enhanced the political power of the Junker official because it meant that he had the backing of the dominant political party. It is obvious that a Conservative *Landrat, Ober-Regierungsrat* or *Regierungs-Praesident* was in a position to accomplish more politically than a Centrist or National Liberal official because he was working in harmony with the Conservative party and, for the most part, also with a Conservative government.

When we come to consider the influence of the Junker official and of the Junker in general upon the policies of the Conservative party we find that it had declined. Altho the Junkers still joined the Conservative party almost without exception and altho Junker officials made a definite and valued contribution to its strength their position had been weakened by the adoption of the modern organization and the new policies and tactics which had been forced on the party by the new, militant agrarian faction.

The most significant development within the Conservative party during our period was, of course, the formation of the Agrarian League in 1893. This League was organized for the express purpose of protecting landowners, particularly those with large holdings, from unfavorable agricultural prices and the Caprivi commercial treaties and promoting agrarian interests in general. It was, therefore, definitely a narrow economic pressure group, but despite its limited and materialistic objectives it was able by 1894 to force the *Kreuzzeitung* group under Stoecker and Hammerstein out of control of the Conservative party and to assume the party leadership. Thus the extreme agrarian wing of the party was able to dominate the party councils and it renovated the party structure and principles along modern demagogic and materialistic lines. The old principle of monarchical loyalty combined with independence of conviction was offset by narrow economic interests and self-centred stubborness.[6] Altho the

---

5. See, *inter alia,* Fuerst Chlodwig zu Hohenlohe-Schillingsfuerst (33) *Denkwuerdigkeiten der Reichskanzlerzeit,* pp. 10, 523; Graf Kuno Westarp (43) *Konservative Politik . . .,* v. 1, pp. 291-92, 390.

6. See, *inter alia,* Arthur Dix (61) *Der Bund der Landwirte, . . . ,* p. 47; Hans Delbrueck (128) "Die Massregelung der Beamten-Abgeordneten", *Preuss. Jb.,* 1899, p. 182; Heinrich Heffter (74) Die *Kreuzzeitungspartei . . . ,* p. 257.

Agrarian League reiterated its loyalty to the Crown it also insisted that
the King and his government give it unqualified support—otherwise
it threatened to go into opposition. As von Ploetz-Doellingen, an
executive director of the Agrarian League, said, ". . . we support
authority but only if it is the right authority."[7] Because of its intransigeant promotion of its own interests the Agrarian League
frequently dragged the Conservative party into opposition to the
King's government.

This ruthless and extreme agrarian type of leadership was not
congenial to all Junkers nor even to all conservatives.[8] The demagogic
and rabble-rousing tactics of the League, its narrow and sordid
economic interests and its tendency to oppose the government over
the slightest issue were repugnant to the old and loyal Junker of
principle. There were many Junkers who were not repelled by the
League, however. Those who were more modern, more aggressive
and more self-assertive welcomed and supported this forceful agrarian
movement and some of these men acquired positions of prominence
and leadership within the League. Thus we find among its executive
directors such men as the aforementioned Berthold von Ploetz-
Doellingen, also Baron Konrad von Wangenheim-Klein Spiegel,
Count Kanitz-Podangen as well as Elard von Oldenburg-Januschau
and others. In fact, in spite of its mass methods the Agrarian League
was controlled by an aristocratic and economic elite, i.e., by large
landholders, both noble and bourgeois, for bourgeois agrarians such
as Ruprecht, Roesicke and the journalist, Dr. Hahn, took their place
alongside Junkers and other nobles in the direction of the Agrarian
League. The presence of these commoners in the most dynamic and
strategic councils of the Conservative party together with the aloofness
of some of the old-fashioned Junkers is not without its significance
for the political influence of the Junkers.

7. Dix (61) p. 19.
8. Wilhelm von Massow (97) *Die deutsche innere Politik unter Kaiser
Wilhelm II*, pp. 246-47, writes "Die besonnenen konservativen Kreise bewahrten
sich ihr warmes Herz fuer die landwirtschaftlichen Interessen, aber sie waren doch
zum Teil erschreckt ueber die demagogische und masslose, der konservativen Grund-
saetzen widersprechende Art, in der der Bund der Landwirte in den Kaempfen um
den Zolltarif seine einseitigen und weitgehenden Ansprueche gegenueber einer wohl-
wollenden und entgegenkommenden Regierung vertrat."

Actually, so far as I can tell, the proportion of Junkers within the Agrarian League does seem to be somewhat smaller than for the Conservative party as a whole. Out of the first Executive Committee of seven members only two were Junkers.[9] In 1901, 21% of the Directors and 20% of the Executive Committee were Junkers[10] and out of a committee of twenty-five in 1903, eight or 32% were Junkers.[11] It is therefore apparent that the rise of the Agrarian League to control of the Conservative party tended to diminish the influence of the Junkers upon it, either by alienating them and crowding them out of the party councils or by converting them to a thoroughly material and selfish point of view which left little room for old Junker principles.

Nevertheless, there can be no doubt that the Junkers and particularly the Junker officials in the party made a very considerable contribution to its strength and to that of the Agrarian League. Altho the latter was a modern political pressure group exploiting the technics of mass propaganda and parliamentary strategy, it also welcomed every opportunity to further its ends, particularly at election time, thru the administrative officials who supported it and were its members. In fact, we would expect the Agrarian League to be quick to take advantage of this interior position. There are many indications that considerable numbers of administrative officials in the east belonged to the League, and used their offices to promote its interests. Count Westarp writes of joining it while *Landrat* of Kreis Bomst, "The leading Germans in the Circle Assembly and the landowners with whom I associated socially and on hunting parties were preponderantly members of the Agrarian League. I also soon joined it." And he adds, "When in 1899 over twenty *Landraete* were dismissed for not voting for the Canal Bill, we *Landraete* were asked to withdraw from the Agrarian League." Westarp refused to comply at that time but he later resigned.[12] It was at such times when the Agrarian League ruthlessly opposed the Government that the agitation to prohibit officials from belonging to the League was most ac-

9. J. Croner (55) *Die Geschichte der agrarischen Bewegung in Deutschland,* p. 137.

10. *Materialien zum Zolltariff* (98), *Hefte* 1-12.

11. *Agrarisches Handbuch* (9) p. 198.

12. Westarp (43) v. 1, p. 4.

tive.[13] In 1899, at the height of the Canal crisis, Viktor Schweinburg told Chancellor von Hohenlohe that "a dissolution [of the House of Deputies] would have no favorable results with these officials in office as long as the organs of the Government went hand in hand with the Agrarian League"[14] and Hohenlohe himself added in a letter to his son, "To dissolve the Chamber without first tearing the officials away from the League would not do much good. Above all, the administration must be cleaned out."[15] But resolutions to rid the service of its League members failed. In March, 1900, even the Crown Council decided that officials should be forbidden to be members of the Agrarian League or to work for favors for it with their superiors, but Hohenlohe writes, "This did not take place, but an honest and trusty agrarian explained that the Conservative party *couldn't* separate itself from the Agrarian League. It had too great need of the latter, and this seems to be the opinion of the *Landraete* as well."[16] Here the reason for failure seems to have been that to break with the Agrarian League would bring the downfall of the Conservative party and this the government would not or could not contemplate.

We can expect that Junker officials who were members of the Conservative party and of the Agrarian League as well would use their position and influence to promote the interests of their party and of this agrarian pressure group. Since the party had been modernized in program and tactics in large part by the League, and since party discipline had been tightened, it is even probable that many of these Junker officials acted as the tools of the party whereas in earlier days a Junker's support of the Conservative party was based rather on his own political principles and his individual attitude toward the government. Technically, officials were more and more expected to be impartial and non-political, devoted only to the Crown. But we may assume that actually large numbers of the Conservative party men were promoting the interests of their party under the guise of non-partisanship. As Max Weber has said, "Domination by officials is

13. Hans Herzfeld (76) *Johannes von Miquel*, v. 2, p. 328; Chlodwig von Hohenlohe (33) p. 567.
14. Chlodwig von Hohenlohe (33) p. 522.
15. *Ibid.*, p. 523.
16. *Ibid.*, p. 567.

in no way no party domination."[17] In this disguised party rule the Conservatives insisted on all the advantages. Altho they maintained that the government should favor them against its will they often refused to support the government against their will, as, for instance in the commercial treaties, the canal bill or the Prussian electoral reform. Thus we have the paradox of a Conservative party opposed on principle to a responsible ministry and yet threatening to defeat any government which tried to govern against or without it. To be a Conservative official meant, then, to work for the party as well as for the government and to have the support of the party even against the government. This would tend both to counteract the bureaucratizing effect of officeholding upon the Junker official and to increase his capacity for political influence but it would also curtail his independence and freedom of political action.

If we review the actual numbers of Junkers holding administrative offices, which give us our most concrete evidence of the extent of the Junker officials' potential political influence, we are again struck with the fact that they are small—much smaller than one is led to expect from a study of the general literature on the period.[18] They give positive evidence that, after all, the Junkers were not, numerically speaking, the prevailing social and political group in the Prussian administration. Moreover, the figures show very definitely that the Junker power in the administration was sectional. Even Junkers in the regular administration were assigned more frequently to posts east of the Elbe than to the west. The relatively high concentration of the small numbers of Junker officials in one area put them in a position of dominance in that part of Prussia, however, and it also tended to check the bureaucratizing effect of officeholding by fostering the "feudal" atmosphere there. But it was counterbalanced by the predominance of middle-class, non-partisan and even liberal officials in western Prussia.[19]

17. Max Weber (156) "Parlament und Regierung im neugeordneten Deutschland," *Gesammelte politische Schriften,* p. 181.

18. The numbers of Junker officials were small even in 1888 at the close of the Puttkamer regime when, according to all reports, the administrative service had been filled with conservatives.

19. Our figures substantiate the following comment by Gustav Schmoller, (148) *Schmollers Jb. f. Gesetzgeb.,* 1910, p. 1269, on the character of Prussian officials in the east and in the west, "Freilich haben wir im Osten noch heute [1910] viel

It is, of course, true that the potential political influence of the small numbers of Junker officials was enhanced by several of the imponderable factors referred to above. The actual numbers of officials exerting a Junker influence were undoubtedly increased by the practice of "feudalizing" the bourgeoisie. The capacity for influence of Junker officials was also extended by their affiliation and cooperation with the dominant political party. In those instances where the individual official owned land and, in particular, where he also possessed a robust and ruthless personality the incentive for an aggressive political exploitation of officeholding was great. But over against these factors which contributed to the capacity for political influence of the Junker officials we must set those influences which detracted from it such as the bureaucratizing effect of officeholding which reduced the numbers of officials exerting a Junker influence, the loss of land-ownership, which removed the incentive for aggressive political action, and the loss of control of the Conservative party by the Junkers, which weakened their influence on policy-making.

Furthermore we must take into account the important fact that the numbers of Junkers in the administration were slowly but definitely declining during our period. The statistics show a slight but persistent decrease in the proportion of Junker officials in almost every department of the government. This decline was, as we know, not due to any consistent effort on the part of succeeding governments to reduce the numbers of Junkers in the administration. It was the result, rather, of the inevitable progress of the age. The increasing amount and complexity of the work which multiplied the offices and increased the requirements for trained technicians and the pressure of the rising tide of the bourgeoisie in a middle-class world at the end of the 19th century made inevitable a relative decline in the numbers of Junker officials.

The findings both as to the actual numbers of Junker officials and their decline make necessary a re-evaluation of the frequent vehement outbursts of contemporary liberal critics such as Max Weber against the "Junker regime" in the administration. The many attacks on the

---

konservative Landraete und Regierungs-Praesidenten, und manche moegen dem Bunde der Landwirte naeher stehen als der Regierung. Aber dafuer ueberwiegt in den Mittleren und Westprovinzen der liberale oder neutrale Character."

Junkers have their value insofar as they indicate that the presence of the Junkers in office was a serious obstacle to political progress. Also the contrast between the fury and persistence of these attacks and the actually quite small numbers of Junker officials gives weight to the conclusion that the numbers of Junker satellites must have been large. In general we must say, however, that these complaints by the liberals give an exaggerated impression of the actual numbers of Junkers in office. But we agree with them in their basic claims that the Junkers exercised great political power in Prussia. For even after one has taken into account all the qualifying factors one must conclude that the Junkers were a strong organized minority and that they drew their power not only from the advantages of their traditional and constitutional position in Prussia, their influence over the Officers Corps and their political arrangements, such as the *Sammlung*, with the National Liberals and the Centrists, but also from their position in the administration where the numbers, altho small, were distributed by the government in such a way, both geographically and among the offices, as to give a high degree of political effectiveness. They undoubtedly formed a powerful barrier to the progress of democratic reforms in Prussia before the last war.

Moreover, the Junker's power was remarkably slow to weaken. That the Junker with his feudal, patriarchal, and privileged attitude toward society should decline in power and influence in a modern, industrial and businessman's age is not surprising. The falling-off in the numbers of Junkers in the administration—and also in the Officers Corps[20]—was actually but a part of a fundamental, thoroughgoing and inevitable altho still sub-surface weakening of the Junkers' traditional social, political and economic position in the Prussian State. What astonishes us is that the Junkers, who were an anachronism both politically and socially, could retain so much power and influence down into the 20th century. Many of the complex and confusing characteristics of present-day Germany spring from the fact that the Junker barrier was strong enough to hold back the course of progress. Whatever our views on Junker principles and policies we cannot but admire the toughness and tenaciousness of the Junker grip on the sources of social and political power. Not their decline

20. Karl Demeter (59) *Das deutsche Heer und seine Offiziere, passim.*

GLOSSARY

The terms, both German and English, which are used in the text are listed alphabetically in the left-hand column. Definitions or German equivalents are given in the right-hand column.

Abiturienten examination	Examination offered at conclusion of the course in the Gymnasium or secondary school
Agrarian League	*Bund der Landwirte*
Assessor	Official of lowest rank in the higher administrative or judicial service; legally qualified for all higher posts
Cabinet	*Kabinett; Geheimes Kabinett*
Central Audit Chamber	*Ober-Rechnungskammer*
Chamber for War and Domains	*Kriegs- und Domaenenkammer*
Circle	*Kreis*
Circle Assembly	*Kreisversammlung; Kreistag*
Circle Delegate	*Kreisdeputierter*
Circle Director	*Kreisdirektor*
Circle Executive Committee	*Kreisausschuss*
Contribution	Land tax introduced by Elector in the 17th century
Counsellor	*Rat*
Diet	*Landtag*
District administrative court	*Verwaltungsgericht*
District Committee	*Bezirks-Ausschuss*
Eastern Marches Association	*Ostmarkenverein*
Ensign	*Faehnrich*
Evangelical Supreme Church Council	*Evangelischer Ober-Kirchenrat*
Forest Inspector	*Forstmeister*
Forstrat	Official of intermediate rank in the forestry service of the higher administration
General Supreme Finance, War, and Domains Directory	*General Ober Finanz-, Kriegs- und Domaenendirektorium*
Gerichts-Assessor	Official of lowest rank in higher judicial service; corresponds to *Regierungs-Assessor* in administrative service

235

Gerichts-Referendar	Apprentice in higher judicial service, training to become *Gerichts-Assessor*
Governmental district	*Regierungs-Bezirk*
Gutsherr	Owner and cultivator of a *Gutsherrschaft*
Gutsherrschaft	Large landed estate cultivated by the landlord himself thru the use of peasants attached to the soil, later of agricultural laborers; peculiar to eastern Prussia
Herrenhaus	Upper house of the Prussian Diet
House of Deputies	*Abgeordnetenhaus*
Judge	*Rat*, e.g., *Oberlandesgerichtsrat*
Kammerpraesident	Head of a Chamber of War and Domains; later called *Regierungs-Praesident*
Knight's estate	*Rittergut*
Kreuzzeitung	News organ of the Right Wing Prussian Conservatives
Kultusministerium	Ministry for Religious, Educational, and Medical Affairs
Landesdirektor	Same as *Landeshauptmann*
Landeshauptmann	Executive head of provincial self-government, elected by Provincial Diet
Landrat	Official, of same rank as *Regierungsrat*, in charge of a Circle; acted both as agent for the Prussian State administration and executive head of Circle self-government
Landratsamt	Office of *Landrat*
Landschaft	Co-operative land credit institution
Light Infantry	*Jaeger*
Ober-Praesident	Official of Prussian State administration who acted as political and administrative head of a province
Ober-Praesidialrat	First assistant of an *Ober-Praesident;* somewhat above rank of *Ober-Regierungsrat*
Ober-Praesidium	Unit of government, headed by an *Ober-Praesident,* which administered a province for the central government
Ober-Regierungsrat	Official superior to a *Regierungsrat* who assisted and collaborated with a *Regierungs-President* or served in a Ministry
Owner of a knight's estate	*Rittergutsbesitzer*
Provincial Council	*Provinzialrat*
Provincial Executive Committee	*Provinzial-Ausschuss* or *Verband*

Provincial Supreme Court	*Oberlandesgericht*
Provincial Synodal Committee	*Provinzial Synodal Vorstand*
Public prosecutor	*Staatsanwalt*
Rat	Counsellor; judge in such cases as *Oberlandesgerichtsrat*
Referendar	Apprentice in higher administrative or judicial service, training to become an *Assessor*
Regierung	Unit of government, headed by a *Regierungs-Praesident,* which administered a governmental district, subdivision of a province, for the central government
Regierungs-Assessor	Official of lowest rank in the higher administrative service; legally qualified for all higher administrative offices
Regierungs-Praesident	Administrative head of a governmental district, subdivision of a province, for the central government
Regierungsrat	Administrative official, immediately superior to a *Regierungs-Assessor,* who served in all branches of the Prussian State administration
Regierungs-Referendar	Apprentice in higher administrative service; training to become a *Regierungs-Assessor*
Ritterschaft	Name given to *Landschaft* in Brandenburg
Rittmeister	Cavalry Captain
Royal Household	*Hofstaat*
Serfage	*Leibeigenschaft*
Staatsministerium	Prussian Government or Council of Ministers
Staendestaat	Mediaeval form of the State in which the upper social groups were divided into Estates—each with its own functions, obligations, and privileges—which claimed and exercised the right to rule along with the prince
Staendisch	Of or pertaining to the feudal Estates and to the political and social principles basic to the feudal Estates system.
Steuerrat	Administrative agent of Chambers of War and Domains in cities, corresponded to *Landrat* in Circles
Supreme Administrative Court	*Oberverwaltungsgericht*

Surveyor   *Baurat*
Top Forester   *Oberfoerster*
Village   *Landgemeinde*
Vortragender Rat High-ranking administrative official in a
                    Ministry who was qualified to make re-
                    ports directly to the Minister

BIBLIOGRAPHY

OFFICIAL PUBLICATIONS

The most important official source of information about the personnel of the Prussian Administration is the *Handbuch ueber den Koeniglich preussischen Hof und Staat*, a publication of the Prussian State which has appeared annually since 1795. Other official publications follow:

1. Germany, Reichstag, *Der Reichshaushalts-Etat.*
2. Germany, Kaiserliches Statistisches Amt, *Statistisches Jahrbuch fuer das deutsche Reich*, 1880-.
3. Prussia, *Gesetzsammlung fuer die Koeniglich preussischen Staaten*, 1810-1923.
4. Prussia, Landtag, *Der Staatshaushalts-Etat.*
5. Prussia, *Rangliste der Koeniglich preussischen Armee*, Berlin, 1855-.
6. Prussia, Statistisches Bureau, *Jahrbuch fuer die amtliche Statistik des preussischen Staates*, vols. 4-5, Berlin, 1876, 1883.
7. Prussia, Statistisches Bureau, *General-Register zum Gemeinde-Lexicon fuer das Koenigreich Preussen*, 2 vols., Berlin, 1898.
8. *Verhandlungen* of the Provinzial-Landtag of Brandenburg, East Prussia, Pomerania, Posen, Saxony, Silesia, and West Prussia.

UNOFFICIAL HANDBOOKS

9. *Agrarisches Handbuch*, ed. Bund der Landwirte, 2nd edition, Berlin, 1903.
10. *Gothaisches Genealogisches Taschenbuch: der Graeflichen Haeuser*, Gotha, 1826-.
11. ——: *der Freiherrlichen Haeuser*, Gotha, 1848-.
12. ——: *der Uradeligen Haeuser*, Gotha, 1900-.
13. ——: *der Briefadeligen Haeuser*, Gotha, 1907-.
14. *Handbuch des Grundbesitzes im deutschen Reiche*, 10 vols., Berlin, 1888-1912.
15. *Jahrbuch des deutschen Adels*, ed. Deutsche Adelsgenossenschaft, 3 vols., Berlin, 1896-1899.
16. *Koesener-Korpslisten, 1789 bis 1904*, ed. Karl Ruegemer, Starnberg bei Muenchen, 1905.
17. Ledebur, Leopold, Freiherr von, *Adelslexicon der preussischen Monarchie*, 3 vols., Berlin, 1855.
18. Mueller-Jabusch, Maximilian, *Politischer Almanach*, Berlin, 1925.
19. *Wer Ist's*, ed. H. A. L. Degener, Leipzig, 1905-.

20. Zedlitz-Neukirch, L., Freiherr von, *Neues Preussisches Adels-Lexicon*, 4 vols., Leipzig, 1836-1839.

AUTOBIOGRAPHICAL WORKS

21. Bismarck, Otto, Fuerst von, *Bismarckbriefe, 1836-1872*, ed. Horst Kohl, 6th edition, Bielefeld and Leipzig, 1897.

22. ———, *Gedanken und Erinnerungen*, 2 vols., Stuttgart and Berlin, 1905, Volks-Ausgabe.

23. Braun, Otto, *Von Weimar zu Hitler*, 2nd edition, New York, 1940.

24. Buelow, Bernhard, Fuerst von, *Memoirs*, trs. F. A. Voight and Geoffrey Dunlop, 4 vols., Boston, 1931-32.

25. Dallwitz, Hans von, "Aus dem Nachlass des ehemaligen Kaiserlichen Statthalters von Elsass-Lothringen, frueheren Preussischen Ministers des Innern von Dallwitz," ed. Albert von Mutius, *Preussische Jahrbuecher*, v. 214 (1928) pp. 1-22; 147-166; 290-303.

26. *Die politischen Testamente der Hohenzollern nebst ergaenzenden Aktenstuecken*, eds. Georg Kuentzel and Martin Hass, 2 vols., Leipzig and Berlin, 1911.

27. Eckardstein, Hermann, Freiherr von, *Lebenserinnerungen und politische Denkwuerdigkeiten*, 3 vols., Leipzig, 1919-20.

28. Ernst von Ernsthausen, A., *Erinnerungen eines preussischen Beamten*, Bielefeld and Leipzig, 1897.

29. Eulenburg, Philipp, Fuerst zu, *Aus 50 Jahren*, ed. Johannes Haller, Berlin, 1923.

30. ———, *Mit dem Kaiser als Staatsmann und Freund, auf Nordlandreisen*, 2 vols., Dresden, 1931.

31. Gerlach, Hellmuth von, *Von Rechts nach Links*, ed. Emil Ludwig, Zurich, 1937.

32. Hohenlohe, Alexander von, *Aus meinem Leben*, Frankfurt, 1925.

33. Hohenlohe-Schillingsfuerst, Chlodwig, Fuerst zu, *Denkwuerdigkeiten der Reichskanzlerzeit*, ed. Karl Alexander von Mueller, Stuttgart and Berlin, 1931.

34. Hutten-Czapski, Bogdan, Graf von, *Sechzig Jahre Politik und Gesellschaft*, 2 vols., Berlin, 1936.

35. Jagemann, Eugen von, *Fuenfundsiebzig Jahre des Erlebens und Erfahrens*, Heidelberg, 1925.

36. Lucius von Ballhausen, Robert, Freiherr von, *Bismarck-Erinnerungen*, Stuttgart and Berlin, 1921.

37. Oldenburg-Januschau, Elard von, *Erinnerungen*, Leipzig, 1936.

38. Reischach, Hugo, Freiherr von, *Under Three Emperors*, tr. Prince Bluecher, London, 1927.

39. Schweinitz, Hans Lothar von, *Denkwuerdigkeiten des Botschafters General von Schweinitz*, ed. Wilhelm von Schweinitz, 2 vols., Berlin, 1927.

40. Valentini, Rudolf von, *Kaiser und Kabinettschef*, ed. B. Schwertfeger, Oldenburg, 1931.

41. Waldersee, Alfred, Graf von, *Denkwuerdigkeiten des General-Feld-marschalls Alfred Grafen von Waldersee*, ed. Heinrich O. Meisner, 3 vols., Stuttgart and Berlin, 1923-25.

42. Wermuth, Adolf, *Ein Beamtenleben*, Berlin, 1922.

43. Westarp, Kuno, Graf von, *Konservative Politik im letzten Jahrzehnt des Kaiserreiches*, 2 vols., Berlin, 1935.

44. Wilamowitz-Moellendorf, Ulrich von, *Erinnerungen, 1848-1914*, 2nd edition, Leipzig, 1929.

45. Wilhelm II, Kaiser, *Ereignisse und Gestalten aus den Jahren 1878-1918*, Leipzig and Berlin, 1922.

46. Zedlitz-Truetzschler, Robert, Graf von, *Twelve Years at the Imperial German Court*, tr. Alfred Kalisch, Garden City, New York, 1924.

SECONDARY WORKS

47. Altmann, Paul, *Die Verfassung und Verwaltung im deutschen Reiche und Preussen*, 2 vols., Berlin, 1908.

48. Altrock, Walter von, *Der Landwirtschaftliche Kredit in Preussen*, Berlin, 1914.

49. Arnim, H. von, and Below, G. von, *Deutscher Aufstieg, Bilder aus der Vergangenheit und Gegenwart der rechtsstehenden Parteien*, Berlin, 1924.

50. Bergstraesser, Ludwig, *Die preussische Wahlrechtsfrage im Kriege und die Entstehung der Osterbotschaft, 1917*, Tuebingen, 1929.

51. Bitter, von, *Handwoerterbuch der preussischen Verwaltung*, 2 vols., 3rd edition, 1928.

52. Bornhak, Conrad, *Preussisches Staatsrecht*, 2 vols., Freiburg i.B., 1888.

53. Brentano, Lujo, *Familienfideikommissee und ihre Wirkung*, in *Volks-wirtschaftliche Zeitfragen*, Heft 258, Berlin, 1911.

54. Bruenneck, Wilhelm von, *Die Pfandbriefsysteme der preussischen Landschaften*, Berlin, 1910.

55. Croner, J., *Die Geschichte der agrarischen Bewegung in Deutschland*, Berlin, 1909.

56. Crueger, Hermann, *Chronik des preussischen Herrenhauses*, Berlin, 1885.

57. Daniels, H. G. *The Rise of the German Republic*, New York, 1928.

58. Delbrueck, Clemens von, *Die Ausbildung fuer den hoeheren Ver-waltungsdienst in Preussen*, Jena, 1917.

59. Demeter, Karl, *Das deutsche Heer und seine Offiziere*, Berlin, 1935.

60. Dewitz, Hermann von, *Von Bismarck bis Bethmann, Innenpolitische Rueckblicke eines Konservativen*, Konservative Schriftenvertriebs-stelle. 1918.

61. Dix, Arthur, *Der Bund der Landwirte, Entstehung, Wesen und politische Taetigkeit,* Berlin, 1909.

62. Erdmannsdoerffer, Bernhard, *Deutsche Geschichte vom Westfaelischen Frieden bis zum Regierungsantritt Friedrichs des Grossen, 1648-1740,* 2 vols., Berlin, 1892-93.

63. Eschenburg, Theodor, *Das Kaiserreich am Scheideweg: Bassermann, Buelow und der Block,* Berlin, 1929.

64. Fontane, Theodor, *Briefe an seine Familie,* in *Gesammelte Werke,* vol. 2, Berlin, 1924.

65. ——, *Der Stechlin,* 13th edition, Berlin, 1906.

66. Ford, Guy Stanton, *Stein and the Era of Reform in Prussia,* Princeton, 1922.

67. Frank, Walter, *Hofprediger Adolf Stoecker und die christlichsoziale Bewegung,* 2nd edition, Hamburg, 1935.

68. Gerlach, Hellmuth von, *Die Geschichte des preussischen Wahlrechts,* Berlin, 1908.

69. Gerloff, Wilhelm, *Die Finanz- und Zollpolitik des deutschen Reiches nebst ihren Beziehungen zu Landes- und Gemeindefinanzen, von der Gruendung des Norddeutschen Bundes bis zur Gegenwart,* Jena, 1913.

70. Gothein, Georg, *Agrarpolitisches Handbuch,* Berlin, 1910-11.

71. Grimm, Jacob and Wilhelm, *Deutsches Woerterbuch,* 4 vols., Leipzig, 1854-1911.

72. Hammann, Otto, *Der neue Kurs,* Berlin, 1918.

73. ——, *Um den Kaiser,* Berlin, 1918.

74. Heffter, Heinrich, *Die Kreuzzeitungspartei und die Kartellpolitik Bismarcks,* Leipzig, 1927.

75. Herrfurth, Gustav, *Das gesamte preussische Etats- Kassen- und Rechnungswesen,* 5 vols., 4th edition, Berlin, 1905.

76. Herzfeld, Hans, *Johannes von Miquel,* 2 vols., Detmold, 1938.

77. Heuss, Theodor E., *Friedrich Naumann,* Stuttgart, 1937.

78. Hintze, Otto, *Einleitende Darstellung der Behoerdenorganisation und allgemeinen Verwaltung in Preussen beim Regierungsantritt Friedrich II,* in *Die Behoerdenorganisation und die allgemeine Staatsverwaltung Preussens im 18. Jahrhundert,* vol. 4:1, Berlin, 1901.

79. ——, *Historische und Politische Aufsaetze,* 4 vols., 2nd edition, Berlin, 1908.

80. ——, *Die Hohenzollern und ihr Werk,* Berlin, 1915.

81. Hue de Grais, Graf, *Handbuch der Verfassung und Verwaltung,* 17th edition, Berlin, 1906.

82. Jaeckh, Ernst, *Kiderlen-Waechter, der Staatsmann und der Mensch,* 2 vols., Berlin and Leipzig, 1925.

83. James, Herman Gerlach, *Principles of Prussian Administration,* New York, 1913.

84. Jordan, Erich, *Friedrich Wilhelm IV und der preussische Adel bei Umwandlung der ersten Kammer in das Herrenhaus, 1850 bis 1854,* Berlin, 1909.

85. ——, *Die Entstehung der konservativen Partei und die preussischen Agrarverhaeltnisse von 1848,* Munich and Leipzig, 1914.

86. Kardorff, Siegfried von, *Wilhelm von Kardorff, ein nationaler Parlamentarier im Zeitalter Bismarcks und Wilhelm II, 1828-1907,* Berlin, 1936.

87. Kehr, Eckart, *Schlachtflottenbau und Parteipolitik, 1894-1901,* Berlin, 1930.

88. Keyserling, Eduard von, *Abendliche Haeuser,* Berlin, 1923.

89. Koch, Walter, *Volk und Staatsfuehrung vor dem Weltkriege,* Stuttgart, 1935.

90. Kohn-Bramstedt, Ernst, *Aristocracy and the Middle Classes in Germany: Social Types in German Literature, 1830-1900,* London, 1938.

91. Kroeger, Karl H., *Die Konservativen und die Politik Caprivis,* Rostock, 1937.

92. Lamprecht, Karl, *Deutsche Geschichte,* 12 vols., Berlin, 1894-1909.

93. Leuss, Hans, *Wilhelm, Freiherr von Hammerstein,* Berlin, 1905.

94. Lorentz, F., *Geschichte der Kaschuben,* Berlin, 1926.

95. ——, et al., *The Cassubian Civilization,* London, 1935.

96. Marcks, Erich, *Bismarcks Jugend, 1815-1848,* in *Bismarck, eine Biographie,* v. 1, 17th edition, Stuttgart and Berlin, 1915.

97. Massow, Wilhelm von, *Die deutsche innere Politik unter Kaiser Wilhelm II,* Stuttgart and Leipzig, 1913.

98. *Materialien zum Zolltariff,* ed. Bund der Landwirte, Hefte 1-12, 1901.

99. Mauer, Hermann, *Das Landschaftliche Kreditwesen Preussens agrargeschichtlich und volkswirtschaftlich betrachtet,* Strassburg, 1907.

100. Meier, Ernst von, *Franzoesische Einfluesse auf die Staats- und Rechtsentwicklung Preussens im 19. Jahrhundert,* Munich, 1908.

101. ——, *Die Reform der Verwaltungsorganisation unter Stein und Hardenberg,* Munich, 1912.

102. Meinecke, Friedrich, *Radowitz und die deutsche Revolution,* Berlin, 1913.

103. Nadolny, Rudolf, *Germanisierung oder Slavisierung?* Berlin, (?, after 1925).

104. Neumann, Sigmund, *Die Stufen des preussischen Konservatismus* (*Historische Studien,* ‡190) Berlin, 1930.

105. Ompteda, Georg, Freiherr von, *Eysen,* Berlin, 1903-05.

106. Petersdorff, Hermann von, *Hans von Kleist-Retzow,* Berlin, 1907.

107. Polenz, W. von, *Die Grabenhaeger,* 3rd edition, Berlin, 1903.

108. *Pommersche Lebensbilder,* ed. Landesgeschichtliche Forschungsstelle fuer Pommern, 2 vols., Stettin, 1934-36.

109. Preuss, Hugo, *Die Junkerfrage*, Berlin, 1897.

110. Puttkamer, Albert von, *Staatsminister von Puttkamer: Ein Stueck preussischer Vergangenheit, 1828-1900*, Leipzig, 1928.

111. Reventlow, E., Graf von, *Kaiser Wilhelm II und die Byzantiner*, Munich, 1906.

112. Ritter, Gerhard, *Die preussischen Konservativen und Bismarcks deutsche Politik, 1858 bis 1876*, Heidelberg, 1913.

113. Rothfels, Hans, *Theodor von Schoen, Friedrich Wilhelm IV und die Revolution von 1848*, Halle, 1937.

114. Scharfenort, von, *Das Koeniglich preussische Kadettenkorps, 1859-1892*, Berlin, 1910.

115. Schmidt, Walter, *Die Partei Bethmann-Hollweg und die Reaktion in Preussen, 1850-1858*, Berlin, 1910.

116. Schmoller, Gustav, *Zwanzig Jahre deutscher Politik, 1897-1917*, Munich and Leipzig, 1920.

117. Schnabel, Franz, *Deutsche Geschichte im Neunzehnten Jahrhundert*, 4 vols., Freiburg i.B., 1937.

118. Thompson, James Westfall, *Feudal Germany*, Chicago, 1928.

119. Tims, Richard W., *Germanizing Prussian Poland: The H-K-T Society and the Struggle for the Eastern Marches in the German Empire, 1894-1919 (Studies in History, Economics and Public Law, #487)* Columbia University, New York, 1941.

120. Tuempel, L., *Entstehung des brandenburgisch-preussischen Einheitsstaats im Zeitalter des Absolutismus*, Berlin, 1915.

121. Vollrath, Wilhelm Otto, *Der parlamentarische Kampf um das preussische Dreiklassenwahlrecht, 1849-1918*, Bonn and Leipzig, 1931.

122. Zechlin, Egmont, *Staatsstreichplaene Bismarcks und Wilhelm II, 1890-1894*, Stuttgart and Berlin, 1929.

123. Ziekursch, Johannes, *Beitraege zur Charakteristik der preussischen Verwaltungsbeamten in Schlesien*, Breslau, 1907.

124. ——, *Hundert Jahre schlesischer Agrargeschichte*, Breslau, 1915.

CONTEMPORANEOUS ARTICLES

125. Conrad, Johannes, "Die Fideikommisse in den oestlichen Provinzen Preussens," *Festgabe fuer Georg Hanssen*, Tuebingen, 1889, pp. 259-300.

126. ——, "Der Grossgrundbesitz in Ost Preussen," *Jahrbuecher fuer Nationaloekonomie und Statistik*, v. 57 (1891) pp. 817-44.

127. ——, "Die Latifundien im preussischen Osten," *Jb. f. Nationaloek. u. Stat.*, v. 50 (1888) pp. 121-70.

128. Delbrueck, Hans, "Die Massregelung der Beamten-Abgeordneten," *Preussische Jahrbuecher*, v. 98 (1899) pp. 180-84.

129. Evert, Georg, "Die preussischen Landtagswahlen des Jahres 1903 und fruehere Jahre," *Zeitschrift des Kgl. preussischen Statistischen Landesamtes,* Ergaenzungsheft 23 (1905).

130. ———, "Die preussischen Landtagswahlen des Jahres 1908 und fruehere Jahre," *Z. d. Kgl. preuss. Stat. Landesamtes,* Ergaenzungsheft 30 (1909).

131. Helldorf-Bedra, Otto Heinrich von, "Der Fall des Sozialgesetzes," *Deutsche Revue,* v. 25, nos. 1-2 (1900) pp. 273-84.

132. Hintze, Otto, "Der Beamtenstand," *Gehe-Stiftung zu Dresden, Vortraege,* v. 3 (1911) pp. 95-175.

133. Hoepker, H., "Die Fideikommisse in Preussen im Lichte der Statistik bis zum Ende des Jahres 1912," *Z. d. Kgl. preuss. Stat. Landesamtes,* v. 54 (1914) pp. 1-98.

134. ———, "Die preussischen Landtagswahlen des Jahres 1913," *Z. d. Kgl. preuss. Stat. Landesamtes,* Ergaenzungsheft 43 (1916).

135. Kardorff, Wilhelm von, "Herr von Kleist-Retzow," *Deutsches Wochenblatt,* Jg. 5 (1892) pp. 245-47.

136. Kuesel-Koenigsberg, Otto, "Rudolf von Brandt, Landeshauptmann der Provinz Ostpreussen. Ein Lebensbild aus Anlass seiner 50 jaehrigen Dienstjubelfeier am 10. November, 1907," *Altpreussische Monatsschrift,* v. 45 (1908) pp. 136-48.

137. Leweck, "Bon, General-Landschaftsdirektor in Ostpreussen, 1887 bis 1905," *Altpreussische Monatsschrift,* v. 43 (1906) pp. 3-28.

138. Lotz, Albert, "Politische Beamte in Preussen?" *Schmollers Jahrbuch fuer Gesetzgebung, Verwaltung und Volkswirtschaft im deutschen Reiche,* v. 24 (1900) pp. 931-55.

139. ———, "Ueber die Notwendigkeit der Reform der Verwaltungsorganisation in Preussen," *Schmollers Jb. f. Gesetzgeb.,* v. 26 (1902) pp. 227-62.

140. May, R. E., "Der Anteil der Arbeiter, der Angestellten und der Selbstaendigen am deutschen Volkseinkommen des Jahres 1900," *Schmollers Jb. f. Gesetzgeb.,* v. 27 (1903) pp. 173-208.

141. Meyer, Alexander, "Die Kanalvorlage und die Beamten," *Die Nation,* Jg. 16 (1898-99) pp. 506-07.

142. Meyer, Rudolph, "Adelstand und Junkerklasse," *Neue deutsche Rundschau,* v. 10 (1899) pp. 1078-90.

143. Miltitz, Dietrich, Freiherr von, "Adel und Staatsdienst," *Der Kunstwart,* v. 27 (1913) pp. 273-79.

144. Mirbach-Sorquitten, Julius, Graf von "Die konservative Partei," *Deutsches Wochenblatt,* Jg. 10 (1897) pp. 546-49.

145. Poellnitz-Weimar, von, "Der Adel in der Armee," *Die Grenzboten* #15 (1910) pp. 49-54.

146. Preuss, Hugo, "Verwaltungsreform und Politik," *Zeitschrift fuer Politik,"* v. 1 (1907) pp. 95-126.

147. Rauh, H., "Die Landarbeiterfrage und die evangelische Geistlichkeit in Ostelbien," *Soziale Praxis*, v. 4 (1895) pp. 1007-09.

148. Schmoller, Gustav, "Die preussische Wahlrechtsreform von 1910 auf dem Hintergrunde des Kampfes zwischen Koenigtum und Feudalitaet," *Schmollers Jb. f. Gesetzgeb.*, v. 34 (1910) pp. 1261-79.

149. ——, "Noch ein Votum ueber die 'politischen' Beamten," *Schmollers Jb. f. Gesetzgeb.*, v. 24 (1900) pp. 113-17.

150. Schulte, F. von, "Adel im deutschen Offizier- und Beamtenstand. Eine soziale Betrachtung," *Deutsche Revue*, 21 Jg., v. 1 (1896) pp. 181-92.

151. Soetbeer, Adolf, "Volkseinkommen im preussischen Staate, 1876 und 1888," *Jahrbuecher fuer Nationaloekonomie und Statistik*, v. 52 (1889) pp. 414-27.

152. Sokal E., "Die buergerliche Erwerbstaetigkeit des Adels in Deutschland," *Die Gegenwart* #28 (1903).

153. Weber, Max, "Deutschlands aeussere und Preussens innere Politik," *Gesammelte politische Schriften*, Munich, 1921, pp. 94-106.

154. ——, "Entwicklungstendenzen in der Lage der ostelbischen Landarbeiter," *Gesammelte Aufsaetze zur Sozial- und Wirtschaftsgeschichte*, Tuebingen, 1924, pp. 460-509.

155. ——, "Der Nationalstaat und die Volkswirtschaftspolitik," *Gesammelte politische Schriften*, Munich, 1921, pp. 7-30.

156. ——, "Parlament und Regierung im neugeordneten Deutschland," *Gesammelte politische Schriften*, Munich, 1921, pp. 126-260.

157. ——, "Wahlrecht und Demokratie in Deutschland," *Gesammelte politische Schriften*, Munich, 1921, pp. 277-322.

158. Zedlitz-Neukirch, Octavio, Freiherr von, "Neueinrichtung der preussischen Verwaltung, *Preussische Jahrbuecher*, v. 107, (1902) pp. 24-43.

SUBSEQUENT ARTICLES

159. Below, Georg von, "Adel," *Handwoerterbuch der Staatswissenschaften*, 3rd edition, Jena, 1919, v. 1, pp. 141-48.

160. Brinkmann, Carl, "Die Aristokratie im kapitalistischen Zeitalter," *Grundriss der Sozialoekonomik*, v. 9, part 1, Tuebingen, 1926, pp. 22-34.

161. ——, "Wustrau, Wirtschafts- und Verfassungsgeschichte eines brandenburgischen Rittergüts," *Staats- und sozialwissenschaftliche Forschungen*, Heft 155, Leipzig, 1911.

162. Dorn, Walter L., "The Prussian Bureaucracy in the Eighteenth Century," *Political Science Quarterly*, v. 46 (1931) pp. 403-23; v. 47 (1932) pp. 75-95; 259-273.

163. Fay, Sidney Bradshaw, "The Hohenzollern Household and Adminis-

tration in the Sixteenth Century," *Smith College Studies in History*, v. 2, #1 (1916) pp. 1-64.

164. Goltz, Ruediger, Freiherr von, "Ruediger von der Goltz," *Pommersche Lebensbilder*, Stettin, 1934-36, v. 1, pp. 279-87.

165. Hartung, Fritz, "Verantwortliche Regierung, Kabinette und Neben-regierungen im konstitutionellen Preussen, 1848-1918," *Forschungen zur brandenburgischen und preussischen Geschichte*, v. 44 (1931-32) pp. 1-45; 307-73.

166. Hass, Martin, "Friedrich der Grosse und seine Kammerpraesidenten," *Festschrift zu Schmollers siebzigsten Geburtstag*, Leipzig, 1908, pp. 191-220.

167. Hintze, Otto, "Die Hohenzollern und der Adel," *Historische Zeitschrift*, v. 112 (1914)pp. 494-524.

168. ——, "Der Ursprung des preussischen Landratsamts in der Mark Brandenburg," *Forsch. z. brandenburg. u. preuss. Gesch.*, v. 28, part 1 (1915) pp. 357-422.

169. Kehr, Eckart, "Das soziale System der Reaktion in Preussen unter dem Ministerium Puttkamer," *Die Gesellschaft*, Jg. 1929, v. 2, pp. 253-274.

170. ——, Zur Genesis des Kgl. preussischen Reserveoffiziers," *Die Gesellschaft*, Jg. 1928, v. 2, pp. 492-502.

171. Martiny, Fritz, "Die Adelsfrage in Preussen vor 1806 als politisches und soziales Problem, erlaeutert am Beispiele des kurmaerkischen Adels," *Vierteljahrschrift fuer Sozial- und Wirtschaftsgeschichte*, Beiheft #35, Stuttgart, 1938.

172. Meyer, A. O., "Hans von Kleist-Retzow," *Pommersche Lebensbilder*, Stettin, 1934-36, v. 2, pp. 122-43.

173. Priebatsch, Felix, "Die Hohenzollern und der Adel der Mark," *Historische Zeitschrift*, v. 88 (1902) pp. 193-246.

174. Poschinger, Heinrich von, "Aus den Denkwuerdigkeiten Wilhelm von Kardorffs," *Deutsche Revue*, Jg. 33, v. 2 (1908) pp. 152-60.

175. Rosenberg, Hans, "The Rise of the Junkers in Brandenburg-Prussia, 1410-1653," *American Historical Review*, v. 49 (1943-44) pp. 1-22; 228-242.

176. Savorgnan, F., "Das Aussterben der adeligen Geschlechter. Statistisch-soziologischer Beitrag ueber die Fruchtbarkeit der Souveraenen und mediatisierten Haeuser," *Jahrbuch fuer Soziologie*, v. 1 (1925) pp. 320-40.

177. Schmoller, Gustav, "Die Entstehung des preussischen Heeres, 1640 bis 1740," *Umrisse und Untersuchungen zur Verfassungs-, Verwaltungs- und Wirtschaftsgeschichte, besonders des preussischen Staates im 18. und 19. Jahrhundert*, Leipzig, 1898, pp. 247-88.

178. Strantz, Kurd von, "Beitrag zur ritterlichen Besiedlung der Mark

in der Wittelsbacher Zeit. Die Strantz von Tuellstedt aus Thueringen," *Brandenburgia,* Jg. 37 (1928) pp. 5-14.

179. Thimme, Friedrich, "Bismarck und Kardorff. Neue Mitteilungen aus dem Nachlass Wilhelm von Kardorffs," *Deutsche Revue,* Jg. 41, v. 4 (1916) pp. 31-40; 131-48; 255-77; Jg. 42, v. 1 (1917) pp. 46-59; 162-85; 278-88.

180. Toennies, F., "Deutscher Adel im 19. Jahrhundert," *Neue Rundschau,* Jg. 23, v. 2 (1912) pp. 1041-63.

INDEX